THOMAS WOLFE

Ulysses and Narcissus

THOMAS WOLFE: Ulysses and Narcissus

by William U. Snyder

Ohio University Press
Athens

Library of Congress Catalog Card Number: 78-141381
ISBN: 8214-0087-8
Printed in the United States of America
Ohio University Press
Athens, Ohio 45701

To the memory of my brother
LUTHER HENRY SNYDER, M.D.
from whom I borrowed Of Time and the River,
and therein discovered the satisfactions
of reading the books of Thomas Wolfe.

CONTENTS

Preface xi

Introduction: Some Biographical Highlights xix

PART I

ULYSSES THE FAR-WANDERER—WOLFE'S RELATIONSHIPS WITH MEN 1

CHAPTER 1. Father and Son 3
The Theme of the Far-wanderer 19

CHAPTER 2. Brothers, and a Preoccupation with Death 28
Frank 28
Fred 31
Ben 37
Wolfe's Preoccupation with Death 44

CHAPTER 3. Friendships and Loneliness 51
Kenneth Raisbeck 55
Olin Dows 60
Inadequacy, Social Isolation, and Loneliness 64

CHAPTER 4. Wolfe and Maxwell Perkins and the Search for a Father 74
The Break with Perkins 82
The Search for a Father 93

PART II

NARCISSUS AND THE SPLIT IMAGO—WOLFE'S RELATIONSHIPS WITH WOMEN 99

CHAPTER 5. Mother and Son 101
Signs of Narcissism 113
Dependency and Counter-dependency 122

CHAPTER 6. His Sister Mabel, and His Sexual Tendencies 126
Wolfe's Oral Sexual Tendencies 135

CHAPTER 7. Some Other Women in His Life 138
Margaret Roberts 138
Clara Paul 141
A Boston Girl 143
"Ann" 145
A School Principal 148
Thea Voelker 151
Elizabeth Nowell 154

CHAPTER 8. Aline Bernstein and Wolfe's Sexual Attitudes 158
Tom's Need for Aline 169
Aline's Need for Tom 172
The Break with Aline 175
Wolfe's Sexual Attitudes 179

PART III

DIAGNOSIS AND PROGNOSIS 183

CHAPTER 9. Diagnosis 185
Wolfe's Pathological Defenses 185
His Need for Catharsis 187
Compulsive and Obsessive Behavior 189
Manic-Depressive Behavior 196
Paranoidal Tendencies 207
Summary 219

CHAPTER 10. Prognosis 220

Selected References 229

Charts

1. Thomas Wolfe's Family xx
2. Thomas Wolfe's Principal Publications xxii
3. Wolfe's Periods of Elation and Depression, and the Concurrent Events in His Life 200

Illustrations following page 104

PREFACE

WHEN I WAS WRITING THIS BOOK, SOME FRIENDS ASKED ME how it was possible to make a psychological analysis of a person simply by studying what he had written and what others had written about him. Certainly I was helped considerably by the fact that Thomas Wolfe was probably the most autobiographical novelist of this century, if not of all time. Critics and biographers, his family, his editors, and Wolfe himself admitted, almost without exception, that his work was primarily autobiographical. Even though at the beginning of *Look Homeward, Angel*, he made a gesture at denying this, Wolfe later reversed himself. By the time he was working on his second book, *Of Time and the River*, he went so far as to say—as he was to do many times later—that practically all good writing is autobiographical. In addition to his novels—four of which are heavily autobiographical—Wolfe wrote voluminous letters. Though he had no intention of publishing them, two volumes which include over seven hundred of these letters have been published. One comprises the letters to his mother, while the other is a selection of his more interesting letters to a variety of correspondents. And recently thirty-six of his diaries and notebooks have been published.

Moreover, Wolfe's mistress, Aline Bernstein, devoted two of her four books—*Three Blue Suits* and *The Journey Down*—to

Wolfe. The first contains a long story about Wolfe entitled "Eugene"; the second is her account of their love affair. Comparing her version with Wolfe's account of their relationship in *The Web and the Rock* and *You Can't Go Home Again* is like comparing the texts of two of the Gospels—an identical story told in rather similar form by two different authors who both participated in the same events. To carry the biblical analogy further, a reader need only turn to Wolfe's *Letters* or *Notebooks* to find the concordance which elaborates the text of the gospels, and ties down the identification of the characters.

In addition there have been many book reviews as well as critical essays about Wolfe. Leslie Field in his collection of critical essays (*Thomas Wolfe: Three Decades of Criticism* [New York: New York University Press, 1968], p. xi) estimates that five hundred essays appeared by 1960. By 1968 five or six biographies of Wolfe had been published, of which three—those by Elizabeth Nowell (1960), Richard Kennedy (1962), and Andrew Turnbull (1967)—must be considered excellent works. For this book, I have drawn the factual data primarily from Wolfe's letters, using his novels and the books about him to supplement what is revealed in the letters.

One difficulty in interpreting events in a study of this sort lies in the effect of the individual's perception of events on the way in which he reports them. As an individual develops from birth, he learns certain beliefs, attitudes, and habits, which create a characteristic life style. This, in turn, influences further learning and change, for one tends to learn what is consistent with one's past learning and to reject new experiences which do not fit. Thus one views the world from one's own particular perspective. In a study of a person such as Thomas Wolfe, one must be aware of his particular distortions—such as his paranoid projections of blame onto others—if one is to obtain an accurate account of events. Obviously it was helpful to have reports from other observers: his mistress, his mother, his sister, his editor, among others, since they make it possible to check his account of various incidents and to achieve a good approximation of the "truth."

But why another book about Thomas Wolfe? If such a book is to justify itself it must offer something which the others do not. It should not be simply another biography, for the three mentioned above are fine studies of Wolfe's life, each from a different vantage point. Elizabeth Nowell knew Wolfe very well and worked closely with him for about five years. Her biography captures the man as someone loved, respected, and admired—a very human Wolfe. Kennedy wrote what he himself called a literary biography, and while he offers some good psychological insights into Wolfe as a man, he addressed himself primarily to Wolfe's creative powers. Turnbull's biography is the most factual of the three, with emphasis on chronology, although he also added some psychological insights.

In this book I have attempted what is primarily a psychological study of Wolfe. Indeed, I would not hesitate to call it a psychobiography, and if the word did not have a very specific meaning of a different sort I would even call it a psychoanalysis. That is, I have attempted to direct upon the writings by and about Thomas Wolfe the insights into personality of a professional clinical psychologist, and to describe the personality which becomes evident. Since my primary interest in the field of psychology has been in the areas of psychotherapy and interpersonal relationships, it is from this vantage point that I have attempted to analyze Wolfe's personality. I have been most concerned with his relationships with the important people in his life, and with what these tell us about his personality.

But why should this be done for an author now dead for over thirty years, who wrote only four long novels, some short novels, and about a dozen short stories, all published within one decade? To begin with, I found the project interesting myself and was convinced that others would share my interest. Also relevant is the fact that many consider Wolfe to have been one of the most important American writers of this century. To this day his four major novels are selling as well as they did thirty or forty years ago, which suggests that Wolfe was far from being the short-lived meteor on the literary horizon that some critics took him to be. Though it is easy to point to literary weaknesses in his work, the fact remains that his books continue to interest not only serious literary scholars but the reading public at large. My assessment of the reasons for this phenomenon is that Wolfe was for my generation—the middle aged of today—what Salinger became for the next generation. For us he captured the trials, the agonies and ecstasies of young Everyman in a poignant and valid way that continues to evoke a deep response. Moreover, he was capable of ascending to heights of lyric prose, of achieving in some of his works an epic form which almost rendered them a saga of American life. Everyone who ever thrilled to a ride on a crack railroad train, with all of its promise of adventure and discovery, reacts with nostalgia to Wolfe's frequent descriptions of train rides. And so it is with many elements of his writing. Few try to read his books as if they were a story in the usual sense; one is more likely to read them as if they were anthologies, savoring certain passages over and over again because of the pleasure they give.

I am not concerned with the question of whether Wolfe was a great writer. He may or may not rank with Faulkner and Hemingway, Sinclair Lewis or Fitzgerald, but certainly these leaders of that literary generation, as well as many critics, willingly placed him within their ranks. Is my purpose, then, to debunk Wolfe—to strip him of his glory by examining his human qualities under the psychological microscope? I can only answer this by saying that while I am aware of his many personal and literary faults, I derived deep pleasure from reading about Eugene Gant, and, later, about George Webber. They were the Holden Caulfield of my youth, much more real to me than my father's

Horatio Alger or my mother's Louisa May Alcott. I admired Thomas Wolfe's writing, and still do. If in my analysis I show him to have been less than a completely self-actualized man, I do so without any sense of disdain, but rather with compassion. I feel as though I have lived intimately with him and his family and associates for several years, and I have come to think of him almost as if he were a brother. So it is only with the most sympathetic probe that I try to elicit the quality and scope of his personality.

Can psychobiography be considered a valid method of personality analysis? I believe that the answer is an unqualified yes. Gamaliel Bradford tried to make such a study of Robert E. Lee in 1912, but probably did not know enough psychology (hardly anybody did at that time) to do a thorough piece of work, with the result that his psychobiography—and he used that term—is really only a biography. But Freud in his studies of Leonardo and Moses clearly demonstrated that a psychologist could apply the tools of "projective analysis" to a man's writings, and learn about his personality. Henry A. Murray showed the same thing in his study of Herman Melville, in the introduction to Melville's *Pierre*, and Ernest Jones analyzed Shakespeare by analyzing *Hamlet*. Erik Erikson's study of *Young Man Luther* is a masterpiece of psychobiography, and indeed, inspired my own efforts in this field. But long before I had read Erikson's book, I had become acquainted with the writings of Harold McCurdy, who has devoted a professional career to this kind of endeavor, as shown by his analysis of the writings of D. H. Lawrence and Shakespeare.

In general I have tried to write this book in nontechnical language and to avoid too heavy a reliance upon rather obscure theoretical concepts. It should be said, however, that the personality theory which influences my own thinking about Wolfe is an eclectic one drawing upon the best that is to be found in Freudian psychoanalysis, together with those constructs about personality which have been derived from the learning theory developed in psychology laboratories. In addition I have been somewhat influenced by the system of "needs and presses" described by Henry Murray.

The title of this book reveals my indebtedness to Freudian theory, but I have never allowed myself to follow it blindly in those cases in which it has seemed to come into conflict with the principles of learning which have been derived from the laboratory. There is not too much of existential psychology in this book, although it will be noted that the concept of self-actualization appears more than once. The professor from whom I learned the most about psychotherapy, Carl Rogers, leaned strongly toward the phenomenological approach to personality, but the teacher from whom I learned most of the rest of my clinical psychology, David Shakow, was a student of Murray's, and an adherent of psychoanalytic theory within the context of synthesis with experimental laboratory findings. Thus the theoretical orientation of this book is very similar to what appears to be emerging among the majority of clinical psychologists, and is characterized by a healthy and thoughtful eclecticism, which is a synthesis of the contributions of the different schools of psychology.

Note to the Reader References are not cited in the notes when their source is obvious; thus if there is mention of a letter which Wolfe sent to his mother in 1928, no footnote reference is given, since it would obviously appear in Terry's edition of *Thomas Wolfe's Letters to His Mother*, and could be located by the date. All other letters by Wolfe appear in Nowell's edition of *The Letters of Thomas Wolfe*, unless otherwise indicated. Letters from Perkins to Wolfe appear in Maxwell Perkins's *Editor to Author*. Occasionally the titles of Wolfe's two best known books have been shortened to *Angel*, for *Look Homeward, Angel*, and *River*, for *Of Time and The River*. Footnote references to Wolfe's four major novels give the chapter rather than the page number, since there are numerous editions of each of these books. For purposes of simplification certain abbreviations, given below, have been used in the notes.

Kennedy	Kennedy, Richard S. *The Window of Memory: The Literary Career of Thomas* Wolfe. Chapel Hill: University of North Carolina Press, 1962.
Letters	*The Letters of Thomas Wolfe.* Edited by Elizabeth Nowell. New York: Charles Scribner's Sons, 1956.
Letters to His Mother	*Thomas Wolfe's Letters to His Mother.* Edited by John Skally Terry. New York: Charles Scribner's Sons, 1943.
Notebooks	*The Notebooks of Thomas Wolfe.* Edited by Richard S. Kennedy and Paschal Reeves. Chapel Hill: University of North Carolina Press, 1970.
Nowell	Nowell, Elizabeth. *Thomas Wolfe: A Biography.* New York: Doubleday and Company, 1960.
Perkins	*Editor to Author, The Letters of Maxwell Perkins.* Edited by John Hall Wheelock. New York: Charles Scribner's Sons, 1950.
Turnbull	Turnbull, Andrew. *Thomas Wolfe.* New York: Charles Scribner's Sons, 1967.
Wheaton	Wheaton, Mabel Wolfe, and Blythe, LeGette. *Thomas Wolfe and His Family.* New York: Doubleday and Company, 1961.

Acknowledgments I am indebted to a number of people for

valuable help in making this book possible. My wife, June, contributed much more than the routinely acknowledged support and comfort. She spent many hours assisting with reading the background materials and coding and collating the references. We also discussed at length the ideas and concepts involved, and she contributed much to their formulation and maturation. And she helped to edit the manuscript. I was given encouragement and moral support by Dr. and Mrs. John D. Walmer, Dean George R. Klare, Dr. and Mrs. Frank Semans, and Drs. Ila and Scott Gehman. The Gehmans also located an idyllic cottage for me in a woods near a pond in North Carolina, with all the amenities of comfortable living, and easy access to an important library. Much of the book was written there. Drs. Frank Auld, Jr. and Oscar Cargill read the manuscript and contributed useful and significant suggestions. It was Dr. Auld who brought to my attention the relevance of the concept of the symbiotic family. Mrs. Barbara Lindsey and Mrs. Sandra Hunter typed the final draft of the manuscript. I am indebted to the following publishers for graciously permitting me to include quotations from materials by or about Thomas Wolfe: Charles Scribner's Sons, Harper and Row, Doubleday and Company, Grosset and Dunlap, *Saturday Review of Literature* and The University of North Carolina Press. Mr. William S. Powell, Curator of the North Carolina Collection of the University of North Carolina Library, kindly permitted me to read printed materials available in the Thomas Wolfe Collection of that library. Sincere appreciation is extended to Mr. James Meehan of the Pack Memorial Library in Asheville for making most of the photographs available for inclusion in this book. Finally, I am grateful to Ian MacKenzie, Director, Mrs. Fannia Weingartner, and the staff of the Ohio University Press, for their helpful editorial work.

INTRODUCTION
SOME BIOGRAPHICAL HIGHLIGHTS

THIS BOOK APPROACHES THOMAS WOLFE'S PSYCHODYNAMics through an analysis of each of the major relationships he developed in the course of his life. To introduce the members of his immediate family—covering a span of two generations—a family tree is included (see chart 1). This is in no way a genealogical chart; it is merely a means of clarifying the family-unit relationship and of indicating how their lives overlapped.

Thomas Wolfe was born in Asheville, North Carolina, in October of 1900, the seventh surviving child, and the last, of William Oliver Wolfe, then forty-nine, and of Julia Elizabeth (Westall) Wolfe, who was forty at the time. Tom attended the Orange Street Public School from 1905 to 1912, when he entered a private school called the North State Fitting School, run by J. M. and Margaret Roberts. Although it was a small school, with only about thirty boys enrolled, the Roberts gave Wolfe a thorough education in the classics and history, and a deep appreciation of literature. Wolfe was a superior student, and also a bookish boy, whose principal interests were reading and, later, writing. He matriculated at the University of North Carolina in 1916, and majored in drama and literature; he was a successful student in college and although considered quite eccentric, was popular. Tom excelled in literary and dramatic extracur-

CHART 1

Thomas Wolfe's Family; Their Names in *Look Homeward, Angel* (in parentheses)

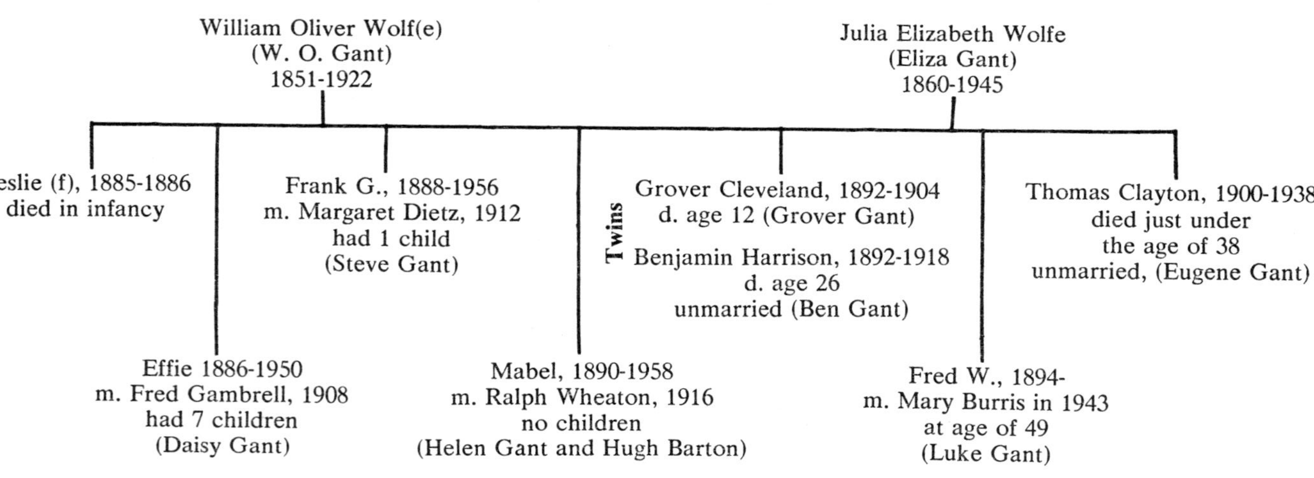

ricular activities, holding top editorial positions on three student literary publications, and being one of the original members of the since-renowned Carolina Playmakers, a student dramatic group.

After his graduation, Wolfe took a Master's degree in drama at Harvard University, under the tutelage of the highly respected English and dramatics professor, George Pierce Baker. Having completed the work for this degree, Wolfe reluctantly accepted a position teaching English Literature and Composition at New York University, where he taught intermittently from 1924 to 1930. Thereafter, he supported himself solely by his earnings as an author, supplemented for a while by financial gifts from his patron and mistress, Aline Bernstein. Wolfe's first book *Look Homeward, Angel* was published in November, 1929. His principal writings, listed on chart 2 (page xii), consist of four major autobiographical novels, several collections of stories, two volumes of notebooks, and two volumes containing most of his collected letters. He never married or owned a home; he died of cerebral tuberculosis in September, 1938.

Wolfe's parents were ambitious middle-class people; his father was a tombstone maker, and his mother had been a country schoolteacher before her marriage. Mrs. Wolfe also carried on some real estate operations, and after 1906 ran a boardinghouse known as the Old Kentucky Home. It is estimated that the Wolfes eventually became relatively prosperous middle-class people. Their marriage was an unhappy one, and the establishment of Mrs. Wolfe's boardinghouse constituted a virtual, but not total, division of the household, with part of the family remaining with her husband, and Tom going with her. This event had profound effects on the personalities of the children, and particularly on Tom.

Asheville was a small city in the poorer western part of North Carolina, noted primarily as a blossoming health resort and mountain vacation center. The milieu was essentially provincial

CHART 2

Thomas Wolfe's Principal Publications

Title	Type	Publication Date	Period In Life
Look Homeward, Angel	Novel (autobiographical)	1929	1900-1920
Of Time and the River	Novel (autobiographical)	1935	1920-1925
From Death to Morning*	Collected Stories	1935	1918-1932
The Story of a Novel	Autobiographic Essay	1936	1929-1935
The Web and the Rock	Novel (autobiographical)	1939 (posthumous)	1925-1928
You Can't Go Home Again	Novel (autobiographical)	1940 (posthumous)	1929-1937
The Hills Beyond†	Collected Stories and Essays	1941 (posthumous)	1904-1937
Thomas Wolfe's Letters to his Mother	Collected Letters	1943 (posthumous)	1909-1938
The Letters of Thomas Wolfe	Collected Letters	1956 (posthumous)	1908-1938
The Notebooks of Thomas Wolfe	Notebooks and Diaries	1970 (posthumous)	1920-1938

***Includes biographical material about Wolfe's relatives and Aline Bernstein based on their reminiscences. These stories predate the autobiographical ones in the book.**

†Includes some autobiographical essays and stories, and a short novel bearing the same title, which is actually a collection of biographical folk tales and legends about Wolfe's maternal ancestors, covering the years 1593 to 1881.

southern and Victorian Protestant, and Tom acquired all of the attitudes and prejudices inherent in such a setting. His parents were socially mobile, probably moving from lower-middle to upper-middle class, a mobility which also characterized Tom's career, although his social group eventually became the somewhat bohemian one of artists and writers, and he came to feel contempt and scorn for the materialism and business attitudes of his mother and his siblings.

Wolfe's life spanned both the Roaring Twenties and the Great Depression of the 1930s. To be relatively poor was typical for most of the generation who lived through the Depression. But from the beginning Wolfe chose a life of financial austerity, even precariousness, rather than taking up the more secure existence of a teacher. His devotion to his art was an all-consuming passion; he never considered himself anything but a writer. At first he hoped to write plays, but it became apparent that his style of writing did not lend itself to dramatic productions; he was, indeed, one of the first of the American group of stream of consciousness writers who modelled their work after that of James Joyce. His books were novels only in a fairly loose sense of that term, at least for their time. Almost devoid of plot, they might more appropriately have been called character studies. Despite their relatively small number, Wolfe's novels have had a great deal of influence on American literature, and continue to be widely read.

Wolfe's siblings played a key role in his life, and they and his parents became the principal subjects of his writing. Yet his relationships with them, as discussed throughout this book, were anything but tranquil. He felt closest to his brother Ben who died when Tom was only eighteen. Grover had died when Tom was four. Of the two oldest children, Tom always hated Frank, and had little affection for Effie. In many ways his closest siblings were Mabel, who was ten years older, and Fred, who was six years his senior.

Tom Wolfe developed only a few deep friendships in his life, and for most of the time after he went to college he lived alone, except for the three or four years when he and Aline Bernstein lived together. His home was usually a fairly bleak apartment in New York, but he made seven trips to Europe, and actually spent about a fourth of his adult life abroad. For eight years after *Look Homeward, Angel* was published he did not visit Asheville, feeling that he was bitterly disliked there because his book had revealed so much that was uncomplimentary about many of the local citizens. He was very much a wanderer, and a lonely one, at that. He wrote often about his loneliness, as in "God's Lonely Man," a subjective account of what it felt like to be an intensely lonely person.[1]

---

1. Published in *The Hills Beyond* (New York: Harper & Row, 1941), pp. 145-54. Originally published as "The Anatomy of Loneliness," *American Mercury* (1941).

PART

I

ULYSSES THE FAR-WANDERER: WOLFE'S RELATIONSHIP WITH MEN

1

FATHER AND SON

WOLFE'S RELATIONSHIP WITH HIS FATHER, WILLIAM OLIVER, or W. O., can be characterized as ambivalent. Until puberty Tom was deeply fond of his Papa, but when he reached adolescence this affection changed for several reasons. To begin with Tom had the not uncommon experience of perceiving that the object of his love and veneration had "clay feet." Then he began to become aware of other things that eroded the rapport he had enjoyed with his father. Ultimately, Tom came to be indifferent to him—an indifference that bordered on dislike.

W. O. Wolfe, known even to his wife as Mr. Wolfe, was an unusual man whose personality was a curious amalgam of the gentle and the rough. His father, a German Pennsylvania farmer, had married a Pennsylvania Dutch girl and had tried, not very successfully, to run a farm. He died when W. O. Wolfe was still a boy, leaving his wife to manage the farm and a large family during the Civil War. According to Julia Wolfe, W. O.'s father was a heavy drinker and not a very good provider.[1]

---

1. Major sources of information about W. O. Wolfe are "The Web of Earth," in *From Death to Morning* (New York: Charles Scribner's Sons, 1935), *Angel*, *River*, and Wheaton.

W. O. could recall being sent to the tavern to fetch his father, and finding it difficult to get him safely home to bed. After the elder Wolf's death (it was W. O. who added the final *e* to the surname) his widow, perhaps because of her rugged and impoverished life, was said by W. O. to have become somewhat "hard on us children." At fourteen, W. O. worked as a mule tender, but after a year decided that he would rather work as a stonecutter, and left for Baltimore, where for four years he learned this trade. During this period he lived in a boardinghouse where—according to his daughter, Mabel—he picked up the colorful but rough language that was to be one of his most prominent characteristics. At the end of the four years he migrated to Raleigh, North Carolina, to work as a stonemason. Later he set up his own shop as a monument carver, which remained his occupation for the rest of his life. He really liked only one aspect of this work, the actual carving of the stone, but hated the business part of it. He was considered to be quite artistic and did beautiful work.

According to his wife, Julia, he would like to have been a lawyer. Intensely fond of poetry, drama, and oration, he had memorized long passages from the English classics, which he would declaim constantly, without invitation, to anyone who would listen. He also loved to read, and to travel, and was interested in politics, being a Yankee Republican in the postbellum South. Interspersed with his declamations were his many Merciful God's and his tirades and invectives against the various persons he felt were making life more difficult for him; among these perhaps the most frequently mentioned was his third wife, Julia, who was Tom's mother.

W. O. Wolfe first married a woman some years younger than himself. According to Julia it was a "forced marriage," although apparently no children were born of it. It was an unsuccessful marriage which lasted only a few years. Then his wife obtained a divorce and left him, although his daughter, Mabel, stated that W. O. probably continued to love her, and always carried her picture in his wallet. Following the divorce, W. O. boarded with a widow who had an older unmarried daughter; he was becoming somewhat known for his rather strong sex drive, and it was not long until another forced marriage took place, this time to the daughter, Cynthia, who was a milliner. It was decided, according to Julia's account, that Cynthia should have an abortion, and she was sent to Washington for it, although apparently a miscarriage actually took place while she was returning to Raleigh. W. O. had already begun his drunken sprees by this time. Cynthia was ill with tuberculosis, and in an effort to improve her health, and perhaps to escape the hostile attitudes of some of the citizens of Raleigh toward this rather profligate Yankee in their midst, the Wolfes moved to Asheville, which was then becoming a well-known health resort. W. O.'s mother-in-law went with them, and shortly after they arrived, his sister-in-law, who was having trouble with her husband, also joined the Wolfe menage. She was said to be a seductive woman, and although Cynthia died only a few years later, it was not before W. O. and his sister-in-law were openly engaging in a sexual relationship, for which W. O. later professed almost lifelong guilt feelings, and for which he blamed his drinking sprees. But Wolfe's brother-in-law heard about this situation, came back with a gun, and by threatening to kill Wolfe forced his wife to leave W. O. and rejoin him. By this time W. O. had built a small house and had a small shop, and was reluctant to return to boardinghouse life. He had met Julia Westall, a younger schoolteacher originally from a country town in the mountains north of Asheville, and after a brief courtship they were married. Although they lived together for forty years, and Julia bore him "a dozen children"[2] of whom seven lived beyond infancy, it was, in most senses of the word, a love-

---

2. See *From Death to Morning*; and Wheaton.

less marriage. These two people were remarkably mismatched, as Thomas Wolfe makes clear in *Look Homeward, Angel* and *Of Time and the River*. W. O. was a generous, loud, drinking man who visited the community prostitutes, and who disliked the acquisition of property. He loved his children, but his usual phrase for Julia was "miserable woman," a derogatory designation for a rather prim, teetotalling ex-schoolteacher, who was at heart a frustrated real estate agent. Julia's real ambition was to be as successful as her two contractor brothers, who had risen from abject postbellum country poverty to become leading citizens of the community. Eventually she managed to earn a good deal of money in the trading and developing of real estate. During the early years of their marriage, W. O. bitterly opposed the acquisition of property, perhaps because it would have limited his freedom to leave Asheville. After all, he had a history of leaving a community whenever circumstances became too complicated for him to handle. However, as age and illness overtook him, W. O. became more concerned about financial resources, and his attitude toward property became somewhat similar to Julia's. While their marriage lasted until W. O.'s death from cancer in 1922, by the year 1906 Julia had decided to leave W. O.'s bed and board and bought a large separate house, which she ran for over two decades as a boardinghouse called the Old Kentucky Home. Julia took with her Tom, then six but sporting curls appropriate to a much younger child; the other children spent most of their time at the family home which W. O. maintained until just before his death.

Tom was to recall again and again his happiness as the baby in this large family during the first six years of his life. He particularly remembered the tremendous meals, for his father possessed a gargantuan appetite, and loved to provide huge meals for his family and guests. Tom sat next to his father at the table, and W. O. would constantly ply him with more food, shouting, "Eat up, boy." W. O. was delighted with Tom's quick mentality, for he was talking by the age of one, and by the time he was two or three, he was parroting and pretending to read books which had been read to him. W. O. would buy him books, and, like the other members of the family, would read to him endlessly. And later he would give him money to buy dime novels or candy. Tom remembered with much nostalgia the great roaring fires his father would build as soon as he came into the house in the evening, and also the first thing in the morning, after which he would call to the children, "Get up, boys," and they would rush downstairs to dress by the huge fire. W. O. would often hug and kiss the boy, or would talk philosophically to him in his monument shop; and if his children were victims of any slights either from adults or their peers, W. O. would charge out of his shop and accost the offending person, demanding immediate restitution of the children's rights.

Thus, in Tom's early childhood, his relationship to his father was a happy, loving one. Tom had not yet learned to be upset by his father's sprees, the periods of great oaths and invectives, or the constant bickering between W. O. and his miserly wife, Julia.

It is of interest that so many of the rewards Tom received in those earliest years were for cognitive and verbal learning. His efforts to read were highly praised and brought him much attention from the various members of his family. His happiest times seem to have been either when someone was reading to him, or when he was trying to read. This early intellectual stimulation was fortunate in that it aided the development of his innate potentialities. However, it is significant that the emphasis was on verbal learning rather than sensory-motor or social learning. This orientation appears, then, to have initiated a major pattern in Tom's life. Once the reading skill was developed, Tom built on it, learning much through his reading, and generally neglecting physical activities. In terms of Tom's personal adjustment, it is unfortunate that much of the material he chose to read was fantasy, from which he acquired unrealistic concepts about the nature of life.

Two traumatic events that occurred within the first six years of Tom's life must have pressed heavily upon the developing personality of the boy. When Tom was about four, Julia took most of her children to St. Louis for the summer, and ran a boarding house there during the Exposition. All of the children had to help out by working at various odd jobs, and late in the summer, Grover—one of the twins—who was then twelve years old, developed typhoid fever and died. This was a severe blow to both W. O. and Julia. Apparently both bright and attractive, Grover had been a favorite of both parents. The effect of the parents' deep grief on the other children, and the invidious comparisons made between them and this paragon dead child must have weighed heavily on Tom. Over thirty years later he wrote a story about it, "*The Lost Boy*,"[3] and visited the house in St. Louis where they had spent the summer. It is hard to believe, however, that a four-year-old would have been overly affected by the loss of just one sibling out of six if the parents had not made a major issue of the matter.

The other traumatic event was Julia's departure from the family home to open the boardinghouse, coupled with her decision to take Tom with her. The rest of the children stayed with their father, and none of the family liked the boardinghouse or the boarders. Tom would continually go back to the family home on Woodfin Street to play with his friends and siblings, to eat the bountiful food now prepared by his sixteen-year-old sister, Mabel, and to feel the warmth of a home which was not cluttered by strangers—some of whom were not very endearing people, if we are to believe Wolfe's descriptions of them. At the end of the day Julia would telephone for Tom, and would shame him for "running away." This breakdown in family unity was

---

3. In *The Hills Beyond*, pp. 7-38.

almost certainly one of the critical psychological influences in Wolfe's life, and one which was to account for much of his unhappiness, loneliness, and difficulty in relating to people. To begin with, it made it more difficult for Tom to establish his masculinity, since he missed having a strong father figure after whom to pattern his behavior. And as an adult Tom was less masculine than his father. Moreover, the new situation deprived him of the security a child derives from living with his family and having a regular mode of life. W. O.'s ritualistic ways of dealing with daily events were much missed by Tom when he left the Woodfin Street house for the weakly structured milieu of the Old Kentucky Home.

One might ask why W. O. permitted Julia to take Tom with her and, eventually, to make him almost exclusively "her child?" Julia's need for Tom was quite strong, but W. O. need not have acquiesced to her plans, and probably would not have done so had his need for Tom been equally strong. Probably it was the particular combination of circumstances at that crucial time that determined how Tom's life would develop, for although Julia had been quite overprotective of him during those early years, it was W. O. whom Tom seemed to prefer, and to whom he returned whenever he could after the move to the Old Kentucky Home. Had the family stayed together, Julia's influence on Tom could not have been as strong.

It is likely that when she first announced her intentions, Julia stated that she would take Tom with her because he was still just a baby needing a mother's care, and moreover, that she would be lonely if she didn't have some member of the family with her. This would have seemed a reasonable argument. W. O. probably did not feel qualified to take care of Tom, nor would he have felt that Mabel, who at that time was just sixteen, should be burdened any more than she already was, running the household on Woodfin Street.

Once Julia and Tom were established in the Old Kentucky

Home, Julia's possessiveness would have been harder for W. O. to counteract. Since Julia was a very determined and persistent woman, it would have required equal persistence from W. O. to force her to allow Tom to grow up more like other boys. But W. O. did not have such a strong need, partly because most of the children were more fond of him than they were of Julia. Also, Fred, of whom he was quite fond, still lived with him. Mabel has described how desperate W. O. had felt when Fred had typhoid fever at the age of eight, and how proud he was of Fred's ability as a young businessman, selling magazines. It is interesting, too, that W. O. sent Fred to college, the latter being the only one of the Wolfe children, besides Tom, to go. Eventually, W. O. named Fred as one of the two executors of his will, again demonstrating his affection for this son. So it is apparent that W. O.'s need for affection was met by several of the children, and especially by Fred. W. O. was fond of Tom when he was a small boy, and was proud of his intellectual ability, but W. O. seems to have had mixed feelings about Tom as he grew older and became fairly bookish and showed a lack of ability to relate to people. Perhaps, the fact that Julia made Tom her child cooled W. O.'s fondness for him. Since Tom became identified with Julia, W. O. may have generalized toward Tom some of the negative feelings he had toward his wife.

W. O. Wolfe was forty-nine when Tom was born, and already having trouble with his health. As Tom reached adolescence, his father's health began to deteriorate seriously. A victim of cancer of the prostate, W. O. also suffered from rheumatoid arthritis, and at one time had shown signs of having tuberculosis. All three conditions required trips away from home to obtain cures, and once or twice W. O. was apparently sent away to dry out from his alcoholic bouts. But it was the prostatic cancer which produced the spectre of death that hung over him for a decade. Tom Wolfe called his father Oliver Gant in *Look Homeward, Angel* and *Of Time and the River*, but made a point of saying that this was a modification from his real name of Gaunt. The slight modification of the father's name—W. O. Wolfe had taken such a step himself—is interesting not only as the sort of identification marker that Wolfe made for most of his characters, but also as a play on the word *gaunt*. For W. O. became a shadow of his earlier self, and the great, hearty, life-loving, generous, father figure became irritable, petty, melancholy, gaunt, and at times irascible. At other times, especially later in his life, he seemed lifeless, disinterested, and preoccupied with himself and his morbid condition. This usual dysphoria would, however, be interspersed with an occasional return to sprees of wild drinking and whoring which were the source of dreadful embarrassment to all of the family. Many terrible scenes occurred in the presence of the boarders or the neighbors, and often the sons had to fetch their father from the saloon, drag him home, either helplessly drunk or fighting mad, and try to put him to bed. Then Mabel would take him in hand, and by a combination of tender ministrations of hot soup, sharp slaps, and curt invectives, would get him to bed where he could sleep it off. At this period Julia began to assume greater control over the family, and particularly of Tom, probably because of W. O.'s declining health. W. O. no longer cared enough to try to assert his masculine prerogatives in dominating the family much of the time. The strong father figure had become a weak and impotent old man, a pitiful hulk of his former self and a disappointment to his children. All of his sons had to work (while Mabel helped Julia with the boardinghouse), which suggests that W. O. was less able to provide his family with a very adequate living, although he always managed to have a wallet full of money at Christmas, or when he was about to go on a spree.

During Tom's adolescence another source of friction developed between Tom and his father. With the encouragement of Mr. and Mrs. J. M. Roberts, Tom was sent to their private school for his high school years. This decision proved tremendously important in shaping his literary and professional career. When Tom went to the Roberts's school, however, none of his siblings was very sympathetic, all of them feeling that he was receiving special privileges, and becoming stuck up. Tom did so well at the school that the Roberts persuaded his parents to send him to college. The Roberts wanted him to go to Virginia, or Princeton, which Tom also wanted, but W. O., who was going to foot the bills, insisted that Tom go to the University of North Carolina to study law so that he could become a politician. Even after his second year there, Tom still considered himself forced to attend the state university. He did write with some pleasure to W. O. to tell him of his election to a fraternity, and also to ask for money for the initiation. By the time of Tom's graduation W. O. was barely able to attend the ceremonies, and although he rallied fairly well when Tom was receiving various special honors, by the end of the visit W. O. was again a sick old man, begging to be taken home. And he adamantly refused to pay for Tom's graduate education in English and drama at Harvard; it was Julia who had to dole out pittances to permit her son to advance his career as a writer by taking graduate work. When Tom refused to make law his career, W. O. was greatly disappointed since through Tom he had hoped to fulfill his own lifelong desire to be a lawyer. This may have led to the final break in their formerly close relationship.

The sense of the loss of his father was one of the important themes in Wolfe's writing. He himself designated it as one of the two main themes of his second book, *Of Time and the River*; Elizabeth Nowell considered it the major theme of all of his writing.

Why did Tom feel such a strong sense of loss? The objective evidence suggests that such a response was unwarranted. For although Julia Wolfe took Tom with her when she moved to the boardinghouse, Tom's father did not die at that point; he was still available, and after school Tom visited him often at his marble shop, and then went to the Woodfin Street house, where he had meals with W. O. and the rest of the family. Thus it might seem that Tom had little reason to feel that he had lost his father.

What Tom had lost was the wonderful sense of security gained from being the adored baby of the family. Both of his parents and several of his siblings spoiled him greatly during his six years at the Woodfin Street house. During this period, it was W. O. Wolfe who had been the dominant figure in the family, and it was his love which was warm, open, and uncritical. During those early years W. O. doubtless protected Tom from harm, solved his problems for him, and shielded him from Julia's excessive demands and from the teasing of his siblings. When Tom moved to the Old Kentucky Home, all of this changed. He saw much less of W. O., and of his siblings, and at the Old Kentucky Home it was Julia who was the dominant figure. Although Julia loved Tom as her "baby," it was a possessive love, with demands attached, rather than W. O.'s uncritical love. Moreover, at the boardinghouse Julia's need for money came first, so that she and Tom had the meanest of the rooms, and typically kept moving from one room to another with the result that Tom had no place to consider his own. Because Julia was kept very busy taking care of the house and the boarders, she had little time for Tom except in the evening, and then she expected him to fill the emotional void in her life caused by her unsatisfactory love relationship with her husband.

We can assume that as time passed, Tom's perception of W. O. gradually changed for a number of other reasons as well. In the early years, in an attempt to win Tom's love all for herself, Julia made many critical remarks about W. O., deriding him for his lack of success in business, for his drinking sprees, and for his whoring. This meant that at an early age Tom was confronted with the fact that his father was not the wonderful and seemingly perfect person that he had felt him to be. Then, too, as Tom grew older, he himself became aware of some of W. O.'s problems because of the scenes they caused. Finally, as W. O.'s health grew increasingly worse his behavior changed, and as he became morose and self-concerned he could not be the same loving, concerned father he had once been.

Thus in his writing Wolfe was not referring just to the father who died at the time Tom was twenty-two years old, but to the lost father of his childhood. Even in his last major work (published posthumously) in the Gant-Webber chronology, *You Can't Go Home Again*, he returned to this theme and indicated in the final pages that one of the things one can't go home to is the lost father of one's childhood, as well as to one's father's land of origin. The fact that Tom continually wished he could recapture life as it had been in those early years suggests that from the time he moved to the Old Kentucky Home, life was unpleasant for him, yet he was ill-equipped to do anything to change his circumstances.

Two of the most moving passages in Wolfe's writings relate to his sense of loss of his father. Both occur in *Of Time and the River*. The first is the account of the last time Eugene sees his father alive, when he visits him in a ward at the Johns Hopkins Hospital in Baltimore: Oliver Gant is slowly dying and Eugene (Tom) tries to reach through to his father, but does so only momentarily when Gant recounts some memories from his own childhood. But at the end of the visit Gant is unable to respond to Eugene as a father should; he kisses him perfunctorily and tells him to be a good boy. The other passage recounts the circumstances of Gant's death a year after this visit. In this scene, Gant finally expresses regret to his wife, Eliza (Julia), for the hard life he has given her. She is deeply moved by this admission, and they discuss their differences. Eugene does not arrive at home until after his father has died (but Wolfe described the events leading up to and including the death in poignant detail). Eugene then discloses his own reactions, describing how the only things that seemed real about his father's corpse were his tremendous, gaunt hands. After the funeral Eugene again leaves Altamont (Asheville)—as Tom did—knowing that he can never really return there, and that the place now holds little to draw him back. Both his father and his favorite brother are dead, and his favorite sister, Helen (Mabel), has married. This account clearly reflects Tom Wolfe's actual feelings after his father's death. He could not be happy with his niggardly mother, and Asheville had become a sort of ghost town for him, haunted mainly by the ghosts of W. O. and Ben Wolfe.

There was much about Thomas Wolfe's life style that was closely patterned after that of his father. The zest for life, the enormous appetite and interest in food, which he recounts ad infinitum in each of his books, the propensity to become the rhetorical, declaiming actor on a stage, the tendency toward alcoholism, the periods of intense elation followed by periods of near-psychotic despair, the love of books and poetry, are all characteristic of W. O. Tom's strong sex drive, coupled with an inability to form deep affectional relationships with women, his tendency to see women as either madonnas or whores—mostly the latter—also reflected the pattern of W. O.'s life. Though Tom inherited certain qualities from his mother's family, as will be seen later, he was undeniably his father's son in many ways, both good and bad. His literary leanings were more those of his father than of his mother, but so also were his more neurotic character traits. That Tom patterned himself as much as he did after his father is probably due to the happiness of the first six years of his life when W. O. was the dominant figure in the family. After that, Julia Wolfe managed to dilute W. O.'s influence on Tom, but was never able to change its course radically.

To understand the affectional change in Wolfe's feelings toward his father, it is necessary to go beyond the obvious reasons. It is not enough to say that Tom was disillusioned to find that his father was not really a great, virile hero, but a very human person with real weaknesses, and later, a chronic invalid. Wolfe revealed what he was looking for in a father in a number of his letters—particularly those to his editor, Maxwell Perkins—as well as in his books. He had a lifelong yearning for emotional nurturance; he wanted to have someone to whom he could confide his troubles, and who would help him by providing emotional support and assistance. This dependency seems never to have left him, or at least not to have abated much until shortly before his death in 1938, and clearly W. O. was not able to respond to it as well as he once had after he became ill. It was this need that was fulfilled in part by his older brother Ben, and by his editor, Maxwell Perkins, who both became, for a time, father surrogates.

More than is normal, Tom needed to be constantly reassured that he was a superior, even a great writer. When he had written a book he would wait for reassurances that it was not just good, but brilliant; favorable criticism elated him, but the mildest of aspersions or just faint praise sent him into abysmal states of depression and melancholy. His ego was terribly sensitive, and as he said in numerous places, but particularly in *You Can't Go Home Again*, he thought that all men are driven remorselessly by the need for fame and love. It is certainly unlikely that all men seek fame; Wolfe was projecting his own need in this regard onto the rest of mankind. It was in fulfilling this need for Tom that W. O. was most lacking. He never could truly appreciate Tom's literary ability. Instead, he was disappointed that Tom was not studying to become a lawyer.

Despite the lessening of Wolfe's admiration for his father, he always retained a sense of appreciation for the man as he had been in the vigor of his manhood. Shortly after W.O.'s death, Tom wrote his mother a note, begging her, "For God's sake, Mama, save all Papa's letters," for he felt that his father had been a rare and unusual character, a great giant of a man. He said that he would not need to invent speech for this wonderful character when he wrote about him, for W. O.'s speech was almost epic in its quality and needed no fictionalizing. He went on to say that his father had been a great man, such as America would seldom see again, and that it was imperative that he be preserved for posterity through the medium of Wolfe's biographical writing. W. O. was still an idealized father figure for Tom, up until the time of his own death, sixteen years later.

Several other characteristics of the relationship between Wolfe and his father deserve mention. The first is the degree to which Tom displayed or copied his father's manic-depressive and paranoid personality traits. Tom Wolfe's strong tendencies toward manic-depressive and paranoid behavior are discussed in detail in chapter 9, Diagnosis. W. O. Wolfe's was almost certainly a classic manic-depressive personality; he was a man of extremes of mood, whose behavior was seldom temperate. On the one hand, he would rant and storm, carouse and drink, and buy up wagon loads of food for his family—more than they could possibly use. On the other hand, he would rave that in his "dying days" he was being abused by his wretched wife and children, and even by the patient jeweler who rented space in W. O.'s shop, listened to his tirades, and often brought him home from the saloon when he was drunk. Evidently he considered his dying days to have begun at a rather early age, for this phrase was frequent in his speech by the time he was fifty years old. Similarly, the rather paranoidal character of his thinking was apparent. He would often accost Julia with a phrase such as "Woman, you have sucked my life's blood," following this up with a long list of abuses he claimed to have suffered at her hands. Frequently, these were merely manufactured complaints which reflected his general dislike of the boardinghouse or the boarders, or of Julia's real estate exploits, which usually proved successful, and which W. O. seems to have both envied and despised. He must certainly have felt threatened by her success in business, since this is usually the husband's province.

While W. O.'s heredity and background were probably as good as Julia's—both of them being able to trace their forbears back for several generations in America—Julia continually implied that the Westalls, despite their abject postwar poverty, were aristocrats. This infuriated W. O., who raved about the stinginess and queerness of Julia's more successful brothers. In one generation they had moved up from impoverished conquered mountaineers to successful business men, and the disparity between their success and W. O.'s must have been underscored by the fact that he had started out in business with Julia's brother, Will, but had withdrawn at the end of a year because they did not get along with each other. Subsequently, Will became quite wealthy as a building contractor, while W. O. earned no more than a respectable income as a monument maker. Indeed, W. O. hated Julia's brothers, and the rest of her family as well, and he made this abundantly clear on any number of occasions. In his books, Thomas Wolfe recalls that W. O. would first practice the diatribes he intended to deliver in the evening before he went home. Once there, he would begin by lighting the fire and then he would "light into" Julia with one of his quite paranoid, and frequently unprovoked orations. These were not taken too seriously by the family, who tended to wait them out or to argue back; but they must have hurt Julia, although Tom felt that she took a certain pleasure in the fray, and in a quieter way gave W. O. back in kind. Many times, however, she was reduced to tears. W. O. saw many forces working in collusion to make his life difficult, a feeling to which Tom was no stranger in his later years. Since Julia, too, was a deeply suspicious person, it is hardly correct to attribute all of Tom's paranoid tendencies to W. O.'s influence, but certainly much of it can be ascribed to the pattern which W. O. set for his son by his dour attitude toward life and people, and by his almost daily tirades and invectives against an abusive world.

Another of W. O.'s habits which must have made an impression on Tom in his formative years was his father's constant repetition of the difficulty of his own childhood; at the age of eight he was working as hard as a man. Although much of this may have been true, the Wolfe boys probably did not like their parents' insistence that they become businessmen by their early teens. Each of them carried papers or the *Saturday Evening Post*, and sold produce from the family orchard and garden. They were also expected to "drum up" trade for the Old Kentucky Home by going down to the station when the tourists came in and passing out Julia's business cards. All of them were considered remarkable in the community for their perseverance as salesmen, but Tom, at least, found this type of activity deeply humiliating. In several of his books he wrote cynically about how all fathers must have trudged miles through the snow on their way to school, and must have done a man's work before they were old enough to wear long trousers—passages undoubtedly inspired by W. O.'s bitter reminiscences about his early assumption of adult responsibilities.

His family's emphasis on the importance of work was partially responsible for Tom's lifelong guilt feelings; he couldn't really relax and enjoy himself because he felt he ought to be working at all times.

The Theme of the Far-wanderer

One of the major themes in Wolfe's writing is that of the far-wanderer, Ulysses, or Antaeus, searching forever for a peaceful resolution of an inner conflict, a resolution that can only be attained by returning to his home. Wolfe saw wandering as the masculine part of life, and staying at home as the feminine. Many times in his writing, particularly during the period when he was working on *Of Time and the River*, the wanderer was searching for a father whom he could come home to, and this particular theme is discussed in chapter 4 dealing with Wolfe's relationship with his editor, Maxwell Perkins. At other times Wolfe depicted the father himself as Ulysses, or the far-wanderer, and the protagonist became Telemachus, the son, or sometimes Jason. The apparent confusion of the themes is a reflection of Wolfe's own dilemma for Tom was both searching for his father, the far-wanderer, and emulating him by becoming a wanderer himself.

Wolfe spent an unusually large portion of his life as a traveller. After he left for college, around his sixteenth birthday, he never lived with his family again for longer than a few months. He spent seven years at Chapel Hill and Cambridge as a student, and during this period also spent several summers away from home, once at Cambridge, and once at Norfolk. Then New York became his home though he never felt at home there. Altogether he made seven trips to Europe, between 1925 and 1936, and spent a total of about forty-four months living abroad. He also spent six months on two separate trips to the West, and in addition made many short trips to Vermont, North Carolina, and especially to southern Pennsylvania, which was his father's place of origin. Even when living in New York, Wolfe was restless, making numerous trips out of town for short periods. Sometimes he would take an overnight trip by train up to Albany for a short junket, perhaps to explore, or to visit girls.

Tom never owned a home of his own, or a piece of land. His possessions were kept to a minimum, and people like Miss Nowell or John Terry, who visited his apartments, noted that they always looked like the temporary headquarters of someone who was between trips. This inability to make a home for himself may have symbolized Wolfe's basic feeling that he was, indeed, a person without a home, and that having lost the one home that was important to him, no other could take its place. He seldom lived in an apartment or lodging for more than a year or two, and often it was just for a matter of a few months. When he took his almost annual trips abroad or to the West, he would give up his apartment and then find a new one on his return. Although even as an adult he sometimes called Asheville home, he seemed to want to stay away from it as much as possible, and by his early twenties he frequently wrote to his friends that he was unlikely ever to make his home there again. After he finished college, his family urged him to accept a teaching position at a small college in Asheville, but he refused, making it clear that Asheville offered nothing that would permit his growth, and that it was constricting and stultifying. He did go back to Asheville in 1937, but was unhappy there even during the two months that he managed to stay.

Wolfe came by his wandering naturally. Julia described her husband as coming from "a race of wanderers." "I never saw a man like that for wanderin'. I'll vow! A rollin' stone, a wanderer . . . forever wantin' to be up and gone. . . ."[4] As mentioned previously, W. O. Wolfe left home at fourteen, worked for a year as a mule-trainer in Harrisburg, then migrated to Baltimore, York, Raleigh, and eventually to Asheville, so that his was really a migrant personality. After his marriage to Julia he made trips to Pennsylvania, New Orleans, Florida, Chicago, and around 1899 he made a three-month trip to New Orleans, Texas, and the West Coast, presumably to recover from a case of incipient tuberculosis. This was a fair amount of travelling for a man of relatively humble circumstances in the late nineteenth century. Perhaps his urge to travel was even more significant than his actual number of trips. If Julia's description is accurate, W. O.'s restlessness was a continuous behavior pattern. His various trips to sanitaria and hospitals might also be added to the list of his travels; but it is difficult to say how much these visits represented voluntary or involuntary travelling.

Despite her protestations that she was a more stable person, Julia Wolfe herself also did a great deal of travelling. After she

4. "The Web of Earth," p. 250.

started the Old Kentucky Home she went to Florida almost every winter. Tom was taken along on these trips, and by his early teens had been to New Orleans, Knoxville, Hot Springs, St. Louis, and Washington as well. Julia's trips were motivated in part by her hope of finding relief for her arthritic condition, in part by her eagerness to participate in the land speculation going on in Florida, and probably in part by what she considered the educational quality of travel. Even in her old age she travelled every winter, to Florida, Washington, New York, or Boston. In an age when most families remained fairly close to their homes, the Wolfes were constantly on the go. Tom came quite naturally by his desire to wander.

Just how important this far-wanderer's theme was in Wolfe's thinking and behavior is best demonstrated by references to materials in his letters and books. As early as 1924, in writing to a friend, he compared himself to Odysseus looking for the enchanted isles, or for the lotus, which if eaten could cause him to sink into a drowsy oblivion.[5] In three letters to his mother between 1927 and 1929 he wrote that there was no likelihood that he would ever return to Asheville, which offered no rest and no inspiration. In his note to the publisher's reader, which accompanied the manuscript of *Look Homeward, Angel,* he identified two essential themes or movements. The one, an outward movement, described the efforts of a youth to find freedom, release, and loneliness in a new land; this was contrasted to the downward movement into the buried life of a family in its cyclic movement through genesis, union, decay, and dissolution.

By the time Wolfe began to work on *Of Time and the River,* the wandering theme had become one of the principal themes of his book. In his prologue, he starts the book with the phrase ". . . of wandering forever and the earth again . . . Where shall the weary rest? When shall the lonely of heart come home?

5. *Letters,* p. 64.

What doors are open for the wanderer?" In several letters to Wheelock and Perkins in 1930 he compared the first section of the book to the Antaeus legend and mentioned "the two things that haunt and hurt us: the eternal wandering, moving, questing, loneliness, homesickness, and the desire of the soul for a home, peace, fixity, repose. . . ."[6] The latter force is exemplified in the love of a woman, or what he called "the female principle—the earth again."[7] He told them that wandering seemed to him to be the more male thing, and mentioned the images of the pioneers, the explorers, the Crusaders, and the Elizabethan mariners, adding that wandering was not only the masculine thing, but also represents the quest of a man for his father.[8] He said "I tell why men go to sea, and why they have made harbours at the end . . . we all know we are lost, that we are damned together. . . ." He then mentioned Poseidon, god of the sea and eternal wandering, the father whom Antaeus, the son, searched for but never saw, but who eventually saved Antaeus.[9] In 1931 he wrote to Henry Volkening that he now found himself, as he had been ten years earlier, "a wanderer on the face of the earth, an exile, and a stranger, and, by God, I wonder why!" So while at times he thought he understood his restlessness, at other times he was puzzled by it. The next year he wrote to his uncle, Henry Westall, about his tendency to roam the earth "in search of a peace and security which I must find inside me. . . ."; and he told Julian Meade that he realized he had spent half of his life wandering the earth, impelled by a hunger and desire whose meaning was hard to describe except as a "struggle to find some . . . better life on earth, some sense of peace, certitude, and direction in my own life and some answer to the riddle of this whole vexed swarming and tormented world. . . ."

At the end of *Look Homeward, Angel*, Wolfe has Eugene

---

6. Ibid., p. 234.
7. Ibid., p. 243.
8. Ibid., p. 244.
9. Ibid., p. 279.

tell Ben's ghost that he wants to find a happy land, and an end to his hunger. Ben tells him that neither really exist in the world, and says "*You* are the world,"—that he would have to look within himself for the happiness he sought. At the beginning of *Of Time and the River*—which resumes where *Look Homeward, Angel* left off—Eugene (Tom), about to depart for Harvard, is waiting at the railroad station, excited and full of anticipation at the magnificent prospect before him. In *The Web and the Rock*, George Webber (Tom) reveals that his life has been primarily devoted to an escape from home. He describes his wanderings, comparing himself to Jason without the Golden Fleece, and explains that during his sojourn in Europe he seldom stayed anywhere for more than a few weeks, wandering from city to city, country to country, sometimes taking the next train to leave the station, or the next plane, regardless of its destination.

No place satisfied Tom for long. Several times while he was in Europe he took lodgings and remained there for some months, but this was usually when he had a concrete writing plan in mind, and was at a productive peak, pouring out his ideas. During the unproductive periods he was restless, and forever searching. At one point in *The Web and the Rock*, Esther (Aline Bernstein) asks Webber "And what is it that you want? Do you know? Could you say? Have you the glimmer of a notion what it is you want?"[10] Esther answers for George that he wants to have one woman, and to have a thousand women, to live in a dozen countries and to see the lives of all the people, and to look into her heart and tear her open, to devour her, and then forget about her! He recognizes that in one way he is going abroad in order to get away from Esther, even though he will always love her, but he realizes that his flight is also a desperate, childlike hope of es-

---

10. *The Web and the Rock* (New York: Harper and Brothers, 1939), chap. 41.

caping from himself.[11] At one point he tells himself that he is searching for his father's land—which is how he characterizes Germany—and he wonders whether it is his father's blood in his own veins that endows Germany with such a haunting fascination for him, and leads him to see it as "a kind of second homeland of the spirit."

In the mid-thirties, Wolfe began to show signs of a yearning to return to his native countryside. In 1933 he mentioned to LeRoy Dock that he had a yen to buy a cabin at Balsam, North Carolina, or else in southern Pennsylvania (W. O.'s birthplace), suggesting an evolving desire to return home. In the next year he wrote Robert Raynolds that he had an urge to buy a place in Vermont, which he had recently visited, and the same year he wrote nostalgically to Helen Moore about finding a place in western North Carolina. By 1936, he mentioned to his brother, Fred, that he would like to visit Asheville again if people there could accept him, given their indignation at his description of them in *Look Homeward, Angel.* This wish finally reached fruition and also frustration in the two visits in May and July of 1937. In July and August he rented a cabin at Oteen, a few miles out of Asheville. But he could not find the peace and quiet he sought, partly because of the somewhat disturbing contacts with his family, who tended to draw him back into their internal difficulties, and partly because he was such a celebrity that he could not be free of unwanted visitors who would drop in and stay for the rest of the day and half the night. As a matter of fact, during the last of August Wolfe abandoned the cabin and retreated to a hotel in Asheville.

The Asheville experiences of 1937 culminated in the growing insight that was to dominate his thinking for the final year of his life, and to find expression in the title of the book *You Can't Go Home Again.* After August of 1937 Wolfe mentioned this

---

11. Ibid., chap. 44.

theme in at least eight letters, and in the notes for his book. The book itself, of course, repeated the theme constantly. But what it meant to him was described most poignantly in one of his last letters to his old teacher, Margaret Roberts. He wrote, in March of 1938, that ". . . my discovery that 'you can't go home again' . . . went down to the very roots of my life and spirit—it has been a hard, and at times terrifying discovery, because it amounts to an entire revision almost of belief and of knowledge; it was like death almost, because it meant saying farewell to so many things, to so many ideas and images and hopes and illusions that we think we can't live without. . . ." But that same spring he wrote to his sister Mabel: "I got away [from Asheville] because I had to get away, there was no place for me at home, which is the simple brutal truth."

What psychodynamic purpose did all this wandering serve? Wolfe himself gave two reasons for it. The first was his need to escape from the tedious, the mundane, the constricting, exemplified most by Asheville, and later in life by his close relationships with Aline Bernstein and Maxwell Perkins. More specifically, although he didn't recognize that it was so, when the various parent figures of whom Tom had become fond became too controlling, and limited his freedom, he was unable to deal with the situation. Too dependent to take a firm stand on his own behalf, he felt guilty about doing anything that might hurt them since they had done so much for him. In such circumstances his typical reaction was to leave the scene, travelling to Europe or elsewhere, following the pattern that both W. O. and Julia had set for him.

The second motivation that he recognized was a search for inner peace, which he hoped to find in new surroundings. But this peace was impossible, because he always took his neuroses along with him—he could escape from nothing by moving on, though in a typically neurotic manner he always kept trying. Apparently the experience of anything novel was rewarding enough so that temporarily his inner turmoil would abate. He would become preoccupied with the new situation or new people, which would last for a few weeks at best. What he may have been searching for in his wanderings was someone on whom he could depend in a completely childlike way, a person who would love him completely and uncritically, and who would offer the security of his early childhood.

Whenever his writing was not going well or when his personal relationships were troubled, Wolfe would be overwhelmed by the sense of insecurity. He had a strong need to be recognized as an author of exceptional talent, and whenever this need was frustrated by his inability to write material that pleased him, he became upset. At such times he often felt that by going somewhere else he would get new ideas that would help him get past this hurdle. For a time he had the notion that by some kind of magic, just being in Europe would make him a better writer. Wolfe rationalized some of his wandering, perhaps legitimately, as a search for new material for his work. Certainly he made use in his books of much that he discovered on his trips, and he did this systematically, keeping rather full notebooks and diaries of his impressions. In the post-World War I period many young students of the arts thought that life was richer and more sophisticated in Europe and that one should experience this more interesting life to become a better artist. But those literary critics who try to account for all of Wolfe's restless wandering as a search for material, are unwilling to admit the psychological significance of this behavior, which perhaps in anyone but a writer would be labelled as escapism or a frenetic search for unattainable emotional peace and self-actualization.

2

BROTHERS, AND A PREOCCUPATION WITH DEATH

Frank

WOLFE'S FEELINGS TOWARD HIS BROTHERS RANGED FROM hatred to intense love and dependency. When Tom was born, Frank, the oldest brother, was twelve. Frank himself seems to have disliked all the members of his family, and his only reported reactions to Tom were negative. Tom, for his part, thoroughly despised Frank.

Both parents were fond of Frank when he was a child, and Mabel said that he was "the spoiled one." Julia Wolfe's affection for him continued throughout his life, and even though he often treated her abusively she always defended him, and gave him money, most of which he used on liquor or prostitutes. Frank "played hookey" from school, and eventually—when he was about to be paddled for some misdemeanor—he broke the principal's paddle and marched out of the ninth grade, never to return to school. By this time W. O. had become disgusted with Frank, beat him (according to Tom), and ordered him to get a job. Frank was never very successful at any work; he was constantly starting ventures, none of which amounted to anything. Positive that he was going to "make a killing," he would usually end up in debt, or would be tired of the work within a few months. In *Of Time and the River* Tom described Eugene Gant (himself) as ashamed to tell some of the men of Asheville that Frank was running a poolhall in Indiana, so he referred to it as a tobacco shop. It is ironic, but understandable, that W. O. came to detest Frank, who had all of his father's bad traits—especially his propensity for excessive drinking and sexual promiscuity—but none of his virtues. Both Turnbull and Kennedy refer to Frank as getting involved in minor delinquencies;[1] but in *Look Homeward, Angel*, Eugene (Tom) accuses Steve (Frank) of forging checks on his father's account, and in his letters Tom called him the "criminal element" of the family. Indeed, he wrote to his mother that Frank was emotionally "diseased."[2] His marriage was unhappy, and he quarrelled with his brothers-in-law. Psychologists would probably classify Frank as a sociopath.

Frank's typical life pattern was to attempt some venture for a few months, and when it was unsuccessful to slink home and in a paranoid way blame his failure on his family or some other noncooperative element of society. He would end up asking for a handout, which Julia usually gave him. Then Frank would hang around for a while, usually have an affair with one of the women boarders at the Old Kentucky Home, and make himself so obnoxious that finally even Julia would become exasperated and would remonstrate with him. Thereupon Frank would take offense and drift off to try another unsuccessful business venture. One of these incidents is recorded in *Look Homeward, Angel*. Steve (Frank) is hectoring and blaming his mother for the pains in his bad teeth, when Luke (Fred) comes in and, always quick to defend a woman in distress, starts to fight with Steve. Luke is getting the worst of it when Ben, his older brother, joins the

1. Turnbull, p. 10-11; Kennedy, p. 27.
2. Turnbull, p. 11.

fracas and quickly floors Steve. Meanwhile Eugene (Tom), still a small boy, stands on the sidelines wildly cheering his two brothers who, like St. George, are slaying the dragon.

It might be said of Frank that he had witnessed many of his father's debauches, and that because of the large number of siblings who followed him, he became almost totally self-reliant. In any case, his shaky ego could not see him through the stresses involved in making any undertaking a success. His compensations were obvious; he dressed flashily, and boasted inordinately and inaccurately about his important contacts.

In *Look Homeward, Angel* and *Of Time and the River*, Wolfe painted a very critical picture of Frank. In 1937 when the Wolfe clan held its family reunion and "rite of forgiveness" for Tom, Frank was also present. This was probably the last time they saw each other, for after the publication of *Look Homeward, Angel* Tom made only two trips to Asheville, both in 1937. By this time his family's recriminations against Tom for publicizing their shortcomings had abated as the Wolfes began to bask in his reputation as a successful writer. Turnbull reports that when Frank asked Tom why he had been portrayed so unsympathetically in the book, Tom was embarrassed. Wanting to smooth over hard feelings, he explained to Frank that every novel needs an antihero, and that he had used the character of Steve—a fictionalized exaggeration of Frank—to fill that role.[3] If this was meant to be placatory, Tom certainly negated its effect in the course of another incident (described by Turnbull) during this same family reunion. Frank had been having difficulty in swallowing because of an esophageal constriction, and one day as Tom watched Frank trying to eat he suddenly asked his brother why he didn't just drink enough to kill himself. "After all," he said, "you don't amount to anything. You don't do anything but drink—you never tried to make anything of

3. Ibid., p. 278.

yourself. . . . Why don't you die?" Yet—and this illustrates Tom's ambivalence, or perhaps remorse for his rejection of Frank—Tom then arranged for Frank to be x-rayed, and expressed great relief when a diagnosis revealed that Frank's condition was due not to cancer, but to arthritis.[4]

Certainly no positive influences on Wolfe could be attributed to his brother, Frank. There was, perhaps, the negative effect of having to live with an unpleasant and difficult brother, but there is really no evidence that Tom was unduly influenced by Frank, who was often not home when Tom was most impressionable. And fortunately, there were several affectionate siblings for Wolfe to identify with, so that it was fairly easy to forget Frank, except for the brief periods when he was making a nuisance of himself. Perhaps a rivalry existed with Frank for Julia's affection, since she seemed to have favored both Frank and Tom more than the other children. In Frank's absence, Tom was unquestionably Julia's favorite.

Fred

Fred Wolfe, who was Tom's nearest sibling in age, was six years older. Possibly Fred should have been his closest brother emotionally—and in later life this was true—but as young boys they had ups and downs in their relationship. They shared some mutually pleasant experiences, such as the annual visit to watch the circus being set up so nostalgically described in "Circus at Dawn" in *From Death to Morning*, but at other times they quarrelled. Much is known about Fred, the last surviving member of the Wolfe family. Tom wrote many letters to him, and in the last eight years of his life they shared a rather understanding relationship; more than to any other member of the family, with the possible exception of Mabel, he could confide his deepest

---

4. Ibid., pp. 278, 344.

feelings to Fred with some assurance of being understood. (While Tom also wrote many letters to his mother, as an adult he found it difficult to discuss significant personal matters with her.)

As a boy, Fred was the jolly, cheerful member of the family. Something of a clown, he always seemed happy himself, and tried to make others happy. He was rather goodlooking, and very extroverted. In his teens he managed the local agency for the *Saturday Evening Post*, and employed Tom as one of his salesmen. Fred was described by businessmen as a born salesman, who used the method of hard sell, and was not beyond wearing out his prospective client until the man would give him a dollar just to be left alone. But the businessmen of Asheville admired his enterprising spirit. Tom's personality was very different from Fred's, and he found sales work rather frightening and highly distasteful. Also he resented Fred's authoritarian way of giving him orders. It was Fred's tendency to try to dominate his younger brother that seems to have caused most of the friction between them.

Fred finished high school and entered Georgia Tech in order to study engineering. Tom recounts that Fred did everything well but study, and after several years he dropped out. Later he studied at Carnegie Tech, and finally returned to Georgia Tech and earned a college degree; his adult life was spent as a salesman, and Tom repeatedly remarked that he was one of the world's best.

Fred was inordinately fond of Mabel, for she really acted as a mother surrogate for him. He often defended her, remarking how patiently she had cared for their father both before and during his illnesses. Mabel considered that she and Fred were the Wolfes of the family, whereas she called Frank, Effie, and Tom the Westalls; Ben was more or less unclassified although, because he was generous, she gave him some credit for being a Wolfe at those times when she herself was feeling more magnanimous. There is no doubt that Fred was much attached to Mabel. He did not marry until he was forty-nine, many years after Mabel had married, and after Tom and W. O. had both died.

Fred showed certain neurotic traits in childhood. Like Mabel (and also Tom, when excited) he stuttered, and he remained a bedwetter until his teens. These are signs that the overtly cheerful personality was attained at a considerable emotional cost to himself.

The early sibling rivalry between Fred and Tom tended to continue into their adult lives, and even as late as 1923 Tom wrote to Mabel that while he loved Fred dearly, and thought that they had much in common, they could not stand being together for more than a few days without getting into a brawl. Tom could not accept Fred's controlling behavior (although he could accept Ben's advice), perhaps because he did not perceive in it as large a degree of paternal affection. In many ways Fred was the more mature brother who was given more responsibilities; when W. O. bought an auto it was Fred who was permitted to drive it, though W. O. complained endlessly that Fred would kill them all with his reckless driving. Perhaps significantly, Tom never learned to drive a car, although in *Of Time and the River* there is a scene in which Eugene, now in his twenties, asks permission to drive a car for which Eliza (Julia) has paid $2,000, but which has never been moved from the garage. Significantly, Eliza refuses to let Eugene drive, saying "Why, you're my baby! . . . I'd be afraid to let you. . . ." This tendency of both W. O. and Julia to allow Fred to do things that Tom wasn't permitteed to do probably reinforced the rivalry between the two boys.

Fred apparently showed some paternal affection for Tom, who said in *Look Homeward, Angel* that it was Luke (Fred) who got him released from a South Carolina jail when, as a college boy, he was picked up with some friends who were accused of drunken driving. In the book, Eugene gets into a violent fight with the police, because he believes that he is going to be put in a cell with a Negro prisoner. He is too drunk to be sure that this is really true (and it may have been an hallucination). As Wolfe tells it, Luke, who was to meet Eugene in the same town and take him to visit his sister, Daisy (Effie), is the one to rescue him. According to Turnbull, however, Fred also was drunk, and became enraged at the supposed insult to white Southern manhood, and he too was jailed, until finally another friend had to rescue both brothers.[5] On another occasion, when Fred was in the Navy and stationed near Norfolk, Tom obtained permission to go to the same area to take a summer job. He worked at various jobs as a laborer and earned some money, but when his money gave out he went for days without having anything to eat. When Fred finally found out that Tom was in the area, and what his condition was, Fred treated him to a hearty meal, scolding him for not having asked for help earlier. But Tom seems to have felt that although Fred was most generous with his gifts, he always expected something in return, and Tom found this sense of obligation somewhat annoying.

The camaraderie which was partially latent during Tom and Fred's youth tended to flower in later life after Ben's death. Fred was having trouble earning a decent living as a salesman because of the Depression, and although he had a girlfriend in South Carolina, he had to take a job in Pennsylvania because he could not find one closer to home. During this period Fred made frequent visits to New York to see Tom, and in a way it was Tom who now took over the more nurturant role, showing Fred the city, encouraging him with his work, and offering to lend him money, of which Tom himself had almost none. Occasionally both brothers visited the area around Gettysburg from which their father, W. O., had originally migrated, and sometimes they went as far as Washington to visit Mabel. At this period in their

---

5. Ibid., p. 76.

lives their relationship seems to have been affectionate and genuinely fraternal.

Two other events which suggest that Tom and Fred became rather close as adults occurred when Tom was in his mid-thirties. In 1937, when Tom planned to spend the summer in a cabin at Oteen, near Asheville, he wrote Fred a long and confidential letter, entreating his help in warding off excessive attention from well-meaning friends and relatives. Though Fred did not prove very successful, it is significant that Tom had turned to him for help. Tom made a point of mentioning that his mother could not understand his difficulties in trying to carry on his creative work, or his need for privacy, but he hoped that Fred would understand and would try to explain the situation to the others.

At the last Fred proved his devotion to Tom during the latter's final illness in Seattle, Washington. Tom, although exhausted after covering 5,000 miles in a two-week auto trip through most of the western National parks, took a boat trip to Victoria, British Columbia. On the boat he drank from a bottle which he shared with a "cold shivering wretch" who was actually suffering from influenza or pneumonia. Tom soon contracted a severe case of pneumonia which was not made any better by the fact that, typically, for the next five days he holed up in hotels in Vancouver and Seattle without getting medical help. When his family learned that Tom was quite ill with pneumonia, Fred arranged to take a vacation, and crossed the country in order to care for his brother, who was by this time hospitalized. Fred remained with Tom for more than a month, until he had to return to his job. At that point Mabel replaced him, and found an apartment for Tom to use during his convalescence. However, they used it only one day, after which Mabel brought Tom to the East where he entered the Johns Hopkins Hospital. Here his illness was diagnosed as miliary tuberculosis of the brain and within a few days, on September 15, 1938, he died.

Even as adults, however, Tom and Fred did not always get

along in perfect harmony. During the last year of his life Tom reacted bitterly to something Fred had done. Tom had quarrelled with Maxwell Perkins, his editor, and had had no contact or communication with him since the spring of 1937. He spent the summer in North Carolina near his family and then returned to New York. During the next two or three months Tom felt so melancholy, largely over the break with Perkins, that he did not write his family a single letter; indeed, he did not even let them know that he had arrived in New York. When their letters to Tom remained unanswered, Fred and Julia wrote to Perkins asking him to let them know Tom's situation. Perkins replied that because of their present strained relationship, he himself had had no contact with Wolfe since the spring, and that he could not understand why Tom felt so angry toward him. Fred, in his typical manner, wrote back saying that he could not understand how Tom could ever feel hostile to Perkins, who had done so much for him, unless he were in fact suffering from some sort of mental hallucinations. All of this correspondence was forwarded by Fred to Tom, who was furious and wrote, but never mailed, Fred a critical letter telling him not to meddle in matters which he knew nothing about.[6] He then outlined in great detail the many ways in which he thought Perkins had abused his trust and confidence. The matter was eventually ironed out, and Tom continued to correspond with Fred, his mother, and his sister. But the incident and the letter show that even at the age of 37, Tom could on occasion fly into a rage with Fred.

Although Tom was capable, at least in his adult years, both of receiving love from Fred and of returning it, and although their relationship—unlike most of Tom's other relationships—did not end in recriminations and paranoid feelings on his part, there is little to negate our basic diagnosis that Tom Wolfe's personality was narcissistic. For while Tom never turned against Fred,

---

6. *Letters*, p. 664.

he also apparently never entered into a truly deep relationship with him. Fred was his closest surviving brother, generous, kind, and loyal, but if we consider the character of Luke—Fred's counterpart—in *Look Homeward, Angel* and *Of Time and the River* we find him portrayed as clearly having limitations. Lovable and well-meaning on the one hand, he is also depicted as bumbling, unable to understand life's finer things, and not a "deep" person. His eagerness to please blunts his judgment. For Christmas he gives Gant an assortment of liquors, apparently oblivious that it is the wrong gift for someone who cannot resist periodic drinking sprees. He defended his sister, and then launched into foolish and excessive praise of her. And because of his desire to ingratiate himself he could change his opinion whenever he perceived his listener wanted to hear a slightly different one. These are not heroic traits, and one senses that while Tom was fond of his brother he also found Fred irritating and condescended toward him. Nevertheless he felt more positive toward Fred than toward most of the people who came into his life.

Ben

The affectionate feelings that developed between Tom Wolfe and his brother, Ben, proved to be one of the most important influences on Tom's life. Benjamin Harrison Wolfe was the survivor of the fraternal twins; the other, Grover Cleveland, died at the age of twelve. Ben was eight years older than Tom, but according to their mother they developed an affinity for each other from Tom's birth.[7] Mabel said that Ben could handle Tom more easily than any of his other brothers or sisters. Ben was the quiet, dignified, solemn member of the family, who showed neither the flamboyant characteristics of W. O. Wolfe, nor the

7. Turnbull, p. 12.

parsimony of the Westalls. Why he became the one who "moved like a ghost in their midst," as Tom put it, is a little uncertain, but it may have been because his twin, Grover, was a lively, exuberant, extroverted, and handsome child, whom both W. O. and Julia had described as "the best of the lot," when he died. Grover is reported to have been his father's favorite, a position which Fred was to assume after Grover's death. Perhaps Ben suffered because he felt that he was less loved than Grover; or possibly he developed an unconscious sense of guilt over Grover's death, as sometimes happens if a child has unrecognized hostile or death wishes toward a relative who later dies. At any rate, Ben became a somewhat misanthropic person, critical of all of the family except Tom, and hostile without being abusive or mean. He seemed to feel like a stranger in the midst of the family, and it appears that Julia tended to reject him. Like many rejected children Ben was apparently always trying to win acceptance from the family. It was he, for instance, who always fixed broken things around the house—typically without any publicity. He was also quite generous, and of all the family, the most regular in remembering the birthdays of the others with gifts, sometimes small, but always well chosen. Ben was boyishly nice looking, and women were generally fond of him and felt protective toward him.

According to Mabel, Ben had a good mind, but he may not have done well in school for Tom reported that he was a poor reader. They sometimes shared a room, and Ben would rather haltingly read the stories of Ring Lardner to Tom. Perhaps because of his poor reading, Ben dropped out of school in the ninth grade, although he later regretted this and during the last year of his life, according to Tom, took correspondence courses in an attempt to finish his schooling. After quitting school Ben worked briefly for his father, but did not enjoy the work. He wanted to work on a newspaper and found a job with the local one on which he held various positions, working as a reporter, in the advertising department—where his personal charm served him well in selling space for advertisements—and finally as circulation manager. In 1918 he took a job as circulation manager for a paper in Winston-Salem which he left because he wanted to enlist in the services. Though he tried three times he was rejected each time, apparently because of his bad lungs. He smoked incessantly and probably had had tuberculosis. Mabel said he was hump-shouldered and hollow-chested, very thin, and had a sallow skin and acne. He often worked long hours at night on the newspaper, and Wolfe reported in *Look Homeward, Angel* and *Of Time and the River* that Ben was often up by three in the morning to get to his work.

Ben's love life and his sexual behavior were much more subdued than either his father or older brother. He had quiet and rather intense affairs with several older women, who in turn loved him quite deeply. It is probably significant that he had not married by the time of his death at the age of twenty-six, although his then current mistress, "Mrs. Pert" in *Look Homeward, Angel*, apparently would have liked to marry him.

The close bond between Tom and Ben began when Tom was a very small child, and Ben became, for Tom, the big brother, father surrogate, filling the role that W. O. abdicated sometime during Tom's youth. Because of his strong need for love, Ben turned to the child, who responded warmly. It was as if all the paternal feelings of the maturing youth were directed toward this eight-year-younger brother. This phenomenon is not an uncommon one; the tendency of young men to father younger siblings or other youths is as natural as the tendency for girls to mother their dolls, or their baby siblings. Ben seemed to feel that it was he who must protect the child in the den of wolves, and he did so vigorously. Apparently he didn't want Tom to be treated as he had been. Ben's relationship with his mother was not a good one, for he deeply resented Julia's penuriousness, and many times criticized her for not caring adequately for Tom. "For

God's sake, Mama, can't you give the boy a clean shirt at least once a week!" was the sort of upbraiding which is often quoted by Tom in *Look Homeward, Angel* and *Of Time and the River*. The most memorable of these reported events concerned a pair of shoes which Ben had bought for himself, found too tight and uncomfortable, and so quickly discarded. This was sheer waste in Julia's eyes and she persuaded Tom to start wearing the shoes, even though his feet were already larger than Ben's. Julia rationalized that the shoes would stretch, but they did not, and although Tom bravely continued to wear them for several weeks, and was, in fact, quite proud of the fine leather, they were beginning to cripple his feet. Finally enraged, Ben tore the shoes off Tom's feet, and offered to buy shoes for the boy himself if Julia was too stingy to do so. Typically Mrs. Wolfe never did concede that it was not a waste of good money to discard the fine shoes, while Tom, with his usual penchant for exaggeration, suggested that his feet had been permanently damaged by the incident.

Ben's paternal feelings are revealed in another touching scene, reported in *Of Time and the River*, on the occasion of Eugene's (Tom's) twelfth birthday. At that time Eugene is described as working part-time as a newsboy, while Ben has already become a circulation manager. Ben hands Gene a package, and when Gene seems puzzled, says "Open it, fool!" Gene does so and finds a handsome gold watch inscribed "To Eugene Gant, Presented To Him On His Twelfth Birthday, By His Brother, B. H. Gant October 3, 1912." When Gene, overwhelmed, tries to thank Ben, the latter responds with, "Oh for God's sake! . . . Now . . . try to take good care of it and don't abuse it!" Ben's generosity was usually cloaked by a gruff manner, but his affection was deep and real, and apparent to all of the family.

Ben would give Tom money and presents, would straighten his tie, or tell him to stuff in his shirt, and perform many other fatherly ministrations. While he was at college Tom wanted to get a summer job in Norfolk, and it was Ben who persuaded the family that Tom should be allowed to go, and who gave him some extra money. Similarly, when Tom (Eugene) acquired a venereal infection after his first visits to prostitutes in Durham (Exeter), it was to Ben that he confided his painful circumstances, and Ben, without any lectures or reproaches, took him to the doctor. But interestingly, Tom would not permit Ben to be present during the medical examination.

During the last two years of Ben's life, after Tom had gone to college, they saw each other occasionally and shared a room at the Old Kentucky Home for brief periods. Once Ben invited Tom to visit him in Winston-Salem. By this time Ben had become even more misanthropic, and especially bitter toward his family, and this bitterness took the form of encouraging Tom "to get everything he could" from their parents. According to Tom, Ben constantly reinforced the idea that W. O. and Julia actually had plenty of money, and that Tom should not believe their tales of inability to pay for his educational and other needs.[8] Ben took the position that their parents had denied the other children their opportunity to get an education and make something significant of themselves, and that Tom was the family's last chance, that it was his right and duty to get all the education he could. Obviously Ben was projecting his own frustration, but he was probably correct in his assessment of his parents.

In 1918 Ben's unsuccessful efforts to enlist in the services prompted him to visit a doctor to find out about his physical condition. Once again he was told that his lungs were in poor condition, and that he was medically unfit for military service. This seemed to depress him seriously and Tom quoted him as questioning the doctor about the meaning of life. During the influenza epidemic of 1918 Ben became ill. When a doctor was finally called, he seemed to improve, but then he contracted

8. Ibid., p. 28.

pneumonia and on October 20, he died. Tom, Fred, and Mabel reproached Julia because she had delayed calling a doctor and had not given Ben much attention at first. Not until late in the illness did she move him from a small room at the Old Kentucky Home to a larger one with a fireplace, and although for the last week of his illness another doctor and nurses were engaged, the family felt that by then it was too late.

Tom had been called home from college and was there for the last couple of days. He was profoundly shocked and grieved by Ben's death, and described it in one of the most beautiful and touching death scenes in American literature in what is really the climax of *Look Homeward, Angel*. In 1935 he dedicated his book of short stories to Ben, and significantly it was entitled *From Death to Morning*. One of the stories, "Death the Proud Brother," posits the premise that death, rather than being a dreaded spectre, is really the proud brother who comes to take men from an unhappy existence to a glorious and heroic state of rest and surcease from care. At the beginning Tom tried to deny that Ben had died. When he returned to college he wandered for many nights in a state of deep depression, trying to puzzle out the meaning of life, and of Ben's death. Apparently by 1928 he had become reconciled to Ben's death, for he concluded *Look Homeward, Angel* with a scene in which Eugene is seen wandering alone in the town square in Altamont (Asheville), late in the night, and on the porch of his father's marble shop encounters a stranger who proves to be Ben's ghost. The man denies that he is a ghost and insists that he is Ben. Eugene is puzzled by this paradox, but accepts it, and the two converse about the meaning of life. Again Ben tells him to take from life all that he can get, and not to look for any future in Asheville, because he will not find it there.

What were the psychological dynamics of the relationship between Ben Wolfe and Tom? They seem clearly to have been those between father surrogate or big brother, and son or little brother. At a deeper level it is apparent that Ben provided nurturance for Tom's strong dependency needs, and Tom provided affectional response to a brother who felt rejected. From the earliest years Tom was more dependent than the average boy, and as he began to find himself different, not only from the typical small-town Southern boys of Asheville, but also different from the strange, teasing, quarrelling Wolfe clan, he apparently needed more and more to find someone who could support his ego, could make him feel that he had some worth, and that he could become someone of significance. Ben fostered these sentiments, and also offered love and affection without strings attached, which is what Tom needed. Tom, in turn, gave Ben devotion and affection, along with a feeling of fatherhood which he did not experience elsewhere. All the evidence suggests that, except perhaps for his very early years, Tom loved Ben more than he did even his mother. Later in his life only two other people—Aline Bernstein and Maxwell Perkins—evoked a response from him which approached the intensity of what he had felt for Ben. But from these two people he eventually broke away in a reaction of neurotic hostility and aggression. Only toward Ben, of all the people he ever knew, can it be said that Tom was able to feel unattenuated love. Whether this would have continued had Ben lived longer is hard to say. Since Tom always tended to find shortcomings in his idols, and indeed, in all the people he knew, perhaps he would eventually have decided that Ben, too, had clay feet. However, Ben was to remain the one unmarred love in Tom's life, and the one person toward whom he could feel deep affection and no hostility. In Tom's later life the relationship became somewhat idealized and sanctified; for it is probably easier to show undying devotion to a dead brother, than to a living, demanding person. Tom's major problem was that he could not respond in a satisfactory way to anyone who expected him to reciprocate their affection. Ben, perhaps, never had a chance to reach this level of interaction with Tom, and so their filial-fraternal love could remain beautiful and everlasting.

Wolfe's Preoccupation with Death

One of the most prominent themes in Wolfe's writing is death. His preoccupation with this topic is apparent in all of his books, and frequently also in his short stories, many of which were gathered together into *From Death to Morning*. W. M. Frohock considers Wolfe the most eloquent writer of the century on this topic, but also notes that it was an obsession with him.[9] Miss Nowell thought that Wolfe's account of Ben's death comprised his most beautiful writing, and several literary critics have discussed the frequency and meaning of the theme in Wolfe's work.[10] He wrote eloquently about the deaths of Grover, (twice) Ben, W. O. Wolfe, one of his college roommates, and Aunt Maw. In addition to these highly personal accounts of death, he also wrote about numerous deaths of people he had not known well, but merely observed in dying. One story, "Death The Proud Brother" reports four such deaths in New York. More than just recounting death in very poignant terms, Wolfe also philosophized about it, and some of his apostrophes to death are highly lyrical. His most fully developed philosophical reflections on death are to be found in "Death The Proud Brother," where he addresses a triumvirate of Proud Death, his stern companion Loneliness, and their sister, Sleep. For him the juxtaposition of these three phenomena, one psychological and the other two physical, was deliberate. Wolfe saw them as similar states, differing in degree rather than in kind. Sleep was like a short death,

---

9. W. M. Frohock, "Of Time and Neurosis," *Southwest Review* 33, (1948): 349-60.

10. See J. R. Reaver and R. I. Strozier, "Thomas Wolfe and Death," *Georgia Review* 16 (1962): 330-50.

but not just a pale image, as the term Sister Sleep might imply, for sleep was also called the great dark horses galloping softly over the land. He pointed out that in sleep we lie naked and alone, just as we do in death. Also in "strange and beautiful" sleep we are united at the heart of darkness. While Sleep is the sister of Death and his stern comrade, Loneliness, she is also mild and magnificent, the bringer of peace and dark forgetfulness, healing, and an enchantress offering a "merciful anodyne of . . . redemption." Death, loneliness, and the search for a father were popular literary themes at the time, and Wolfe's preoccupation with them can in part be explained by this.

For Wolfe, Loneliness was perhaps the most dreaded of the three companions, and he called it "dark brother and stern friend, immortal face of darkness and night." But Loneliness was also an heroic friend, blood-brother of Proud Death. His companionship with Loneliness was brave, glorious, and triumphant, because Loneliness had brought him invincible strength, deathless hope, and triumphant joy, as well as confidence for renewed attacks upon the ramparts of the earth. Although of the three Tom seemed to fear Loneliness the most, he also seemed to find a sort of perverse strength in it, which drove him to seek it out, as if he received some spiritual nourishment from the agony it caused him.

The same sort of ambivalence marked Tom's feelings about death. He dreaded it, and was preoccupied with it, but at times admired it. He saw in Proud Death a source of mercy, love, and pity, the bringer of compassionate pardon and release, the retriever from exile of desperate homeless men. Death offers a "stern provender to stay the hunger that grows to madness in search of never-found goals." It honors in glory not just famous men, but also those whose lives were nameless and obscure, because it gives them the awful majesty of its own grandeur. Tom said to Death "I have seen and known you so well, and have lived alone so long with Loneliness, your brother, I do not fear you any longer, friend. . ." (p. 68). Nothing shabby on earth could alter the immortal dignity of proud death for Wolfe, and in *The Web and the Rock* he wrote "Death bent to touch his chosen friend with mercy, love and pity, and put the seal of honor on him when he died."

Wolfe's fear of death may have had its origin in Grover's death, which occurred when Tom was only four years old. As Tom describes it in *Look Homeward, Angel*, Eugene is awakened from sleep by Helen (Mabel) and taken to see Grover's body lying on the "cooling boards." At first he doesn't understand, but then he suddenly recognizes that the still, white form is the same as the loving older brother with the dancing brown eyes, and he is upset. This in itself need not have been an overly traumatic experience. But his parents, who had been especially fond of Grover were quite deeply upset by his death. His mother kept repeating, "He was only twelve." So Tom learned that death can come early, and that when it does it is a tragedy. This early experience, then, had associated death with night and sleep. Julia Wolfe remained disconsolate about Grover's death all through the following winter, so Tom would have been impressed repeatedly with her sense of loss and tragedy. We know that Tom was her baby and that she was very fond of him; we know also that she had experienced the death of a child before, in the loss of her firstborn, so she may have said something to the effect that she hoped she would not lose Tom before he became a man. This is only speculation, of course, but it would be consistent with the rest of the dynamics of the situation. Julia was, herself, morbidly preoccupied with death, and was always talking about the deaths of her relatives.

The year before Ben died, Tom had been so much upset by the death from heart disease of a favorite college roommate, that he never again slept in the room they had shared in Chapel Hill. Tom's feelings about death would have been strongly reinforced by the death of his beloved brother, Ben, when Tom was only eighteen. Many times Tom mentioned to relatives or friends that Ben's death had been the most profoundly disturbing event of his life. The only comparable experiences were his breaks with Aline Bernstein and Maxwell Perkins. Eleven years after Ben's death, Tom told his sister Mabel that he had never forgotten Ben, and never would, and that Asheville had died for him when Ben died.

Apart from this deeply felt loss, there was the fact that the Wolfe family lived with the spectre of W. O.'s certain death for so many years. But although W. O.'s gradual deterioration depressed Tom, he was rather philosophical about it. He wrote to his mother that he was resigned to the probability of his father's death while he was away at Harvard, but could see no escape from the inevitability of the situation, even though the prospects "gouged [his] very soul." But after his father actually died, Tom seemed to brood a good bit about death and in 1923 he wrote to his mother about his distress regarding the mortal, perishable quality of man, and confessed that he dreaded each new year because it meant one less year in which to accomplish his life's goals. He felt that Ben and his father seemed so far away and almost unreal, although at times he also experienced their presence very vividly. Sometimes he felt that all of life seemed like a dream, and said "We soak our bread in tears and swallow it in bitterness. It seems incredible . . . that flesh that once I touched . . . is now unrecognizably corrupted in the earth." So for Tom, death played a significant role from his earliest years.

That Thomas Wolfe was afraid that he might die before he had a chance to write all he wanted to can be explained by several factors. First there was his exposure to the tragedy of early death. Second, there was his strong need to write and to prove himself to his parents and siblings. Third, there was his lack of understanding of the feelings that welled up in him, and his consequent conviction that it would take a long time to express them. And finally, he himself had spit up blood at Harvard and had written to his mother that he had some concern that he might have tuberculosis. Ben's early death, hastened by his having weak lungs, could have made Tom fearful of the same consequence.

In 1924 Tom wrote to his mother about his regret that "The golden years of my life are slipping by on stealthy feet at nightfall. . . . My life is like water which has passed the mill; it turns no wheel." He worried that his health might be crushed from him at any moment, and that life was brutal, with a tragic underscheme. Later that same year he told her that there was only one thing a brave and honest man need be afraid of, and that was death. He wrote that people who said they have no fear of death were liars, for death ends all of man's glories. By this time Tom was living in New York in one of the most lonely years of his life. But ten years later he was still writing her of his concern that though there were hundreds of things he had to say, he would not live long enough to say them.

In March of 1937 Tom once again began to fear that he had tuberculosis and made a new will. During the long, cold winter he had suffered more than his usual number of respiratory illnesses. Mabel remembered that on his visit to Asheville that year Tom spoke to Fred about his fear that he would not live long enough to finish his work, and *You Can't Go Home Again* concludes with a prediction to this effect. But Kennedy[11] says that the valedictory paragraphs of *You Can't Go Home Again* were actually written as the concluding passages of "I Have a Thing to Tell You," which appeared a little earlier in the book; and this would mean that they were written in the fall of 1936. Tom also had a very strong premonition of death during his last illness, in the summer of 1938. At that time he wrote to Max Perkins that he had "seen the dark man very close"; he didn't think he was too much afraid to die, but still wanted desperately to live, but as he said, "I've got a hunch. . . ." It was the last letter he ever wrote.

---

11. Kennedy, p. 437.

Wolfe's fear of death expresses the fatalism of someone who knows that the cards are stacked against him. Probably his frequent exposure to the deaths of those he loved, and his mother's constant talk of death, led him to feel, as he put it to Max Perkins, that he was, in fact, just a grain of dust. Given these fears of premature death, it is all the more paradoxical that Wolfe seems to have gone out of his way to neglect the elementary rules of preserving good health. He paid so little attention to his dress that he did not have heavy clothes to protect him from the winter weather. During his creative periods his obsessive need to keep writing led him to go on until he was exhausted. At such times he would not stop for meals or sleep, and even when he finally went to bed he would be so excited that he could not fall asleep. But if one is tempted to postulate a death wish, this can be countered with the evidence that runs through all his letters that he very much wanted to go on living so that he could go on writing, and so achieve great fame.

Actually, Tom's illnesses were usually minor—bad colds and fever, or the flu. It is pretty certain, however, that he had had tuberculosis at least once in his life before the terminal illness. Julia had always made light of illness, and Tom appears to have acquired this tendency; he visited doctors as little as possible, and ignored the advice they gave him. When he suspected that something might be wrong, he preferred to pretend that the problem did not exist. Thus, when he was extremely ill with pneumonia in Seattle, he waited days before calling for help. This reaction really constituted a sort of denial; if a problem was denied, perhaps it would go away. His delay in asking for medical help may also have been a function of his difficulty in making decisions. A final element may have been his paranoidal feelings about paying excessive fees.

Wolfe's preoccupation with death can be seen as deriving from one of his basic personality characteristics—his tendency to sink into frequent depressions, which was in turn fostered by his fear that he would not have enough time to complete the enormous body of work that he felt compelled to write to achieve fame. This preoccupation with writing, on the one hand, and his inability to relate easily to people on the other, isolated Wolfe from others and led him to suffer much loneliness. Eventually he personalized this loneliness and associated it with the Proud Brother, death. It is noteworthy that Wolfe chose the title *From Death to Morning*, and insisted, to Perkins, that the words appear in that order.[12] This title reflects the progression of a theme the development of which is reflected by the order in which the stories are arranged, starting with "Death The Proud Brother" and proceeding to "The Web of Earth," which Tom perceived as relating to the theme of eternal rejuvenation, as the generations replicate themselves through the reproductive process. In his other books as well Wolfe always depicted some concept of immortality, or an afterlife, as the sequel to his death theme. For a man who rejected formal religion, this seems like a significant vestige of his parents' combination of Episcopalian, Baptist, Presbyterian, and spiritualistic indoctrination. Ben's ghost was not the only one that returned to visit his relatives in Wolfe's books. Grover's ghost visits Oliver Gant (W. O.) when he is dying, and Eliza Gant (Julia) and most of her children claim on numerous occasions that they have seen or heard ghosts talking to them. Thus Wolfe seems to have believed in an afterlife, if not intellectually, at least emotionally. In *Look Homeward, Angel* he described death as "The last voyage, the longest, and the best."

---

12. Ibid., p. 282.

3

FRIENDSHIPS AND LONELINESS

THOMAS WOLFE WAS A LONELY PERSON MOST OF HIS LIFE. In childhood he had a few playmates, mostly neighbors. Once he moved to the Old Kentucky Home with his mother he found it harder to make friends. Occasionally he saw his old friends on Woodfin Street, but it was difficult for him to make lasting friendships with the children of Julia's boarders because they were an essentially transient group. Even at school Tom seemed friendless, perhaps because the other boys teased him about his long curls which Julia did not cut until he was nine. In general his relationships were less intense than is usual for most boys and when he was sent to a private high school, what remained of his early friendships faded altogether. Though he developed some friendships at the private school, one gets the impression that they were rather superficial, and that Tom was usually a hanger-on in the group, rather than a leader, or even a very active participant. Because of his height he was called "high pockets" by the other boys, and his bookish nature did not foster intimate friendships. Moreover, there were differences in social status, since the majority of the other boys in the private school were the sons of the more well-to-do professional or businessmen of Asheville. Writing about an earlier period—before he went to private school—Wolfe saw himself as a hunted and tormented child. He learned early to turn to books for consolation, but his bookishness stunted his development of social skills and deepened his isolation from his peers. At the North State Fitting School, Mrs. Roberts tried, rather unsuccessfully, to encourage Tom's participation in athletics; when he did take part in group sports it was with reluctance.

Wolfe's early years at college were not very different, and once again he found himself something of a misfit. More rural than many of the boys, less sophisticated, and a bit overawed by the significance of going to college, he found the first year difficult. He usually chose to live alone, although at times he had roommates, some of whom he disliked and some of whom he found acceptable. In his later years at college Wolfe became rather popular. He found that he had some of the same talent Fred had for clowning, and he joined everything he could get into. When war broke out many of the students left for the service, and Wolfe became a student leader—editor of the campus newspaper, chief writer for the humor magazine, an associate editor of the literary magazine, and one of the prominent actors in the newly formed and subsequently well-known group of Carolina Players. Nevertheless most of his friendships remained superficial.

While Wolfe tended to blame his loneliness on a sense of being different because of his height and size—he was six feet five inches tall when he entered college—his isolation was actually more a product of his own reclusive tendencies. During his later years he sometimes wrote or visited college friends, but most of the letters and visits were separated by long intervals. As he himself admitted, these were not so much intimate friends as acquaintances. After he became famous, former Carolina and even Harvard friends would look him up, and he might go out and drink with them, but he seldom maintained a steady relationship with them. One poignant example of his feelings about himself and his friends is illustrated in a letter he wrote to Benjamin Cone, a University of North Carolina acquaintance and later a textile manufacturer.[1] Cone wrote to Tom to congratulate him on the publication of the "Angel" story; he was one of the few friends to acknowledge its publication. Wolfe was touched and wrote back to invite Cone to visit him. In the letter, he recalled a day or two which they had spent together in Paris in 1924, and expressed regret that most of his former friends were now married and thus lost to him. He seemed to regard the marriage of a friend as if it were a personal betrayal.

An example of Wolfe's difficulty in retaining friendships was his relationship with John Terry, a friend from his years at the University of North Carolina, although in one letter Wolfe hinted that their college relationship had not been close, but became more so in Terry's memory, after Tom became famous.[2] Later Terry became an English professor at New York University, and so they were thrown together again. At one point Wolfe mentioned to LeGette Blythe that during this period he usually visited with Terry every week or two. It was Terry who eventually edited *Thomas Wolfe's Letters to His Mother*, and in his introduction recalls his first meeting with Mrs. Wolfe at Tom's apartment in New York in January, 1934. The description of the visit certainly gives one the impression that Wolfe and Terry were close friends, and Cargill reports that they were. Mrs. Wolfe also became quite fond of John Terry, and always asked to be remembered to him when she wrote to Tom. Terry greatly admired Wolfe and when the friendship broke up it was under complicated circumstances in which Terry was only indirectly involved. In 1936 Tom met a young Irish boy to whom he gave some manuscripts which the young man was to try to sell

---

1. *Letters*, p. 194.
2. *Letters to His Mother*, p. 323.

for him. Tom also became friendly with this man's family, as had Terry, whom Tom had introduced to them. The Irish boy did sell some of the manuscripts, but did not turn the money over to Tom and, even worse, destroyed some of the works—or claimed that he had done so—because he considered them obscene. Moreover, he threatened to encourage people in Asheville to bring libel suits against Tom. Wolfe felt obliged to protect his name in the courts, and was finally successful in doing so in a court hearing in the spring of 1938. When this unpleasantness began in 1936, Tom wrote to his mother that he could no longer consider Terry as his friend, or have anything to do with him, because Terry continued to maintain a friendly relationship with the boy's family. Tom's letter to his mother was strongly marked by that paranoid quality which was to pervade much of his thinking between 1936 and 1938. Clearly he expected his friends to be so loyal to him that they would cut themselves off from anyone with whom Tom disagreed. Naturally this friendship did not endure under these conditions.

After he became a well-known writer Wolfe carried on extensive correspondence with many people in the literary world and occasionally accepted their invitations. These visits were almost always enjoyable, and Wolfe wrote long letters to his hosts, but never seemed to be willing to give up enough of his time to maintain a really deep friendship with any of these people, either men or women. Somehow he could not relate well to most people except as one-night drinking or sleeping partners.

When Wolfe went to Harvard to study drama, he became more of a recluse than he was at Chapel Hill. The Harvard community was a more sophisticated one, and Tom felt somewhat boorish among the aesthetically-inclined young people who came to Harvard for Professor Baker's celebrated drama classes. He also felt unsure of his tastes in literature, since his classmates seemed not to share his evaluations of various authors. And here the social class barrier was even more of a problem for Tom than at the University of North Carolina. At Chapel Hill most of the students came from middle-class homes so that their values and financial status were not too different from Tom's. But at Harvard many of the students were from upper-class families of considerable financial means. In this new setting, Tom's principal advantage was his intelligence but he experienced more competition than at North Carolina University, so there was little to cause others to seek him out, or to value his friendship.

Kenneth Raisbeck

There were two exceptions to this picture of loneliness at Harvard. The first was Kenneth Raisbeck, who was Professor Baker's graduate assistant, and is identified in *Of Time and the River* as Francis or Frank Starwick. In *Of Time and the River*, Wolfe told of their remarkable meeting, when Raisbeck invited him to go to dinner. Tom's admiration for this sophisticated aesthete was unbounded, and they enjoyed an on-and-off relationship throughout Tom's stay in Cambridge. Later he described Raisbeck as the person whom he valued for the deepest friendship he had ever known, and in fact he did carry on a sporadic correspondence with this friend almost until the time of Raisbeck's death.

To Tom, Raisbeck was a person who exuded the quintessence of charm. When Tom wrote about him (in the late 1920s) he made him sound affected and effeminate, but whether he recognized these traits at the beginning of their relationship is unknown. In *Of Time and the River*, Frank Starwick (Raisbeck) is depicted as a somewhat moody person who would summon Eugene (Tom), often late at night, to go out on a drinking binge, and then ignore him for weeks. Eventually Eugene chides Frank bitterly for this, and for never revealing anything about himself or his past, whereas Frank is constantly plying Eugene with questions about his. Frank becomes abjectly apologetic and tells Eugene that he hadn't thought his own background could possibly be of much interest to anyone—that he comes from a Midwestern middle-class family, and that his great desire in life is to escape from the mediocrity which has engulfed his childhood. He wants above all else to be a famous writer, but is convinced that he lacks the spark of genius which he thinks Eugene has.

What Tom found very appealing about Kenneth Raisbeck was his sophistication and ability to cope with the people at Harvard. He acted as though he were in command of the situation, and even though this was only a facade, he impressed Tom with it. Tom, by contrast, felt quite uncertain of his behavior in this sophisticated setting, and was often ill at ease. Second, Raisbeck admired Tom's ability as a creative writer, and Tom needed this kind of appreciation very much, since his family tended to undervalue his ability. Moreover, praise from Professor Baker's assistant seemed especially significant. Enthusiasm for his creative work was to become a prerequisite for anyone who aspired to a friendship with Thomas Wolfe.

After leaving Harvard Tom wrote occasional letters to Raisbeck, usually recounting his own Bacchanalian exploits. In the summer of 1924 Raisbeck apparently stopped to visit Wolfe once on his way to Europe. Later that fall Tom made his first trip to Europe, where he spent several lonely months wandering in England and Paris, trying to write without much success. Then by chance he encountered Raisbeck on the steps of the Louvre and they resumed their friendship. Raisbeck was staying with two older women, one of whom had deserted her husband, and invited Wolfe to join the menage. Eventually Tom fell in love with one of the women (Ann in *Of Time and the River*) only to discover that she loved Raisbeck. But what made the situation even more painful was Tom's growing realization that Raisbeck was incapable of returning Ann's love because he was a homosexual. The foursome lived a Bohemian life for a month or so in and around Paris, when Raisbeck met Alec, a young French gigolo. The others became alarmed and finally disgusted, but decided to try to patch up their crumbling relationship by making a trip to the south of France or even to Spain, so that Kenneth and Tom could get some writing done. Then Kenneth told them that he intended to take Alec along, to which the others objected. Finally Wolfe decided to leave the group, partly because he was running low on money. He had less than a hundred dollars left, and the older girl (Elinor in *Of Time and the River*) hinted that he was not paying his share of the cost and it hurt Wolfe's sensitive pride to have this truth exposed. According to the account in *Of Time and the River*, on their last evening together Starwick asks to borrow some of Eugene's money, obviously to use it in some way connected with Alec. Eugene agrees to give him money, but then very deliberately toys with Starwick while he eats dinner and drinks some wine. Finally Starwick asks him what is wrong, and Eugene, in a blind rage, accuses him of being a "dirty little fairy," and beats his head against the wall until Starwick is unconscious. Eugene's fury intensifies as he realizes the irony of the situation that while Ann loved Starwick, the latter could not love her. After Eugene brings Starwick back to consciousness he is overcome with remorse and Starwick also tries to patch up their relationship. But Eugene feels that the situation is hopeless. A day or two later he leaves Starwick, saying "You were my brother and my friend [and now] . . . . You are my mortal enemy. Good-bye." As Pamela Johnson notes it is hard to believe that it took Tom so long to discover Raisbeck's sexual inclinations, but perhaps he chose to ignore his suspicions until the Paris encounter when Raisbeck's behavior forced him to acknowledge the situation.[3] Tom had always reacted with great hostility to what he called perverts, and now he acted with unnecessary brutality. To the psychologist, the intensity of his reaction

3. Pamela Johnson, *The Art of Thomas Wolfe* (New York: Charles Scribner's Sons, 1963), p. 63. Originally published under the title *Hungry Gulliver* in 1948 by Scribner's.

suggests an overcompensatory acting out, perhaps because of repressed guilt feelings about the affection he felt for Kenneth, or perhaps because he was jealous that Kenneth cared for someone else more than he did for Tom. Wolfe implied that his anger stemmed from his frustration over his unrequited love for Ann. There may have been some truth to this explanation, but it may also have been a rationalization.

In *Of Time and the River* Eugene and Starwick (Raisbeck) meet only one more time and then by chance. Actually in a letter to Mrs. Mildred Hughes, Tom also mentioned that several months after the quarrel they met in London by chance.[4] Sometime later they exchanged several letters and in one Tom responded to Kenneth's request that they reconcile their differences by saying that he would like to do so. Then in 1929 he helped to get Kenneth's play produced for a short run in New York. Raisbeck died in 1931 under highly suspicious circumstances which led to a police investigation. Wolfe wrote about it to his mother and to Fred, having heard the details from a mutual friend, Olin Dows, who had attended the police investigation. Raisbeck's body had been found in a cemetery in Connecticut, and Tom indicated that although the police suspected foul play, he and Dows were convinced that Kenneth died of natural causes. According to several of Wolfe's biographers, a first autopsy resulted in the finding that Raisbeck died of a cerebral inflammation, but a later autopsy revealed bruises, suggesting that the death may have resulted from a fight or a deliberate homicide. Wolfe wrote his mother and brother that the whole thing was a rather sad and sordid business, which he would tell them about the next time he saw them. He wrote to another friend that his own name had been found on Kenneth's list of best friends, but despite the innuendoes of a tabloid paper he refused to consider himself implicated in any scandal surrounding the circumstances of Raisbeck's death.

---

4. *Letters*, p. 101.

It is difficult to assess the importance of the relationship between Raisbeck and Wolfe. Tom surely enjoyed their companionship during his lonely days at Harvard, even though Kenneth was rather niggardly with his time, and always seemed to have different groups of friends to whom he turned. Turnbull suggests that Kenneth was probably engaged in homosexual activities at Harvard, but had to be more circumspect there than he later was in Europe in order to retain his assistantship.[5] He also experienced homosexual relationships in the southern part of France before going to Paris, and according to Turnbull was sent away by his host Philip Barry who became disgusted with these activities. In *Of Time and the River*, Starwick often hints at dark secrets in his life, especially about his experiences in Europe. That Wolfe felt genuinely betrayed by Raisbeck seems clear enough, but his letters show that he was willing to befriend Raisbeck again, although not necessarily to reestablish any sort of intimacy with him. Since the friendship with Raisbeck, according to Tom's own testimony, was one of the more meaningful ones in his life, it is indeed tragic that it was such an unsatisfactory one, and should have ended with the unfortunate breakup in France. These circumstances certainly did nothing to help Wolfe develop meaningful and affectionate relationships with other males.

To what extent did Wolfe fatalistically pursue the friendship knowing full well of the differences in their sexual proclivities? Typically, Tom was not a contriving person, and it may be that he really did not realize that Raisbeck was overtly homosexual until the events in Paris. Or if he did, he may still have been attracted to this man who seemed to him the most charming and graceful he had met in his life. That they were at one point good friends is undeniable. Turnbull reproduces a portrait of them, with Raisbeck seated, and Wolfe seated beside him with his hand on Kenneth's shoulder. The pose is a formal one, not un-

5. Turnbull, p. 90.

characteristic of the period, but it is significant that it is Raisbeck who appears to be the more dominant of the two. Kenneth was, of course, slightly senior in age and academic rank, but perhaps the photograph also reveals a tendency on Wolfe's part to adopt a somewhat more passive role. Considering the consistency of his passivity in many of his close associations it is likely that his attitude toward both males and females was passive and dependent reinforcing the diagnostic impression of his tendency toward narcissism.

Any indication that Wolfe engaged in homosexual activities has never been reported. On the contrary, his sexual behavior, like that of his father and his brothers, was vigorously and promiscuously heterosexual. It may be argued that this Don Juan behavior is really the overt manifestation of the latent homosexual trying to prove his masculinity—which neglects the possibility that a philandering male may also be trying to prove his heterosexual masculinity. Perhaps he had not passed completely through the narcissistic stages of psychosexual development, and that his promiscuous heterosexuality signified that his sexual needs were expressed in terms of sensuality rather than of relationship.

Olin Dows

The other Harvard friend about whom Wolfe wrote fairly extensively in *Of Time and the River* was Olin Dows (Joel Pierce). Dows, four years younger than Tom, was an art student at Harvard, but he had acted in some of the plays that Tom wrote and produced in Professor Baker's drama course. Dows admired Wolfe, and painted a picture of him. They had only a limited acquaintanceship at Harvard, but afterward, when Tom was teaching at New York University, Dows, who had subsequently gone to Yale, decided to do some work in New York, and wrote to Tom in June of 1924 asking him to get him a room at the

Hotel Albert where Wolfe was living. Tom arranged this, and later mentioned to his mother that he and Dows saw each other frequently that summer. Dows was the son of an enormously wealthy family who owned an estate at Rhinebeck on the Hudson River. According to Wolfe they were neighbors of the Franklin Roosevelts, the Delanos, the Astors and the Harrimans. In July, Wolfe spent one week at the estate, and later described the visit at length in *Of Time and the River*. Except for a slight knowledge of the Vanderbilt estate in Asheville, Wolfe had no previous contact with such people; his awe and amazement at their life style was obvious both in *Of Time and the River*, and in several letters to his mother and to his teacher, Margaret Roberts. The Dows were charming people and Wolfe became immediately fond of both Olin and his sister, and to some extent of his more reserved mother, and his distinguished father and grandparents. He was so impressed by the Dows that he devoted much time to a book about them—which was to have been titled *The River People*, and to have been published after *Look Homeward, Angel*. The book did not develop very satisfactorily, but the part dealing with the Dows comprises one of the more delightful sequences in *Of Time and the River*. Wolfe's descriptions of their enormous refrigerators filled with food attest not only to the Dows' very comfortable life, but also to Tom's oral preoccupation. Another feature of the Dows' home which impressed Tom greatly was their tremendous library. In *Of Time and the River* he recounts that he spent practically an entire night feasting his literary tastes on their wonderful collection of books.

Tom was quite fond of Olin Dows; his description of him, both in the book and in letters, depicts him as a gentle, cultured, charming, friendly person, who is so sympathetic to all living things that he does not even eat meat. However, he was no weakling, and Tom describes his athletic skills with enthusiasm. His letters suggest that he enjoyed Dows' company a great deal, although there was a certain constraint, apparently emanating more from Wolfe than from Dows, because of the tremendous difference in their background and financial resources. Dows already had enough money to make him one of the wealthiest bachelors in the country. At the end of the holiday in *Of Time and the River*, Wolfe has Eugene Gant (Tom), leave Joel (Olin) at the Rhinebeck station with an au revoir which implies that they can never develop the friendship that Joel offers because of the differences in their circumstances. Also, in the book Joel very generously offers to pay the expenses of a European trip for Wolfe. Actually Tom told his mother that Olin had offered to give him many expensive books. In *Of Time and the River* Eugene invites Joel to join him on his trip to Europe but Joel explains that he has to stay in America to help settle some differences between his parents. Wolfe also mentions such differences in a letter to his mother. But he liked both of Dows' parents very much, and the senior Mr. Dows apparently often took his son and Wolfe to the theatre and to magnificent dinners in New York. In the book, the leave-taking between the two young men is presented in a dramatic sequence as a sad farewell preordained by the social and economic gulf that separates them. This was more a fictional device than reality, however, for Wolfe's letters reveal that over the next half dozen years he made numerous visits to the Dows' estate, and one very hot summer occupied the gatekeeper's lodge for several weeks, taking his main meal at the family house, or having it brought to him at the lodge when he was very busy with his writing. Some of Wolfe's visits were made when only Olin was in residence at Rhinebeck, and Nowell says that the young men frequently argued enjoyably and at length about their interests in art and social philosophy.

Wolfe wrote a number of letters to Dows, but two of them are especially significant in understanding their relationship. In both of these letters Wolfe expresses concern that they seem to be drifting apart, and once he asks Dows whether he has said or done something to alienate him. At another point he says he does not know why Dows never seems to accept him fully. Apparently Dows also made frequent trips to Washington, and Tom may have visited him there at least once, and in turn invited Dow to visit him in New York on several occasions. It was also Dows who reported to Wolfe the events surrounding the mysterious death of Kenneth Raisbeck.

How deep was the friendship between Olin and Tom? Wolfe wrote his mother in 1927 "I like Olin Dows very much—a great person."—and a year later "He is a fine person and a true friend." And in writing to his former teacher, Margaret Roberts in 1927, he called Dows "almost as great a saint as you are." But the sense of constraint was always there. Referring to another proposed visit to the Dows, he told Mrs. Roberts, "But I'm afraid of the big house and all the swells." To Olin himself, Wolfe wrote in 1926, "Let me see you more often, Olin. I very honestly would like to have you as my friend; and very honestly I tell you that I have never been wholly sure I had your friendship. This is because you are fundamentally decent and courteous to everyone. . . . It cheers me to think that you may have ever found me interesting or strange or stimulating, but one sometimes grows a bit tired of existing as the Man-Mountain, the Wild-Haired-Wonder, and the like. . . . At any rate, no matter how you feel, I get a great deal of pleasure from seeing you, and I will willingly perform my stunts for you. . . ." In 1927 he wrote that he would gladly write all night if it would bring Olin to see him, and mentioned wondering whether he had offended Olin. Then he added that he wondered "whether you were disgusted at my manner of life. Because, somehow or other, I imagine I may suggest to the thoughtful person the worst excesses of Nero, Caligula, or the most evil devotee of Gomorrhaean lechery. Let me reassure you: you will find me respectable. . . ." Tom was at this time deeply involved in his affair with Aline Bernstein, and was living in lofts and garret apartments. In another letter to Mrs. Roberts, Tom mentioned his visit to the Dows' and the Vincent Astors' estates and said "How they stared at me! I looked very well in my clothes, but they knew I was an alien of some sort. I have a kind of notoriety among them, I believe, as Olin's wild Bohemian friend. . . ." It seems probable that this sense of social alienation was more pronounced on Tom's side than on Olin's. Some of the Dows' friends may have made Tom feel lower-class and inferior, but the only evidence that Olin may have rejected him comes from the implication in Tom's letters that he felt he had to push the friendship harder than Olin did, particularly in the later years. Whatever Tom's doubts may have been, they remained friends and may have gotten together as late as 1936.[6] But the relationship seemed to be typical of Wolfe's relationships with his friends: he could remain on friendly terms with many people of both sexes, but could never maintain deep interpersonal relationships with them. In the case of Dows, the socioeconomic differences may have accentuated the problem, but Wolfe's literary fame would probably have balanced Olin's wealth. Perhaps a more basic feeling of personal inadequacy made it impossible for Wolfe to maintain deep friendships, and this, in turn, might well have been an outgrowth of the basic narcissism which seemed to be a major dynamic of his personality. Dows offered Tom a constant veneration and faith in his literary promise, and this was the meat which sustained Wolfe's strongest appetite—his desire for fame. Without this faith in his literary skill, no friendship with Thomas Wolfe was able to survive.

Inadequacy, Social Isolation, and Loneliness

Thomas Wolfe's most pervasive theme both in his writings and in his life was his sense of deep loneliness, inextricably tied

6. *Letters to His Mother*, p. 336.

to his sense of personal inadequacy and of social isolation. These feelings are manifested in his creative work and in his letters; a number of reasons make these aspects of his personality understandable.

One reason for Tom's feeling of inadequacy, which he commented on many times, was his sense of having a poor body image. His main physical difference was his height, six feet six inches, which made him feel like a giant. One of his stories, "Gulliver," in *From Death to Morning*, develops the theme of what it feels like to be so tall. He mentions that nothing is manufactured to fit the tall person, so that he must always adapt himself to small furnishings. A particular annoyance was the difficulty of finding beds which were long enough. Finding well-fitting clothes was yet another problem. When he became more affluent Tom had his clothes tailored, often in England, but when he was a young man his clothes never seemed to fit. Finally, he experienced a constant barrage of witticisms about his size, each person fancying his comment original. Wolfe learned to tolerate the boredom and isolation that this raillery imposed on him, and eventually came to accept it—often, as a sort of distinction—but throughout his life he remained tremendously sensitive about his height.

Tom also suffered from a persistent eczema on his neck, and by letting his hair grow long, perhaps he hoped to cover up this blotch which he claimed both incurable and hereditary. Scratching, or using sandpaper however was not a very effective cure.

There are a number of accounts, both in his books and in the reminiscences of acquaintances, which suggest that Tom was inclined to be excessively concerned and displeased with his body image. He mentions gazing at himself naked in a mirror, and several other persons commented on his tendency to look at himself in a mirror for prolonged periods.[7] (These signs of preoc-

---

7. William Braswell, "Thomas Wolfe Lectures and Takes a Holiday," *College English* 1 (1939): 11-22.

cupation with his body image are treated later in the discussion of Tom's narcissism.) Basically, he was far from repulsive; however he was disturbed by his sallow skin, his awkward and ungainly limbs and large hands and feet, and the smirk or contemptuous smile which he thought played constantly on his face. The sense of adequacy or inadequacy of one's body image is usually attained at a very early age, and several circumstances might have contributed to Tom's negative self-image. His mother kept him wearing long curls until he was nine which evoked much teasing from his peers. Then he became very tall and thin,—aspects of his physique which were constantly pointed out to him. Mabel often called him a freak, and he was teased about his large feet. Furthermore, he was notoriously unsuccessful at all sports, reinforcing his inadequacy regarding his masculinity.

Fears of sexual inadequacy also began during his childhood. Turnbull notes that as a schoolboy Wolfe was accosted by peers who doubt his masculinity, until eventually he opens his fly to refute their aspersions.[8] Tom dreaded recess at school because the stronger boys would pick on him, and he would often buy his peace by giving them his lunch so that they would not torment him. As an adult, Tom visited prostitutes, and acquired something of a reputation for this activity, but in his books the prostitutes are often depicted as critical or patronizing toward Eugene because of his sexual ineptness, sometimes causing Eugene to withdraw from the situation.

In college Tom was criticized and teased for his slovenly appearance, and he was aware that other students were critical of him for neither bathing nor changing his clothes frequently enough, and for not cutting his hair. However, he seemed to feel no need to conform; instead he seemed challenged to defy them.

Other feelings of inadequacy stemmed from his sense of an inferior class background, of lacking social sophistication. Even

---

8. Turnbull, p. 10.

as a small child he felt that some of his neighbors looked down on him. For example, some nearby neighbors who were quite wealthy considered the Wolfes beneath them socially, and erected a fence in order to keep the Wolfe children off their property. Once—so Wolfe wrote later and Mabel confirmed—their horse stepped on Tom, but as Tom reconstructed it, the neighbors showed no concern for him, and just ignored the incident. Tom, like his siblings, was deeply embarrassed and threatened by his mother's boardinghouse, and by some of her clientele. As a college student Tom was embarrassed when his mother visited and tried to drum up trade among his fraternity brothers, and he told Mabel that his mother was ruining his career at school.[9] The Wolfe children's sense of social inadequacy was further aggravated by W. O. Wolfe's drinking and whoring, which was well known in the community. When he was older, Ben would not even walk near his father, and refused to go and bring him back from the saloon. Only Fred and Mabel could accept their father's behavior, but did so by denying that he had had more than "a little nip." Interestingly enough, everyone in the family seemed to consider W. O.'s visits to prostitutes as a form of behavior that was to be expected. In *Angel* Tom recounts that one of Helen's (Mabel's) friends paid for her brothers' visits to whores, because she felt that a sexual outlet was necessary for a man's health.[10] Another sign of Tom's sense of social inferiority was revealed in his attitude toward the church. The family attended the Presbyterian church, but Tom felt that the other boys in that church were socially above him, and he had no other contacts with them except in Sunday School. In his adolescence he refused to attend church.

In college Tom felt terribly gauche and inadequate, but later he made an effort to join groups. When he went on to Harvard,

---

9. Wheaton, p. 165.
10. *Angel*, chap. 12.

he felt very insecure among the other more self-confident graduate students. Though he sneered at their artificiality, he confessed that this was probably because he was afraid of them. He wrote to his mother in 1921 that he suffered a great deal because he was a youth in a class of mature men, and revealed that he spent most of his time by himself.

A major source of Tom's sense of inadequacy stemmed from his uncertainty about his ability as a writer. He tended to compensate for this uncertainty by writing boastfully to his mother or to Mrs. Roberts that he would make a name for himself in drama or literature. Some of his letters reflected his insecurity. To Professor Baker he once wrote that he knew he would never be a dramatist, and on several occasions he wrote to Max Perkins or to other staff members of Scribner's indicating that he was abandoning his career as a writer because he was not fitted for it. This self-criticism usually followed criticisms of his plays and books by either peers or professionals. We must conclude that his own strong feelings of insecurity were often handled by overcompensatory boasting, but that when his life experiences caused him to feel that he had failed, his insecurities were reactivated, and that he then felt completely inadequate, and consequently, depressed. He was inordinately sensitive to criticism, revealing depressed and paranoid-like feelings in his letters (see also chapter 9). Tom never felt that his family really had any confidence in his skill as a writer, or any appreciation of the effort it took for him to write. When he was a small boy his siblings criticized him for spending so much time reading, and his early writing efforts in high school were usually the source of mockery by his siblings, even though they typically earned him school prizes. Tom's father had little sympathy with his desire to write, since he wanted Tom to become a lawyer and politician. And the family, in general, measured success by the criterion of income earned; by that standard it was a long time before Wolfe was able to reach the level of his business-oriented peers and siblings.

Then, when he finally earned some royalties, the family unrealistically overestimated them, and felt that his money came easily and with little work. Wolfe's total lifetime income probably did not amount to more than forty or fifty thousand dollars, although the posthumous earnings to his literary estate must have been many times that amount.

When Tom finally published his first book, its nature caused his family and townspeople to reject him for exposing them to embarrassing publicity, and consequently it was eight years after the publication of *Look Homeward, Angel* before he felt that it was appropriate for him to visit Asheville again. While the family and the people of Asheville eventually forgave Tom for writing about them, and though later his books were so favorably reviewed that he became a celebrity, and Asheville's most famous son, his family probably never really understood or appreciated his writing.

In New York, during his relationship with Aline Bernstein, Tom felt uncomfortable with her theater friends. He always felt that they were putting on airs, that they were unaware of him, or worse, that they denigrated him. Although he detested their social values (and in *You Can't Go Home Again* implied that it was for this reason that he broke off with Aline) he admitted in his books that he was actually jealous of their successes and self-assurance. Even in his teaching he felt very unsure of himself and somewhat afraid of the students. He was tremendously surprised and pleased when one of his classes presented him with a pipe at the end of the semester. But although he considered himself a faithful teacher, he seems never to have realized that he was probably also an inspiring one.

Tom's feelings of social inadequacy caused him to hold back in social situations for fear that others would be as critical of him as he was of himself, and would reject him. A person who is expecting criticism or rejection is often defensive with others, and his uneasiness makes others similarly uneasy. As previously discussed this general attitude interfered with Tom's social relationships, and made it difficult for him to establish close friendships.

A person's perception of the world and of himself is learned through his experiences. These experiences give him a frame of reference for judging his own adequacy and for deciding whether the world will satisfy or frustrate his needs. The two perceptions—of self and of the world—combine to determine the person's feeling of security. Tom learned to perceive himself as of questionable quality and the world as threatening rather than basically friendly. He came to doubt his loveableness and his competence, causing intense insecurity.

Thomas Wolfe's loneliness was his most pervasive personality characteristic. He began to suffer from this as a very young boy, and he never overcame his sense of social isolation. Probably when his mother took him to live with her at the Old Kentucky Home, he felt his first severe sense of loneliness. Once he wrote to Mrs. Roberts that he had had two roofs and no home from the time he was a little boy. Although Tom was somewhat lonely the first year at college his last three years at North Carolina were among the happiest of his life. But at Harvard his almost continuous loneliness began, with only two brief periods of happiness, or of relating to people, later in his life—the periods when he was close to Aline Bernstein (from 1925 to 1928), and with Max Perkins (from 1930 to 1936).

In his letters Tom wrote more than a hundred times that he felt himself to be one of the loneliest of persons, and in his books, his literary protagonists, Eugene Gant and George Webber, mirror Wolfe's own feelings in their descriptions of states of desperate loneliness. As early as 1920 Tom wrote to his mother that he was alone and on a perilous sea. By 1924 he wrote her at least four times that he was one of the loneliest of men; and in 1928 he reported that one of the ugliest feelings in the world was to be alone in a foreign country and to come away from the mail window empty-handed. In 1933 he mentioned to her that he had lived alone most of his life, and that this was very hard at times. He wrote similar poignant and very dramatic letters to Max Perkins, Henry Volkening, and John Wheelock. To his mother in 1924 he wrote, "I am utterly lonely; there is no one in all the world to whom I can talk, but in my loneliness I am strong. I shall survive and triumph." And three years later he wrote her, "Strangers we are born alone into a strange world. We live in it . . . alone and strange, and we die without ever knowing anyone. . . ."

An entry in his diary in 1935 reads, "I came away 'abroad' to be alone, but what I am really tired of, what I am sick to death of, what I am exhausted and sickened and fed up to the roots of my soul with, is being *alone*."[11] One is prompted to ask, why, if Wolfe was so unhappy in his loneliness, didn't he do something about it? He did indeed try, but because of his early experiences his need for love and acceptance was so strong that it could not easily be satisfied. Moreover, although he was miserable when he was alone, he was too uncomfortable with people to take the necessary steps to alter the situation. His feelings of inadequacy and his basic dependency made it difficult for him to make friends; and his poor family relationships had made him wary of people. As he wrote to Mabel in 1929, "I live alone more than any person I have ever known. . . . I must spend a large part of my day alone. I hate crowds and public meetings. . . . But this is the only life I can lead. Sometimes I love to go out and join in with the crowd, and have a good time. But not often. The truth of the matter is that most people I meet bore me until I could cry out. . . . And I am not often bored with myself or with my reading or writing. . . . about the only real satisfaction I have had has been in work. . . ." In 1933 he told her that it was not good for a little child to be told that he is selfish, unnatural and inferior in gen-

---

11. *Notebooks,* p. 741.

erosity, because he may in time come to believe it, "and that is when he begins to live alone and wants to be alone and if possible to get far, far away from the people who have told him how much better they are than he is. . . . the habit of loneliness, once formed, grows on a man from year to year and he wanders across the face of the earth and has no home and is an exile, and he is never able to break out of the prison of his own loneliness again, no matter how much he wants to." Other personality characteristics which made it difficult for him to form friendships, and so relieve his loneliness, were his lack of social skills, and his basic narcissism. Neither of his parents was competent enough socially to teach Tom the good manners and etiquette which might lead to easy social relationships, and once Tom left the provincial setting of Asheville, he was unsure of himself. His constant concern with his own feelings and needs interfered with his ability to be concerned about the feelings and needs of others. This combination of narcissism and lack of social skill led him to constantly do and say things that were inappropriate, or even offensive to others.

In 1929 he wrote to his mother, "But in many ways I have the tastes of an old man—I don't like crowds, I don't like parties and going out, and most of the time *I want to be alone*." In 1930 he wrote to Max Perkins from Switzerland, "I have been entirely alone since I left New York. . . . Something in me hates being alone like death, and something in me cherishes it: I have always felt that somehow, out of this bitter solitude, some fruit must come. I lose faith in myself with people. When I am with someone like Scott [Fitzgerald] I feel that I am morose and sullen—and violent in my speech and movement part of the time. Later, I feel that I have repelled them." In 1937 he wrote to both his mother and his brother Fred that he desperately needed peace and quiet, and to be away from people, prompting him to rent the cabin in the woods at Oteen.

One may wonder whether Wolfe ever overcame his tendency

toward self-isolation. As his books were published and favorably reviewed, his confidence in his writing ability was strengthened to some extent. Moreover as he became famous, many people sought him out, so that he himself did not have to initiate social contacts. When he was being entertained as a literary lion he felt more appreciated and generally more responsive to people. However, even these experiences were not all positive, since Tom learned that those who sought him out were often only trying to increase their own importance rather than wishing to praise him for his achievements. Thus one gets the impression that Tom began to feel a bit more at ease with people, but never totally appreciated.

Actually Wolfe learned to satisfy his needs for companionship primarily through members of his own family, particularly in his early years. At the same time, these relatives were the source of much of his anguish, so that he was both drawn to them and repelled by them. And because he never learned how to relate easily to others he was constantly lonely. At times when he was lonely and upset he would make efforts to get in touch with one of his family; when, as usual, conflict arose, he would go off on his own again for a time. This was his typical pattern, except for the periods in his life when he related primarily to Aline Bernstein, or to Maxwell Perkins. Perhaps he was least lonely during the period from 1930 to 1936 when he enjoyed the companionship of Max Perkins and drew continual reassurance from him.

4

WOLFE AND MAXWELL PERKINS, AND THE SEARCH FOR A FATHER

THE SYMBIOSIS WHICH DEVELOPED BETWEEN WOLFE AND Maxwell Perkins was an intensely personal author-editor relationship. They met in January of 1929 after Perkins, an editor for Scribner's, read the manuscript of *Look Homeward, Angel*, while Wolfe was in Europe. Perkins had been impressed by the first passage of *Angel*, but then grew weary of a subsequent and labored theme development which seemed to him irrelevant to the plot, and turned the manuscript over to an assistant.[1] Not long after this he was shown one of the more vivid scenes later in the book, and from that time on he and his entire staff read the book avidly, and were tremendously impressed by it. Perkins then wrote to Wolfe and invited him to visit Scribner's on his return from Europe. However, Tom did not rush back from Europe immediately, although he did write to express his pleasure that Perkins and Charles Scribner's Sons were interested in the book. He had received enough rejections from producers and publishers not to allow himself to become overly excited, but in his

1. Maxwell E. Perkins, "Thomas Wolfe," *Harvard Library Bulletin* 1 (1947): 269-77.

letter from Vienna he repeated to Perkins what he had written in his Introduction to the Publisher's Reader, namely, that he wanted direct criticisms and advice from an older and more critical person who would be interested in talking over his huge "monster."

Perkins is considered by many literary people to have been one of the greatest American editors of the century. He was a somewhat eccentric person, who lived and breathed little else but his work, which he considered to be the development of promising undiscovered young writers. He had no use for social life, and even music and the other arts bored him; literature was his total preoccupation. The father of five daughters, he had a deep need to experience a father-son relationship, according to Nowell and Kennedy, and this need was met vicariously through his work with such famous authors as Hemingway, Fitzgerald, and Wolfe. He was an erudite man, and although brusque and direct in his manner, he was actually a gentle and very kindly person. He had the reserve and canniness typical of the traditional New Englander (which he was by descent), although he could also be impulsive, and on occasion uninhibited and colorful in his speech. He is depicted by Wolfe—somewhat caricatured—as Foxhall Edwards in *You Can't Go Home Again*. Perhaps his most noted eccentricity was his habit of keeping his hat on all the time he was at work in his office.

In Perkins, Wolfe found someone who could meet several of his more pressing needs: act as a father-figure; help him turn his prodigious writings into publishable book form; and last, but far from least, someone who would have unlimited faith in his artistic skill and promise. Perkins, in turn, was not only looking for good writers to add to the Scribner's list, but also for someone through whose efforts he could exercise his own never fully satisfied ambitions to be a writer.[2] Moreover, Tom fulfilled Perkins's apparent need for a son-surrogate. Thus Perkins, too, found

2. Kennedy, p. 335; Turnbull, p. 130.

several of his important needs satisfied in the seven years during which he and Wolfe shared a working relationship.

Unconsciously Wolfe was searching for a father, and that he saw Perkins as a father surrogate is clear from his letters both to Perkins and others. In 1929 he wrote to Fred that he thought of Perkins as a father, and cared for him as such;[3] and at Christmas during the same year he wrote to Perkins: "Young men sometimes believe in the existence of heroic figures, stronger and wiser than themselves, to whom they can turn for an answer to all their vexation and grief. Later they must discover that such answers have to come out of their own hearts; but the powerful desire to believe in such figures persists. You are for me such a figure: you are one of the rocks to which my life is anchored." On many other occasions he made similar remarks to Perkins, or told other people of his affection for Perkins. He dedicated his second book, *Of Time and the River*, to Perkins in a touching tribute to the latter's patience, help, and friendship. Indeed the dedication was worded less strongly than he really felt, for he had originally written a much longer and more adulatory one which he had shortened at Perkins's request, because of the latter's fear that such a long paean of devotion might injure Wolfe's reputation as a writer. Wolfe said that one of the main themes of *River* was man's search for a lost father: "all of us are wandering and groping through life for an image outside ourselves, for a superior and external wisdom we can appeal [to] and trust. . . ." Elizabeth Nowell, Tom's friend and biographer, believed that this search for a father was the main theme of Wolfe's life. More likely it was not the major or only theme, but it was assuredly a very important one. In his prologue to *Of Time and the River* he wrote: "And which of us shall find his father, know his face, and in what place, and in what time, and in what land?" By a somewhat ironic coincidence, it was Perkins who suggested

3. Kennedy, p. 335.

this theme to Wolfe, when on one of their many walks together he outlined a possible plot in which a boy searches for, and perhaps finds, an absent father. Wolfe immediately asked if he might use the theme, and Perkins assented, not realizing that it was to become a major theme of Wolfe's next book, and in fact was to appear in much of his subsequent writing.[4]

Eventually Wolfe's dependence on Perkins as a father figure caused him to turn to the editor to help him find apartments, to take care of his money for him, to discuss his problems in dealing with women, and to provide almost daily companionship. For a period of more than a year they worked together every evening, after Perkins's regular workday was over, as well as on weekends, hammering out problems in the development of *Of Time and the River*; or they would go out to drink together, or to take long walks, sometimes all around Central Park. Many times Wolfe spent the night at the Perkins's home, both when Perkins lived in Connecticut, and later when he moved into New York City. As Wolfe wrote to Percy MacKaye in 1933 in regard to this type of relationship, "I think we never lose entirely the hope that we have in childhood and that persists strongly in the first years of our youth that we will meet someone of such invincible strength and wisdom and experience that all the grief and error in our lives will be resolved by him."

Perkins, in turn, reciprocated with a friendly, reassuring paternalism. His original impression of Wolfe caused him some apprehension, for when he first saw "his wild hair and bright countenance" he thought of Shelley. However, he also feared he had a Moby Dick to deal with, for word of Wolfe's engaging in a serious brawl at the Munich Oktoberfest (see chapter 8) had already reached Perkins. But as he later wrote, eventually he came to love Wolfe. Much of his time with Wolfe was spent in gently reassuring Tom; and some of his letters reveal this patient,

4. Ibid., p. 201.

everlasting, and gentle paternalism; he worried that Tom was not taking adequate care of his health, or that he was letting some critical reviews affect him too much, or that he was becoming too concerned about financial problems. Perkins was, in fact, the person Tom designated as the principal executor of his will, and Max's affection for Tom endured long after the latter had died. In 1937 he wrote "I am your friend, and always will be, I think. . . ." When Tom was ill with pneumonia in Seattle, Perkins wrote to Tom's brother, Fred, and asked him to send a letter, or even a postcard, letting him know how "Old Tom" was. And he mailed Tom, who was too ill to read, three books of pictures which he thought Tom would like, and reassured him that the most important thing for him to do was to take care of himself and try to recover his health, and not to worry about the loss of time away from his writing. Perkins was at the hospital when Tom died in Baltimore, and attended his funeral in Asheville; he reported that his grief was overwhelming.[5] Perhaps his deepest feeling was indicated in a letter to Tom, written in 1935 when he said "Nothing could give me greater pleasure or greater pride as an editor than that the book of the writer whom I have most greatly admired should be dedicated to me. . . ."

The second need which Max Perkins supplied for Wolfe—that of a collaborator who could mold his tremendous outpourings into a coherent book—became the best known aspect of their relationship, and probably also the basis of its undoing. Wolfe could write wonderful prose, but he had great trouble in organizing it, and while he could write a story which had integrity and literary merit, and could also plan an epic, or even a whole series of books, he had trouble deciding how to weld the elements of the story together into a novel. This skill Perkins possessed in abundance, and so the two gradually learned to mesh their talents into the production of the books for which

5. Nowell, pp. 438-39.

they were jointly responsible. In the earlier years, Wolfe was very grateful to Perkins for the help that he so generously supplied and that fitted so well into the pattern of Tom's need; and initially Tom readily acknowledged his debt to his friend and editor. In 1933 he wrote to Mabel that Perkins had been almost desperate trying to figure out how to help Tom solve his major literary problems—his prolixity and his inability to organize—but that finally they figured out a method. When he finally delivered the manuscript for *Of Time and the River* to Perkins he wrote, "I don't envy you the job before you." Wolfe commented that Perkins had often said that if he could just get his hands on some manuscript, he could help him get out of the woods, and then Wolfe said, "Well, now here is your chance. I think a very desperate piece of work is ahead for both of us. . . . But you must be honest and straightforward in your criticism. . . ."[6] Several months later (in 1934) he wrote to Robert Raynolds "I told him [Perkins] the other day that when this book comes out, he could then assert it was the only book he had ever written. I think he has pulled me right out of the swamp just by main strength and serene determination. I am everlastingly grateful for what he has done. He is a grand man and a great editor. . . ." Later he wrote to Percy MacKaye "I have never heard of another writer who had such luck. No success that this book could possibly have could ever begin to repay that man for the prodigies of patience, labor, editing and care he has lavished on it. . . ."

Perkins himself reported the many nights and Sundays of labor during which the two worked together on the book, and said that every cut had to be argued about endlessly.[7] He admitted that since Wolfe never willingly parted from anything, he and Wheelock finally just took the proofs away from Tom and read them for him. In fact in *Story of a Novel*, Wolfe wrote that it

6. *Letters*, p. 399.
7. Perkins, "Thomas Wolfe."

was Perkins who announced when the manuscript was finished, and who started the production of the book over Tom's protests. Wolfe seemed to want to tell practically the entire history of America in each book, and he could not easily distinguish between the material that was relevant to a main theme and that which was not.

Yet later, the editorial prerogatives that Perkins assumed were to become a source of friction between them. Perkins mentioned his role as an editor only occasionally, and guardedly. He told Frere-Reeves, Wolfe's English editor, that he had been unable to make Tom read all of the proofs for *From Death to Morning*, that he would try to do so, but that if Tom would not read them, he would try to get the proofs away from him and put them into pages, unread.[8] To Wolfe he wrote in 1937 that he stood ready to help him at any time; that Tom had asked for his help on *Of Time and the River* and that he had given it gladly. But he also pointed out that Tom had never been overruled on a decision, and commented that he could think of no one who was less prone to be overruled than Tom. Perkins also commented that one of his own main functions was to try to turn Tom's mind away from his sufferings, and to help him achieve equanimity, so that he would not spend so many useless hours in brooding. Tom for his part acknowledged—in *The Story of a Novel*—that Perkins had sustained him during the long ordeal of producing *Of Time and the River*, by his "immense and patient wisdom and a gentle but unyielding fortitude. I think if I was not destroyed at this time by the sense of hopelessness which these gigantic labors had awakened in me, it was largely because of the courage and patience of this man. I did not give in because he did not let me give in. . . ." He told LeGette Blythe, "The amount of labor, patience, and devotion which the editors put in on my huge manuscript is something that can never be reckoned . . . or paid for except in terms of friendship and belief."

---

8. Perkins, *Editor to Author*, p. 106.

This editorial collaboration with Wolfe did, in fact, provide Perkins with a tremendous sense of satisfaction. In 1935 he wrote to Tom that ". . . working on your writings, however it has turned out, for good or bad, has been the greatest pleasure, for all its pain, and the most interesting episode of my editorial life." Later he wrote: "But, although I had moments of despair and many hours of discouragement over it, I look back upon our struggles with regret that they are over. And, I swear, I believe that in truth the whole episode was a most happy one for me. I like to think we may go through another such war together."

Finally, Wolfe acquired from his relationship with Perkins a feeling of reassurance about his competence as a writer. In 1929 Wolfe, writing to his former teacher Margaret Roberts, reported that Perkins thought that *Look Homeward, Angel* would be a critical sensation, although sales might not be so good. In 1935 he wrote to his mother of his great gratitude to Perkins for being such a true friend and for believing in him for all the years they had worked together. Earlier the same year, he had written Percy MacKaye a glowing tribute to Perkins' loyalty to him: "He has never once faltered in his belief that everything would yet turn out well—even when I had almost given up hope myself." And later he said, "Perkins never lost faith. . . ."

In 1930, when Wolfe was in Europe, Perkins wrote encouraging letters telling him that he was "a born writer if there ever was one" and "if anyone were ever destined to write, that one is you." He also reported to Tom that Sinclair Lewis had praised *Look Homeward, Angel* at the time that Lewis received the Nobel prize. In the spring of 1935 Wolfe, with the encouragement of Perkins, had gone to Europe when *Of Time and the River* was about to be published, not only because he was exhausted, but also because he could never stand to wait for the daily reviews of a book. Perkins cabled him that the book was received very favorably, but Tom did not believe him, and went through a phase of deep despair and depression. Perkins then informed him that all of the major reviewers had written favorably about the book, and that the *New York Times* and the *Herald Tribune* Sunday bookreview sections had each given full front-page favorable reviews, and that at the various cocktail parties the name of Thomas Wolfe was the main topic of favorable discussion. He ended the letter by saying "So, for Heaven's sake, forget anxiety, which you haven't the slightest ground for, but every ground for the greatest happiness and confidence, and enjoy yourself." In 1936 Perkins wrote: "You must surely know, though, that any publisher would leap at the chance to publish you." And later that year, he wrote, ". . . I have never doubted for your future on any grounds except, at times, on those of your being able to control the vast mass of material you have accumulated and have to form into books."

Thus Perkins supplied for Wolfe that most important ingredient of ego support, the firm expression of full confidence that Wolfe was a great writer. The story of Wolfe's life reveals that it was only with those people who could supply this reassurance, and could openly demonstrate their faith in him, that Wolfe was able to maintain a meaningful relationship for any significant period.

The Break with Perkins

Since the relationship between Wolfe and Perkins had been so close and productive, the literary world was startled when it began to deteriorate in 1936, and when in late 1937 Wolfe finally broke off his publishing and personal relationship with Perkins and Charles Scribner's Sons, going over to Harpers and the editorship of Edward Aswell. The break developed due to a combination of circumstances. Most seriously Wolfe's reputation came into question as a result of a few unfavorable reviews of *Of Time and the River*, and after the publication of *The Story of a Novel*, an essay in which Wolfe reported how *River* had been written. He had first presented this report at a writers' conference in Boulder, Colorado, in 1935 and both he and Perkins had thought it was worth publishing. But it brought forth from Bernard DeVoto, one of the chief literary critics for the *Saturday Review*, a scathing criticism of Wolfe, entitled, "Genius Is Not Enough."[9] DeVoto took the position that Wolfe's books were not novels because they lacked the unity and plot essential to that form of literary work. He also criticized Wolfe's style, and, most devastatingly, he challenged the possibility of successful collaboration in the writing of novels: "Then Mr. Perkins decides these questions. . . . But such a decision is properly not within Mr. Perkins' power. . . ." Perkins wrote that one critic had used a phrase somewhat like, "Wolfe and Perkins—Perkins and Wolfe, what way is that to write a novel?"[10] Tom couldn't accept even mild criticism, and this very strong, almost brutal attack haunted him for years. It became a cause célèbre—one of the famous literary feuds of the period, and a decade later DeVoto wrote that he couldn't understand how a single review could have become the source of so many comments and articles. The reason was probably that Wolfe was so shaken by the review that it ultimately led to the breakdown of the relationship between himself and Perkins. As the biographers have pointed out, Tom felt forced to demonstrate that he could, indeed, operate independently of Maxwell Perkins. Eventually (1936) Wolfe wrote Perkins a letter of "independence" which filled twenty-one pages of small print. He got to the heart of the matter when he declared: "As you know, I don't have to have you or any other man alive to help me write my books." Probably almost every writer has to believe this about himself, for writing, unlike some other arts, is usually an individual enterprise, and Wolfe was more sensitive than most on this point. Insecure about his talent and

---

9. Bernard DeVoto, "Genius is Not Enough," *Saturday Review of Literature* 13 (1936): 3-4; 14-15.
10. Perkins, "Thomas Wolfe."

skills in most undertakings, he was particularly unsure about his writing, which he considered his most important endeavor.

The relationship between Wolfe and Perkins began to waver when Perkins took the manuscript of *River* away from Wolfe, and went ahead with its publication before Tom thought the book was ready to appear. There are some reasons to defend Perkins for this action. First, Scribner's advanced Wolfe several thousand dollars on the book years before, and naturally felt they had a stake in getting something published. Secondly, they had a natural reluctance to let a promising new author disappear from the public eye, and six years were to elapse between the publication of *Look Homeward, Angel* and *Of Time and the River*. Moreover, Perkins believed quite sincerely that he had to help Tom get over the great hurdle of producing the second book, the traditional breaking point of many would-be writers. Then, too, Tom's insecurity and compulsiveness led him to write and rewrite, and left him unable to decide if the work was finished. Tom himself often recognized that he needed help because of this tendency but in retrospect he seemed to forget this, just as at one point he wrote to Perkins that he had no obligation to Scribner's to produce another book, apparently forgetting the large advance they made him on *Of Time and the River* years before. When Tom read the first printed edition of *River* he was greatly distressed to find some errors that he thought should have been corrected in the proofs, but in fact he had been so unwilling to read the proofs himself that Perkins had to have Wheelock read them. As it was, extensive proof revisions were made and all the personal pronouns changed from first to third person because of a decision to have the book be about Eugene Gant, rather than narrated by him.

When Scribner's later charged Wolfe around $1100 for author's alterations in proof, Wolfe became indignant and claimed that he had not made any such corrections, although he did admit that he should have. At any rate, he felt that the charges were excessive, even though in his contract he had signed the usual agreement to pay for author's corrections. Part of the problem stemmed from the fact that in the case of Tom's first book, *Look Homeward, Angel*, Perkins, aware of Tom's very limited financial resources, and probably feeling that Scribner's had found a very promising author, simply forgave Tom the more than $700 for author's corrections, so that the charge for the alterations in the second book took Tom by surprise.

When *Story of a Novel* appeared, Tom and Perkins once again disagreed. Tom had agreed to accept a smaller royalty than his previous fifteen percent, because he wanted the book to be inexpensive so that students and young authors could buy it; Scribner's shared this desire, but eventually priced the book at a dollar and a half because of increased production costs. Tom was incensed, and wrote a bitter letter to Perkins, implying breach of faith, and asking that his fifteen percent royalty be restored. Although not obligated to do so, Perkins arranged for this to be done to keep Tom happy.

Yet another harassing problem arose when Wolfe became the object of various libel suits, which was hardly surprising considering the very open and critical way he wrote about people. Although Scribner's, like most other publishers, included in his contracts a standard clause freeing them from any liability in such cases, they stood by Tom quite loyally and usually agreed to pay half of the costs. One suit alone was for $125,000 and Scribner's lawyers, who were prestigious and rather high-priced, recommended that this suit be settled out of court for only four percent of the original amount, and the complainant, a former landlady, agreed, even though she had been called "Mad Maude" in Wolfe's book. Scribner's paid half, but with lawyers' fees the suit cost Tom almost $3000, and somehow he managed to blame all this on Scribner's, especially because their lawyers were expensive. Tom eventually became quite paranoid about the entire legal profession, which he saw as an entrenched establishment created and maintained by lawyers largely for themselves, and not their clients. Moreover, Wolfe began to feel that in these lawsuits Perkins was not acting resolutely enough, nor showing sufficient regard for principle. Though in fact Perkins and Scribner's seem to have acted most generously toward Tom he was once again beginning to feel that his idol had clay feet. He wrote to Perkins in 1937, "I cannot bear to see you just a good but timid man. . . . I see you as the noble captain, strong and faithful, and no matter what the cost, right to the end. I have no right to ask it, but you must be the great man that I know you are." Here it is evident that for Tom Perkins was falling short of Tom's image of him as the idealized father-protector.

Driven by the need to demonstrate his ability to function independently, Tom at this point began to resent any editorial assistance, objecting to it as an intrusion on his author's prerogatives. His letters to Perkins and to Scribner's during 1936 and 1937 were paranoid in character. In the most critical one of all he wrote, "Like Mr. Joyce, I am going to write as I please, and this time, no one is going to cut me unless I want them to." And later he wrote, "Restrain my adjectives, by all means, discipline my adverbs, moderate the technical extravagances of my incondite exuberance, but don't derail the train. . . . I'm not going to let it happen." In what was probably his most extreme statement he wrote: "I will go to jail because of this book if I have to. I will lose my friends because of it, if I will have to. I will be libelled, slandered, blackmailed, threatened, menaced, sneered at, derided and assailed by every parasite, every ape, every blackmailer, every scandalmonger, every little Saturday-Reviewer of the venomous and corrupt respectabilities. I will be exiled from my country because of it, if I have to." Such behavior is more indicative of Wolfe's inner needs and conflicts than of the objective situation.

Another source of friction between Scribner's and Tom was the publisher's seeming reluctance to give him a contract for his future writing. After the publication of *River* he came to measure a publisher's devotion by his willingness to write a contract and advance a $10,000 royalty on a manuscript, sight unseen. He had once been made such an offer, and these were indeed the provisions of the contract he signed with Harpers in late 1937. The fact is that Scribner's was also prepared to give him these terms, as Perkins wrote him several times, but from past experience Scribner's knew how difficult Wolfe was to deal with, and how vulnerable he was to libel suits because of the nature of his writing, so that there was some hesitation. Most significantly, Perkins feared that any mention of business matters would threaten his friendship with Tom, and it was this personal relationship that Tom valued most. It was in fact true that whenever legal matters were broached Tom reacted badly because he felt that this intruded on his personal relationship with Perkins, whom he wanted as a close personal friend first, and a devoted editor second. Even after the publishing relationship was severed Tom continued to avow his great friendship for Perkins. But in late 1936 Wolfe wrote, but never mailed, to Perkins, the following statement: "I impeach your virtues and your conduct; may I tell you frankly, plainly, that I do not believe they have achieved and maintained always the quality of . . . faith, good will, and simple direct integrity that you have always claimed for them. . . . And therefore I renounce you, who have already, for so long a time, renounced me and got so safely, with no guilt or wrong, so freely rid of me." He also wrote in December, 1936: "no one has a right in my opinion to mix calculation and friendship, . . . financial astuteness with personal affection." And a year later he wrote to Perkins "maybe for me the editor and the friend got too close together and perhaps I got the two relations mixed." He said that the artist may seem naïve to the businessman because he is playing the game with only one set of chips, while the publisher apparently plays it with two sets, friendship and business acumen.

Wolfe's practically paranoid reaction to Perkins was to reach even more ludicrous extremes when at one point he accused

Scribner's of demanding that "I must now submit myself to the most rigid censorship . . ." in order to have a book accepted by them. He thought such a censorship was planned in order to prohibit him from writing about Perkins or Scribner's, which he had, in fact, started to do; it was a process which he felt "If I agreed to it, would result in the total enervation and castration of my work. . . ." Perkins expressed to Miss Nowell the fear that if Tom revealed some of the inside workings of Scribner's told to Tom in confidence, Perkins would be morally obliged to resign from the editorial staff. Later, in a letter to Wolfe, he tried to explain that this should in no way affect what Wolfe chose to write about, but Tom considered Perkins's comment to Miss Nowell tantamount to censorship. On other grounds, too, there was cause for Scribner's to worry about Wolfe's subjects. His former mistress, Aline Bernstein, had threatened a libel suit if he wrote about her, and Tom was indeed doing just that in *The Web and the Rock*.

Tom conceived the fiction that Max actually enjoyed seeing him suffer during the lawsuits that were brought against him. He said in late 1936: "At times, particularly during the last year or two, the spectacle of the victim [Wolfe] squirming beneath the lash has seemed to amuse you. . . . There is an unhappy tendency in all of us to endure with fortitude the anguish of another man." No evidence is available to justify this notion of Wolfe's. It seems a paranoid projection of his own state of mind, for Perkins appears to have actually been greatly distressed about Tom's anguish.

Similarly, in the summer of 1938 Tom wrote to Miss Nowell that Max instructed the Scribner's salesmen to say critical things about Tom and to discourage the purchase of his books. As Perkins wrote later, a few salesmen might, on their own, have made remarks indicating their annoyance with Wolfe for changing publishers, but Perkins loved him too much to do such a thing, even if it were a good business practice to run down one's former authors, which was doubtful.

A final source of friction between Wolfe and Perkins, was that Tom's political views were becoming more liberal. His background was quite conservative, although he had always, as he said, leaned toward the side of the working man, and was an ardent New Deal Democrat. For a while he had toyed with communism, but he was never in any sense a communist, and he rather despised the card-carrying party man. However he leaned strongly toward a socialistic point of view in the late thirties, as is evident in the latter half of *You Can't Go Home Again.* While he loved and admired the Germans when they lionized him on his visits to Germany in 1935 and 1936 he had come to feel horror over the Nazi movement; this is best revealed in his section of the above book entitled, "I Have a Thing to Tell You" where he exposed the brutal treatment by the Nazis of a Jew who was trying to escape from Germany with some of his fortune, and whose arrest Wolfe witnessed at Aachen. Tom felt that Perkins was too conservative, and was refusing to let him include his more liberal views in his books. Perkins contended that neither he nor Scribner's cared how liberal Wolfe might be, but that in describing the Eugene Gant of the twenties Tom should not make him speak the radical thoughts of the Wolfe of the mid-thirties. By this time, Tom did indeed seem to lean toward more revolutionary concepts of social change than he had earlier, although he maintained his faith that America would eventually weather the political and social malaise of the thirties; but Perkins, as he beautifully outlined in a later letter to Tom, leaned more toward evolution as a means of bringing about social change. These differences provoked frequent political arguments between the two but in themselves would probably not have posed a significant problem; however they may well have contributed to Tom's feeling of disillusionment with the ideal father figure to whom he had attached himself. In the final passages of *You Can't Go Home Again,* Webber (Wolfe), in a letter to his editor, Foxhall Edwards, tries to make plain the irreconcilability of their political and philosophical views, although he is not entirely successful in doing so. However, quarrel Wolfe and Perkins did, and one time at a restaurant, when Wolfe was quite drunk, he even tried to start a fist-fight with Perkins, but was fortunately diverted from it when an admirer happened along, and started a conversation with Tom.

What effect did their professional and personal separation have on Wolfe and Perkins? Both retained a pathetic desire to maintain the friendship, and both suffered misery and agony over the broken relationship. Tom experienced one of his most profound depressions, which lasted for much of the remaining two years of his life. He compared his feelings at the loss of the friendship to the grief he had felt at his brother Ben's death. To numerous persons he wrote in that period "I have been mourning for the dead." In several letters, he wrote to Perkins that he would never cease to respect and admire him, and be devoted to him. In one letter he said, "I am your friend, Max, and . . . want you to be mine." He said that he wanted to see Perkins, but thought that the present time (November, 1937) was not a good time for them to see each other, apparently feeling that they might renew some of their arguments. And Perkins replied to this letter, saying that he, too, was Wolfe's friend, and would always be. In December Wolfe asked Perkins to help him by testifying at a legal trial, and Perkins gladly complied. Wolfe wrote a pathetic statement to a mutual friend saying, "I have just heard [that] the man I know best in all the world wants to see me, and is my friend." In even more touching phrases he wrote to Belinda Jelliffe in February of 1938 that, "it means so much more to me than I can ever utter here to know that in another hour I shall meet again and hear the voice again of the wonderful and noble man who has been, I think, the greatest, best, and most devoted friend that I have ever had; of whose friendship and belief I hope I may be forever worthy."

The last letter Wolfe ever wrote (Aug. 12, 1938) was to Max Perkins. He was very ill in Seattle with cerebral tuberculosis, but he wrote: ". . . I wanted most desperately to live, and still do, and I thought about you all a thousand times, and wanted to see you all again . . . no matter what happens or has happened, I shall always think of you and feel about you the way it was that Fourth of July day three years ago when you met me at the boat. . . ." Perkins wrote back a tender affectionate letter, saying "I remember that night as a magical night," sending Tom the books of pictures, and urging him to take care of himself, so that he would get well. In just about a month Wolfe died.

What, then, are the basic psychological dynamics in the relationship between Wolfe and Perkins? It seems evident that in this relationship Tom's basic dependency again showed itself; his tendency to seek emotional succor was a strong one, and must have stemmed from the early state of marked dependency which his mother first fostered and then left unsatisfied, and which he sought in Perkins. Although Tom was always quite dependent upon someone else for support and reassurance, he at the same time resented what he considered domination. Perkins tended to be the more dominant of the two men, and at first Wolfe welcomed this; later, however, Tom felt the need to express his independence, just as he had to in practically all of his other close relationships. The origins of this dynamic, too, can be seen in his childhood. Most children come to resent overcontrol, and Tom found himself in a life situation in which there was a great deal of it. Julia was a very domineering woman; her strong masculine protest showed itself in many ways, but most obviously in her business affairs, and in her tenacity to get her way in altercations. In one of his early letters, Tom mentioned to Mabel that it wasn't possible to influence Julia much once she had her mind set, no matter how reasonable the arguments might be. We may recall that Tom wrote that even when he was in his twenties Julia wouldn't let him drive her car, maintaining that he was still her baby.

Tom had to struggle to gain his independence from Julia and

try to establish himself as an autonomous person. Since the satisfactions of autonomy were not always as great as those of dependence, he tended to vacillate between these two states. Thus his life pattern became one of searching for parent figures on whom to depend, and then rebelling against their efforts to control him. This was the drama he acted out with Maxwell Perkins.

At the time that Tom first met Perkins and was an unknown author submitting his first manuscript, he was willing to accept editorial help in order to get his work published. Once he became famous, he was unsure whether he could repeat his success. He approached the task of writing a second book with considerable apprehension, and as he wrote, his insecurity increased. Starting with a general idea of what he wished to communicate, he wrote voluminously, but then was uncertain about the quality of his efforts, changed his plan for the book, and again wrote voluminously, continuing to vacillate until he dissipated four years in writing compulsively detailed descriptions of seemingly unrelated memories, feelings, and experiences. At this point Maxwell Perkins responded to Tom's appeal for help by agreeing to try to select from his writing portions that would fit together, and by urging Tom to exclude irrelevant material. Although Tom resisted changes in his work, he agreed to enough of them to allow the second book to be published, but exhibited his resentment by refusing to read the page proofs. This domination by Perkins during 1934 and 1935 was the sort of domination Julia, and later Aline, tried to impose and Tom struggled against. When this period of domination was followed by DeVoto's public questioning of Wolfe's competence as a writer, Tom's deep anxiety about his personal competence was reactivated, which was intolerable for him. It is possible, too, that as his personal involvement with Perkins grew, their relationship began to require some true reciprocity, which Tom simply could not supply. All of these circumstances combined to bring about the severance of their deep relationship. One cannot help feeling that many of Tom's complaints about Max during the last two years of their relationship were manufactured in an unconscious effort to justify the break. Just as in his earlier relationship with Aline Bernstein Tom had been unable to deal with the circumstances in a realistic way, and had had to project the blame for their difficulties onto her, so in his relationship with Max he had to find flaws in Max's conduct which would justify his rebellion and eventual termination of their relationship.

The Search For a Father

The search for a father or father substitute was a pervasive element in Tom Wolfe's life. He had started to feel some loss of his father when he moved to the Old Kentucky Home, but it was probably not until the time of his puberty, when W. O. began to be troubled with his various illnesses, that Tom started to search for a father substitute. Then he turned to Ben, who gratified Tom's dependency needs for a strong male figure until he died in 1918. In 1921 Wolfe wrote to his mother that he would like to return to Asheville and see his father, but that he could not do it because he knew that he would stagnate there. In 1923 he wrote about his nostalgia for the happy mornings he spent as a small boy when the family lived on Woodfin Street, and that same year he wrote plaintively that both Ben and his father seemed so far away, that his whole life with them seemed almost like a dream.

In college Wolfe turned to three of his professors as possible father surrogates, Dr. Williams, the Professor of Philosophy, Dr. Greenlaw, the Professor of English, and to Professor Koch, who directed the Carolina Players. However, these forms of dependency on a parent figure at college were probably no greater than for many young men. Toward Professor Baker, the dramatics professor at Harvard, Tom seemed to direct more of his dependency needs, asking often for advice and support, and even visiting him at his place in New Hampshire for periods of up to a week. But Dr. Baker disappointed Tom too by merely telling him to continue writing without giving him the practical advice and emotional support Tom sought. As Tom complained to his relatives, this sort of advice would hardly feed him, and he went on to explain that Dr. Baker had confused him further by changing his mind on several previous occasions. At one time he advised Tom both against teaching and against going to Europe, and only shortly afterwards suggested both teaching and a trip to Europe as possibilities for Tom as if these were his own ideas.

For a time at Harvard Tom turned to his maternal uncle, Henry Westall, who lived in Boston, as a father substitute, and also to dispell some of his intense loneliness. Westall appears as Uncle Bascom Pentland in *Of Time and the River*, portrayed by Tom as a Dickensian character of the first magnitude. Actually many of the Westalls were eccentric, but Uncle Henry was especially so.[11] Tom visited Uncle Henry many times during those two years, and in *Of Time and the River* he describes a dinner at Uncle Bascom and Aunt Louise's (Laura's), and a tremendous lunch to which his vegetarian uncle treated him. At some point Tom tried to establish a close relationship with his uncle, but he reported that the older man responded only momentarily, and then sank back into his own remote, almost schizoid world. Obviously Tom was looking for a father substitute in Uncle Henry, but his efforts were futile. When Tom left Boston he gave Mr. Westall some money to forward his books to him, but the old man was so undependable that eventually Tom had to collect them himself on a trip to Boston.

In his early days in New York, Tom showed a somewhat more

---

11. It is interesting that in one manuscript Uncle Henry was called Bascom Hawke; the parallel between the names Wolfe and Hawke seems rather remarkable. The name of Tom's maternal grandmother's family was Penland, and in his books Wolfe called the Westalls the Pentlands.

than ordinary dependency on Dr. Watt, the head of the English Department at New York University, and on Professor James Munn, the Dean there, and praised both men highly as always most helpful and considerate. Perhaps the main problem in this case was that Wolfe did not like teaching, although he did his best to perform well in his classes. But the academic world with its firm deadlines and large classes of sometimes dull or critical students was not one he could feel at home in, so he never allowed himself to become really involved in it.

In his work, the theme of the search for the father is first expressed in *Of Time and the River*, which he wrote in the early thirties, although it dealt with the period from 1920 to 1925 in his own life. Wolfe admitted that this search was the dominant theme and in describing the book he refers to the Antaeus legend, in which a son remains faithful to his father, even though he travels and is away from home most of the time. Moreover, the titles "Telemachus" and "Jason's Voyage" are used for two parts of *Of Time and the River*. In the book, Eugene is tremendously excited when the train comes to take him away to the North, which he equates with his father's country. Tom best described the theme of *River* in *The Story of a Novel* when he said "the central legend . . . the deepest search in life . . . was man's search to find a father, not merely the father of his flesh, not merely the lost father of his youth, but the image of a strength and wisdom external to his need and superior to his hunger, to which the belief and power of his own life could be united." Subsequently he again mentioned this point many times in letters to relatives and friends, and in notations to the editor of the book. The similarity of these various statements about the qualities of a father is noteworthy, since they reveal a concept of a father, or father figure, who is loving, wise, and competent—who will protect his son from harm and solve his problems for him. In *River* Eugene turns to Professor Hatcher (Baker) and to his Uncle Bascom Pentland, but neither of these men is able to fill the role for him.

The search for a father figure is also found in *The Web and the Rock*, which describes the period of 1925 to 1928 in Tom's life. George Webber (the new name for Eugene Gant) is very fond of Nebraska Crane, a glamorized all-powerful big brother figure who defends George from the town bullies, and who was probably a fictionalized combination of three or four older boys and men whom Wolfe admired, including his brother, Ben, a neighborhood chum, and a professional ball player whom he met as an adult. The world of George Webber's father (the city) is depicted as good and clean, where men provide companionship and protection. Webber is delighted when he is given the opportunity to revisit his father and his brothers. During the period in which this book was written Wolfe made a note in his diaries that the most terrible thing for a boy to see is that his father is afraid of another man.[12]

The best answer to the search for a father is described by Wolfe in *You Can't Go Home Again*, covering the phase of his life from 1928 to 1936. The character of the editor, Foxhall Edwards (Maxwell Perkins), appears as the idealized father substitute. He is resourceful and competent, and Webber and Edwards have mutual interests and tastes, and great respect for one another. Edwards values work, and thinks it disgraceful not to make a strong effort to achieve one's goals. He has an instant and penetrating understanding of people, but tends to be somewhat contemptuous of women, although always protective toward them; his scornful phrase "Women!" is repeated by Wolfe over and over in the book. Edwards does not like parties, or meeting the right people, and is scornful of businessmen, but friendly to writers. He is concerned with world events, and reads the evening and morning papers as rapidly as they become available. All of these characteristics in fact describe Maxwell Perkins.

---

12. *Notebooks*, p. 586.

Unfortunately Wolfe's constant need to find some older male to nurture and protect him, combined with his inability to enjoy that state of being nurtured because it impaired his independence was acted out with Maxwell Perkins, to the sorrow of both. Had he been content to remain dependent, their relationship might have survived. But Tom could not remain dependent and keep his self-respect. And Perkins was bewildered by Tom's withdrawal from the relationship, because he felt that in providing editorial help and emotional reassurance he was only doing what Tom had asked. Max could hardly know that the idealized father whom Tom required must not only be nurturant toward him, but must do so without becoming dominating or critical, and that even the most loving parent figure would be used by Wolfe as a scapegoat on whom to project his hostility when Tom himself felt inadequate or unloved.

PART II

NARCISSUS AND THE SPLIT IMAGO: WOLFE'S RELATIONSHIP WITH WOMEN

5

MOTHER AND SON, AND SIGNS OF NARCISSISM

JULIA AND TOM WOLFE'S FEELINGS FOR EACH OTHER WERE ambivalent for the better part of their lives. While he was, as he put it, "the last coinage of her womb" (except for a possible later miscarriage), and was generally perceived as her favorite child, Julia was unable to supply him with the unending flow of mother love that often typifies such situations.

Julia Westall came from a very impoverished but proud family of English and Scottish descent, who had lived in the mountain regions of Yancey County, near Mount Mitchell, North Carolina, for many generations before moving to the vicinity of Asheville. Her father and some of his brothers had served in the Confederate army, and the family's fortune had been wiped out by the war. One of a large number of children, Julia showed promise and was able to attend one or two small "colleges."[1] She was twenty-four when she married W. O. Wolfe and had taught school near Asheville for a number of years by then. Of

1. Her children, Fred and Mabel, differed as to whether it was one or two colleges; Kennedy maintains that they were really only secondary schools, and not colleges.

her brothers, Henry—immortalized as Uncle Bascom in *Of Time and the River*—was brilliant but very eccentric; another, slightly younger than Julia, was much admired by her but died shortly before her marriage. Yet another behaved somewhat strangely and may well have been mentally defective. But two of her brothers aroused both her respect and envy when they became highly successful in construction and in real estate. Julia tried to emulate them. By the time she was married, she had already bought one property in Asheville and, according to Rubin, in a period of less than forty years she acquired and sold over forty others.[2] On her almost annual winter trips to Florida she dabbled rather extensively in real estate, particularly during the real estate boom of the twenties. After twenty years of married life, when Tom was only six years old, she purchased a boardinghouse—naming it the Old Kentucky Home—which, despite her denials, provided her with a considerable income.

One of Julia's most obvious traits was her compulsive talking. She would ramble on and on, becoming involved in intricacies of detail dredged up from her remarkably full memory. This trait was acquired by most of her children, and especially by Mabel and Tom. She also believed that she was psychic, had many premonitions, and heard voices of the dead. Some of the members of her large ancestral family were quite eccentric and may indeed have demonstrated recognizable signs of insanity; others were leaders in their communities.

Julia's marriage to W. O. Wolfe was not a happy one, although they had eight children, of whom seven lived beyond infancy. It is likely that they were sexually incompatible, for Julia appears to have rejected sex, and W. O. turned to other women and to prostitutes, naturally compounding their problems. By the time Julia was in her early forties and approaching the end of

---

2. Louis D. Rubin, Jr., *Thomas Wolfe: The Weather of His Youth* (Baton Rouge: Louisiana State University Press, 1955).

her child bearing period, she became weary of living with W. O. Wolfe, who had become more and more difficult because of the increasing frequency of his drinking. In fact, Tom Wolfe states in *Angel* that his parents were on the point of separating around the time when he was born. By that time Julia could be fairly certain that the neighbors were aware of the cross she had to bear so that she probably felt less anxious about provoking social censure for refusing to live with her husband any longer.

Julia ran a successful and profitable boardinghouse in St. Louis during the Exposition which encouraged her in the belief that if she chose she could become financially independent of W. O. By 1906 Tom was old enough to go to school and did not require constant supervision. Mabel had graduated from high school and was capable of handling W. O.'s household—moreover, she was quite fond of her father. All of these circumstances contributed to Julia's decision to move to the Old Kentucky Home at this point in her life.

Julia did seem very eager to keep her youngest child close to her. He slept with her until he was nine, and even longer, when on trips; and he was not weaned until he was over three. She kept his hair in long curls until he was nine, and then had them cut off only because he had acquired lice from some neighbors. On her trips to Florida Julia frequently took Tom along with her, and even after he started school she took him out of school for the winter, and tutored him herself. When she established the boardinghouse, Tom was the only one of her children whom she took with her, all of the others staying with their father at Woodfin Street, except Effie and Frank who left home around that time. Julia referred to Tom as her baby, and on the pretext that he might be hurt, denied him most of the activities of a normal childhood.

In taking Tom with her to the Old Kentucky Home, Julia attempted to meet her need for love. But her need for money and property, as well as independence from W. O.—which required that she be self-supporting—seemed equally pressing. After she moved to the Old Kentucky Home, she often became so involved in meeting the demands of her boarders that she neglected her role as a mother to Tom. Not until she was done with her boardinghouse duties did she become lonely, realize that Tom was not there, and send for him. Julia most likely wanted to make Tom into the perfect male—different from W. O., certainly, and better than her other sons, who had disappointed her in one way or another. She wanted Tom to love her, appreciate her and need her, to be intelligent, to work hard, and to "make something of himself" (which to her meant that he should earn a great deal of money).

When Tom did not accept her economic value system Julia was disappointed in him. While at first he gave promise of meeting her various expectations, as he grew older it became more and more apparent that he was not fully able to do so, for although he depended on and needed her, he was not motivated to become a wealthy businessman. Moreover, once he left her to go to college at the age of sixteen, Tom could no longer supply her with constant companionship and affection. From then on he provided few satisfactions for Julia, who reacted by concentrating more and more intensely on her financial dealings and by expecting Tom to support himself.

During the years when Tom was at the Old Kentucky Home he was constantly made aware of Julia's concern about money, and came to feel that whenever she had to decide between giving him her time and concern, and making money, she chose the latter. Understandably, Tom resented Julia's preoccupation with money and property, which contrasted so sharply with W. O.'s generosity and kindliness. W. O. was always glad to have the children bring their friends home to share supper with the Wolfe family, or to have relatives come to visit. And Mabel describes an occasion when he allowed a poor woman and her child to steal coal from his coal bin one cold winter night without doing any-

Mr. and Mrs. W. O. Wolfe, 1900

Pack Memorial Public Library, Asheville, N. C.

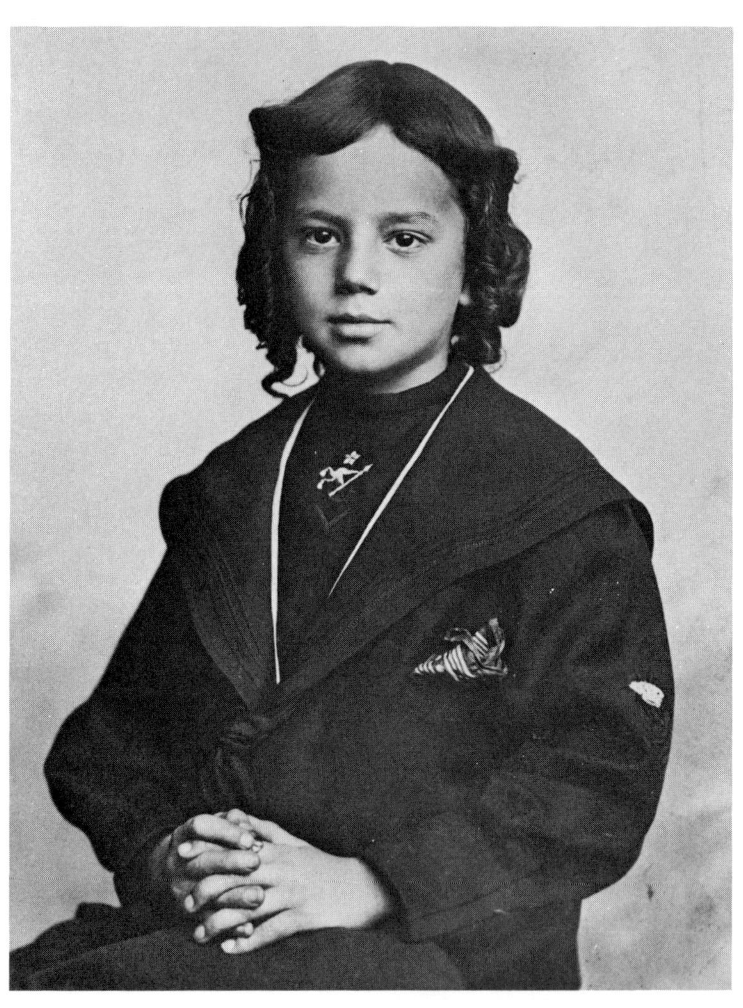

Thomas Wolfe, age eight

Pack Memorial Public Library, Asheville, N. C.

Ben Wolfe at about age fourteen

Pack Memorial Public Library, Asheville, N. C.

The Wolfe family at 92 Woodfin Street, Asheville, July 4, 1899.
Effie, W. O. Wolfe, Mabel, Fred, Grover, Ben, Julia Wolfe,
and Frank

Pack Memorial Public Library, Asheville, N. C.

Thomas Wolfe, June 1938, three months before his death

Pack Memorial Public Library, Asheville, N. C.

Mrs. Margaret Roberts at age 25

Pack Memorial Public Library, Asheville, N. C.

Effie, (top) Julia, Tom's mother, and Mabel Wolfe about 1910

Pack Memorial Public Library, Asheville, N. C.

Maxwell Perkins

Blank and Stoller, Chicago, Ill.

thing to stop them, only exclaiming, "Poor devils." Julia took Tom away from W. O., whom Tom greatly loved, and then instead of making him feel loved and secure, she turned her prime attention to making money.

There are many examples of Julia's frugality. She became well known as a hoarder of many things, including paper and string. Her family found this habit very exasperating, but posterity must be grateful for it since it led her to save practically all of the letters that Tom wrote to her. When the children were young, Julia managed to cultivate a small produce patch on their property and had the children sell whatever food the family didn't need for themselves. Because she was convinced that work "wouldn't hurt the children" she urged them to take jobs from the time they were quite young. Julia never gave Tom a regular allowance, so that when he needed money he usually had to beg her for it.

At the Old Kentucky Home Julia did not give any of the children a space they could consider their own when they visited her. If another paying roomer arrived, the children's rooms were turned over to the paying guest, and they would have to squeeze in somewhere else. In fact, to the great disgust of the rest of the family, Julia even charged her relatives for room and board when they came to visit. Though a good cook, she was careful about portions and did not provide food as bountifully as W. O. Because she was so niggardly about paying them, she had trouble keeping maids with the result that they often left her without giving notice. On those occasions Mabel was summoned to help with the housework, and Tom sent to try to find a new maid in the Negro section of the town. A sign of Julia's willingness to put money before principle was her practice of renting rooms to women of questionable reputation so long as they paid their bills promptly.

Tom's letters to his mother, written when he was in his twenties, frequently discussed money, and also the question of whether or not Julia and his siblings loved him. He stated that he would not ask them for help much longer since they neither bothered to write to him, nor to send him enough money to live on. Often he said how grateful he was for all they had done for him, and then begged them to write to him and send him money. This hope that they would write continued through his life, always accompanied by the recognition that they seldom did. Julia wrote sometimes; Fred and Mabel, later during the thirties, wrote more than they had previously. Tom stopped asking his mother for money after his European trip in 1925. By that time he was earning some money as an instructor in English at New York University, and was also receiving financial support from his mistress, Aline Bernstein, much to his mother's disapproval.

In the thirties the character of Tom's letters to his mother changed somewhat, and he became rather solicitous about the health and finances of all of his family, and particularly of Julia. During the Depression of the thirties all of the family faced financial difficulties, and Tom, although quite poor himself, offered to lend or give them money. In 1931 he wrote to Julia and offered to send her fifty dollars a month if she needed it. He often encouraged her to go to Florida in the winters, largely because the boardinghouse was not properly heated. Actually the Depression may have been an advantage to Tom in one way, for since many competent men were out of work at the time, being poor had little stigma attached to it. If one adds that Julia lost much of her property, whereas Tom's books were favorably reviewed and were earning some income—in fact, enough for him to offer help to his mother and siblings—one can see why at this stage of his life he no longer felt as hostile toward Julia about money matters. At this point he was probably more successful, financially, than she.

Julia's emphasis on money and property led Tom to attribute the breakup of his family to his mother's "mania for property," and to speak disparagingly of it. By contrast he tended to idealize his father's interest in literature and in family life. Tom's hostility to Julia's values may explain why he spent the money she did give him foolishly and why—in his early twenties—he was always asking for more financial aid. It may account, too, for his lifelong inability to handle his financial affairs and for his need to have someone else do it for him—in later years the business department of Scribner's. Julia's preoccupation with business was responsible for Tom's contempt for businessmen and their interests, and probably accounted for his political leanings in the thirties, which expressed his opposition to the exploitative nature of business.

What is most striking is the ambivalence of Tom's feelings for his mother and family in general. For although he became extremely critical of them in his late twenties he never completely cut his ties to them. His continuing dependency on his mother is revealed in the letters he wrote her from New York asking her to visit him, and both seem to have enjoyed the several trips she made to see him. But he also continued to speak of himself as a stranger in his own home and to recall his "alien and unhappy childhood." In later years he claimed that he rose above these unhappy memories, and indeed, he always remained loyal to his family and as he became older showed compassion for them and for his mother. When the publication of *Look Homeward, Angel* shocked his family and friends, he apologized, pointing out how admirable the important critics found them. He seemed to see them as a prototype of American familyhood, rather than his own parents and siblings—who taught him to be a lonely and atypical man, who never felt quite comfortable with others. Tom resented this, but precisely because he had not learned to relate easily to others, he remained quite dependent on his family for love, and did not dare to be too critical of them.

The Wolfes might be described as a symbiotic family unit. That is, almost all of the relationships of the members of the Wolfe family that were psychologically important were relationships with other family members. They did not easily establish independent relationships with outsiders; characteristically, their relationships with outsiders were carried out within the limits of the roles that had been assigned them by the family. For each family member felt that he could not survive apart from the family unit, nor it without him. Tom had the role of baby of the family; Fred that of the favorite boy. W. O. had the role of irresponsible philanderer, and Julia that of put-upon, long-suffering, hard-working, morally-upright woman. Frank became the bearer of the family's negative identity. This close identification with the family and the consequent difficulty in relating to outsiders was to have repercussions in the lives of all the Wolfes.

What were some of the ways in which Julia Wolfe affected her son's personality? First, she thwarted his efforts to achieve independence by trying to keep him as her baby, and consequently robbed him of the opportunity to develop skills which would have made him feel competent. For example, she sent him on sporadic errands, but refused to assign him consistent, specific responsibilities. It is through learning how to handle problems effectively that a child acquires a sense of competence and a feeling that he can deal with the world. Julia never permitted Tom to use his abilities to help him develop needed skills as he was growing up, and consequently kept him dependent on her in many ways. In addition, by keeping him in curls, Julia prevented Tom from looking and acting like other boys, so that during these crucial years of childhood he always felt different and alone. At the same time, she robbed him of a sense of security by taking him to live in the erratic, confused environment of the Old Kentucky Home. Then, too, Julia fostered in Tom a disdain for neatness and material possessions by the way she reared him—by denying him a room of his own, by forcing him to make do with old, ill-fitting clothes, by showing no concern for his or her own appearance. Similarly, Julia's tendency to treat all illness as psychosomatic—which probably contributed to Ben's death—probably bred Tom's lack of regard for the elementary rules of maintaining good health. For instance, Tom later complained that she had not taken the trouble to teach him to care for his teeth. As an adult, Tom seldom went to doctors and paid scant regard to their advice. His reluctance to obtain adequate medical care may well have hastened his death.

Julia's puritanical attitudes toward sex had an undesirable effect on Tom's psychosexual development. She taught him to be ashamed of nudity, and to feel that sex was dirty, and something that no good woman would be interested in. In *Look Homeward, Angel* Tom recounts that whenever W. O. tried to fondle Eliza (Julia) she would push him away and say, "It's too late for that, Mr. Gant." Similarly, Julia spoke disparagingly of W. O.'s or Frank's or Ben's sexual involvement with women, and deliberately discouraged Tom's interest in girls. On several occasions in *Look Homeward, Angel*, Wolfe has Eliza come out on the porch at night to discourage Eugene from talking to a girl by telling him that he ought to go to bed. Later Julia was extremely critical of his mistress, Aline Bernstein, or of any friendships with other women. Julia or Mabel, or both, may have been responsible for Tom's tendency to associate women with housekeeping and with the preparation of food. Julia's prolonged nursing of Tom may have laid the foundation for his strong interest in food and contributed to his confusion of food-acquisition and sexual behavior characteristic of the narcissistic person.

Many of Tom's neurotic traits were learned from Julia: his suspiciousness, his ritualistic counting, self-coerciveness and other compulsions, his tendencies toward magical thinking (assuming unreasonable cause and effect relationships), and his interest in the psychic and the occult. These traits Wolfe discusses in detail in *The Web and the Rock*, and all of them are more characteristic of Julia than of anyone else in his family. Tom's tremendous preoccupation with death may have been in part, at least, also learned from Julia, since from the time of Grover's death, when Tom was four, she talked a great deal about death.

Her incessant recital of the illnesses and deaths of the Westall family were a part of his early life, but of course his own exposure to several traumatic deaths—particularly those of Grover, Ben, and W. O.—must not be discounted as formative influences.

In his early childhood Tom came to idealize his father, perceiving him as a person of extraordinary qualities. Julia challenged this concept by her continuous, even though partially justified, criticisms of W. O. Her complaints about her hard life, her husband's iniquities, and the "awful curse" of his drinking—which most of his sons, as well as Mabel, shared to some degree—made it difficult for Tom to retain his unrealistic image of his father, to develop an accurate idea of normal male behavior, or to have respect for his own masculinity.

Furthermore, Julia was inclined to disparage Tom's intellectual interests, although at times she expressed confidence that he would eventually succeed. It was hard for her to see his efforts at writing as a satisfactory occupation for a man. Tom complained in a letter to Fred that Julia seemed to think that writing was very easy—almost an avocation. She also implied that she was sure that she, herself, could write, but there was always the faint implication that she was too busy with her business. Tom was very bitter about this and about her tendency to measure success by money. He criticized all of the "slick" businessmen of Asheville who became wealthy by cheating their neighbors; and he eventually wrote that the "madness for money" was the source of all of his family's misery. He even wrote to Mabel that he wished Julia would lose some of her property during the "crash," since he thought that this might make her more generous. Later, he became quite worried about his mother's possible losses and reassured her that he would help the family in any way he could. He had legally withdrawn any claim upon her property or estate, but she, in contrast, was the principal beneficiary of his own will. In an earlier will which he changed in 1937 he divided his estate equally between his mother and Aline Bernstein.

Perhaps it was an asset that Julia taught Tom the virtue of working hard in order to "make something of himself," but since in Tom's case it became a drive that prevented him from doing anything but his writing, it became compulsive. Certainly Julia emphasized the middle-class virtues of the Protestant ethic, and in many ways Tom fashioned his life accordingly. W. O. shared this belief in the necessity of hard work, but he was considerably more easy going than Julia about sex and spending money, and also believed in the importance of generosity and fair play. Tom learned something from both parents, but he never learned to relax. Even when he travelled—which can be a hobby for some people—he was restless and driven, compulsively searching for something, and only occasionally able to give himself up to enjoying the moment.

Undoubtedly, some of the traits Tom acquired from his mother—her prodigious memory and love of storytelling—contributed to his skill as a writer. But when they took on the aspect of compulsions, a need to remember every detail, to read every book, to meet every person, they proved a hindrance to his work. One more trait that Tom seems to have acquired from Julia was her love of lawsuits. The difference between them was that Julia always won hers. She would rent her boardinghouse to someone during the winter and then find some pretext to have it taken away from them when she returned. Or she would seize her tenants' suitcases if they fell behind in their payments. She was very suspicious, even paranoid, and it is quite likely that many of the paranoid tendencies that Tom developed later in his life can be traced to his mother's example. In Tom's brushes with the law he was sometimes the plaintiff but more often the defendant, and was involved in his first lawsuit by the age of twenty-three, when he refused to pay a typist's bill for typing a play. Later he refused to pay his dentist's bill. Then he brought suit against his young Irish friend (see page 54) for stealing his manuscripts, and, after his books were published, the libel suits were brought against Tom. In all of this one senses that Julia's passion for litigation was reenacted by her son, as were so many of her traits.

To be fair to Julia, some mitigating circumstances help to explain her personality. There is the possibility, although not much is known about this, that she may have felt somewhat rejected in a large family of mostly male children. She showed signs of intense masculine protest and competitiveness with men, and went to college at a time when few women did, suggesting that she did not think it particularly advantageous to be a woman. This competitiveness might have made it difficult for her to find a husband. Her pictures do not show her as especially attractive, although she was not ugly. Certainly she did not receive from W. O. Wolfe a very significant display of love and affection; it is distinctly likely that he married Julia because he was lonely, wanted to have children, and perhaps because he needed a housekeeper. She soon found him a not very devoted husband; that his ambitions did not correspond with her own, or those of her brothers, did not improve the relationship. W. O.'s inability to take a more masculine role in finances may have aggravated Julia, with her strong drive, to achieve economic success.

Julia grew up in a state of extreme poverty, making her extreme penuriousness more understandable. It is likely that the farm home in Pennsylvania, where W. O. grew up in the pre-Civil War period, provided much more bounteous fare than the farm in the North Carolina hills where Julia grew up just after the Civil War. Finally, when Julia turned to her children for affection she found them rather unresponsive; all of them seem to have preferred their generous, spontaneous father. Julia is said to have been the disciplinarian of the family and this may have produced hostility toward her, so that her need for love was probably not very well met from any source. Presumably, as her need for love remained thwarted she became even more unlovable.

What was Julia's influence on the psychosexual development of Tom Wolfe? There is much evidence to suggest that he felt ambivalent toward her; that he wanted to love her and be loved by her, but that this need was not adequately reciprocated. Kennedy[3] says that all of the signs of the classical Oedipal situation existed in the Wolfe home, with W. O. showing a very obvious preference for his daughter Mabel over his wife, and with Julia favoring her sons, particularly Tom. While this is certainly true, it is probably too simple an explanation of the dynamic of the pyschosexual interplay in the family. Julia was unconsciously quite seductive in her behavior toward Tom, having him sleep with her until he was almost pubescent; however, she was also a rigid moralistic woman. The seductive parent, in such circumstances, unconsciously tempts the child; when the child responds to the temptation, the parent with deep moral sense rebuffs or punishes him. The child feels that he is bad because he has been punished. Typically this kind of experience recurs a number of times, and he learns to expect that he will be punished when he responds to such seductiveness. Such experiences produce confused attitudes toward women and sexuality.

Apparently Julia did devote a great deal of attention and preference to Tom in his early years, but sometime around the period when she started the boardinghouse, she became too involved with her money-making activities and Tom had to start shifting for himself, or to turn to others for love and affection. He consequently turned primarily to Ben and Mabel. (The relationship between Tom and Mabel is discussed in the next chapter, and that with Ben was treated earlier.) It is apparent that Tom developed a considerable amount of affection for Mabel, and seems to have preferred her to his mother by the time he had reached puberty; he also loved Ben deeply. There are numerous signs of Julia's unconscious rejection of Tom after his early

3. Kennedy, p. 131.

childhood. She was, of course, very niggardly with money, and she did not buy him adequate clothing. She made Tom earn money quite early and never gave him an allowance. She derogated Tom's writing, and gave the impression that he should be earning money at a steady job. She apparently remarked unfavorably at least once upon his beginning salary of $1800 for the nine-month year as an instructor at New York University.

One of the most obvious instances of Julia's unconscious rejection of Tom occurred in 1925 when he pleaded for some money while in Europe, where he was making his last major effort to write plays. Julia usually answered his requests only after long delays, and then with less than the amount he would request. On this one occasion when he was desperately in need of money she finally sent a check, after several months delay, but then Tom discovered that it was made out to Julia E. Wolfe, and could not be cashed anywhere in Europe. It took more than another month to get a new check from her, and in the meantime Tom had to borrow money from various sympathetic but strange women. Probably as a result of unconscious annoyance or hostility, Tom lost the useless check and then, in turn, had to reassure Julia repeatedly that no one else could possibly cash it. It might be argued that a man of twenty-five should not ask his mother to help support his European travels. But Tom saw this travel as the necessary culmination of his efforts to establish himself as a writer. Furthermore he was convinced, as was the rest of the family, that Julia had plenty of money in the bank, but was too niggardly to give any of it to her children. She was constantly buying property, and in *River* Tom describes her as having bought an automobile which she never took out of the garage; so that the children's annoyance with her seems understandable.

Julia also insisted on calling Tom "my baby" and even when he was in his thirties she still addressed him as "Child, child." This did little to enhance Tom's self-image as a mature male. Mrs. Wolfe was forty when Tom was born. Usually mothers tend to be quite fond of children born to them late in life, and certainly in his early childhood Tom was treated as a favorite by his mother. Actually however, she tended to be a somewhat castrating mother, who tried to make her sons into copies of herself, rather than their father. With each of her sons, except Ben, Julia seems to have tried to establish a close mother-son relationship, but she always had to compete with W. O. for their affection. As mentioned before, both Julia and W. O. spoiled Frank, their oldest son. Then they turned to Grover, "the best of the lot." After Grover's death, they both focussed on Fred for a time (Julia kept him in curls until he was eight). But Fred gradually became W. O.'s favorite. Again, when Tom was born, both parents lavished affection on him. However, Julia won, that time, by removing Tom from W. O. Toward her two daughters Julia had a more distant relationship regarding them primarily as sources of help with her wifely duties—particularly cooking, and care of the younger children. Emotionally, the girls were closer to W. O.

It is significant that of the sons only Frank, the oldest, married early in life, and to an older woman. Fred was forty-nine when he married, and neither Tom nor Ben married at all. Ben, Frank, and Tom were usually attracted to women who were older than they. The sons' image of marriage must have been one of a very undesirable state; they seem to have suffered from some psychosexual inadequacy which prevented their easily assuming the role of a husband and father. It is likely that Julia produced, by the various combinations of circumstances described above, a condition known as a split-imago problem in the boys. The split imago, a condition in which all females are either seen as too pure to be thought of as sexual objects, or else are seen solely as sexual objects, rather than as desirable human beings and mates is evidenced in Tom. He apparently perceived most women as whores; at least all of the evidence available would support this notion. He saw just a few women as ideal females,—his teacher, Margaret Roberts, probably his mother, and perhaps his sister, Mabel —and perhaps over-idealized them. It is significant, and typical of a split-imago situation, that most of Tom's sexual alliances were with women older than himself.

Matthew Besdine describes what he calls a Jocasta type of mother (drawing the name of Jocasta from the legendary Greek tragedy of Oedipus, who was doomed, though unknowingly, to kill his father and marry his mother, Jocasta).[4] Besdine points out that many men of genius, among them Michelangelo, Leonardo da Vinci, Freud, and even Christ himself had such mothers. In this situation, as conceived by Besdine, the mother, unable to relate to her husband, early devotes massive amounts of attention to her son, who may be an only son, or the last of her children (as Tom Wolfe was). In a warm mother-son symbiosis she instills in him her own values and interests. Frequently she tutors him herself (as Julia Wolfe did Tom). Eventually (Besdine places this around the Oedipal period near the child's sixth year), she becomes frightened by the intimate dependency of the child, and periodically repulses him. He then comes to regard his wonderful and sometimes loving mother as two-faced—both close and tender, and rejecting or suffocating and crippling. His only way of reaching out to this mother and pleasing her is by prodigious creative efforts which will please her by their precocity, and perhaps by her vicariously rewarded sense of creativity. According to Besdine, the sons of Jocastas are unable to have satisfactory sexual and love relationships with other women. The women they relate to are unavailable—as whores, or mental defectives, lesbians, or older women. Real love becomes an idealized expression which may be directed to their works of art. Sometimes there is a strong homosexualization of their love interest, or sometimes this is guarded against by paranoid, masochistic, or guilt-ridden

4. Matthew Besdine, "Mrs. Oedipus," *Psychology Today* 2 (1969): 40-47, 67.

ideation. Usually such men are driven throughout their lives to produce tremendous amounts of work, and they are often among the world's outstanding artists because of the impulse to create superior works.

All of this seems to fit very well the relationship between Thomas Wolfe and his mother, Julia. The Jocasta-Oedipus label is hardly necessary; what is relevant is that the elements of the personalities involved fit the image depicted in the syndrome, and that they make psychological sense as a means of explaining the needs and interrelationship of the two individuals. This Jocasta-Oedipus analogy fits the Wolfe interaction so closely that it is a legitimate prototype for explaining that interaction. Julia was bright, and sexually frustrated in her relationship with W. O. Her last child, Tom, was also very bright, and she attempted at first to build a close, symbiotic relationship with him. She held him to her much more closely than the average mother holds onto her sons. Then she became unable to continue giving this unconditional love, and started to withdraw it. Tom Wolfe showed all of the consequent symptoms: the interest in artistic (literary) creation, the tendency to relate better to males than to females, the great difficulty in establishing a love relationship with suitable women, the corresponding tendency to satisfy lust with inadequate or inappropriate women, the overwhelming drive toward a constant excess of creativity, and finally the suspicious, sensitive, and eventually paranoid, responses to annoyances and frustrations. It is probable, therefore, that Tom's developing libido found no wholly satisfactory object except himself, and for this reason his psychosexual development became primarily narcissistic, or self-oriented.

Signs of Narcissism

There are many signs that Wolfe's main life style was essentially narcissistic. He himself used that word in an earlier draft of *Look Homeward, Angel*:[5] "The sad family of this world is damned all together, and joined, from its birth . . . in the incestuous loves of sons and mothers . . . in the insatiate sexuality of infancy, in our wild hunger for ourself, the dear love of our excrement, the great obsession of Narcissus. . . ." He referred also at that time to "the bare appalling flashes that the great wizard of Vienna has thrown upon" the shore of the invisible, magic world. Kennedy says that Wolfe's familiarity with psychoanalytic thinking was derived from hearing about Aline Bernstein's psychoanalysis, and that he had no deep knowledge of the subject. Wolfe, himself, said that Freud had spoken a century too soon to be comprehended by the rest of mankind.

Earlier we discussed Tom's preoccupation with his body image (see page 66), a pervasive theme in almost all of his books, and even in some of his letters (see Braswell's account of Tom's preoccupation with himself when looking into a mirror).[6] In *The Web and the Rock* Tom describes George Webber gazing at himself in the mirror, convinced that he would become great, and would find "Perfection." Actually, we know Tom was not happy with his body image, and described his dissatisfaction in many passages, dealing especially with his height, or his awkward limbs.

DeVoto, in his criticism of *River* in 1935, was perhaps the first person to discuss Wolfe clinically; and he was actually rather accurate in his perceptions. He says that part of Eugene Gant's condition is explained as an infantile regression.[7] In his famous review of *Story of a Novel* in 1936, DeVoto says that in addition to the desire to recapture the happiness of his infancy, Gant shows another stigma of infantilism, namely that all experiences are for him perceived at an equal level of frenzy, a ride on a train being as exciting as eating a meal, or making love to a

---

5. *Notebooks*, pp. 106-07.
6 Braswell, "Wolfe Lectures," pp. 11-22.
7. Bernard DeVoto, "Review of Boyd's *Roll River*," *Saturday Review of Literature* 12 (1935).

woman, or even reading a book.[8] And even Miss Nowell, who hardly said an unkind thing about Wolfe, describes him as a person who experienced a very prolonged adolescence. She feels that he only moved into adulthood at the age of thirty-seven, the year before his death. This was when he severed his relationship with Perkins, and also showed signs of becoming interested in a social philosophy, rather than being primarily interested in autobiography. But she admits that in many ways he never grew out of his childhood emotionally.[9]

Wolfe's major signs of narcissism were his inability to form sustained love relationships with other persons, his tremendous preoccupation with his inner experiences, his need to tell all of his thoughts publicly and in writing, his drinking, his preoccupation with good food and physical sensuality, and most significant of all, his desire to achieve great fame.

Wolfe expressed his conviction that he would be great many times. In his effort to handle his insecurity he developed the defense mechanism of overcompensatory boasting. The person who feels competent doesn't brag; it is the person who is uncertain who bolsters his own sagging self-confidence by loudly proclaiming his past or present successes. Tom was constantly preoccupied with his efforts to achieve personal fame, but was uncertain about his ability to do so. As early as 1920 he wrote his mother of his need to complete much writing before he died. A year later he wrote that he was confident that by the time he was twenty-five, he would have written a good play. That year he again wrote that he had something important to say in his plays, and that his work would be talked about by the time he was twenty-five. Two years later, when he asked his mother to save all of his father's letters, he said that he believed he could capture the character of his father in his writing in a way that would "knock the hearts

8. DeVoto, "Genius is Not Enough," pp. 3-4, 14-15.
9. *Letters*, pp. xvi-xvii.

out of people by its reality." And that same year he declared that nothing could stop him but insanity, disease, or death. That year he wrote to Professor Baker of his belief in the innateness of his own genius, although shortly thereafter he also said that he was going to destroy his manuscripts (he never actually destroyed manuscripts) and become a teacher, which he considered tantamount to defeat. He mentioned to Albert Coates that he wondered whether he would ever cease to be a child, and that he was unwilling to revisit Chapel Hill yet because he did not, after three years, have any achievement to show, for he had not yet sold one of his plays. Apparently he did not consider a Master's degree in drama and English literature as a significant accomplishment.

In 1924 Wolfe wrote his mother that nothing lasts but beauty, but that he would create beauty. He chided her for not understanding him, and reminded her that he would be great if he did not die too soon, and that she would become known as his mother, for he would survive and triumph. In the next year he expressed pleasure that the people at New York University had enough confidence in him to hire him, but felt that he was not yet saying what was twisting his brain and what he needed to say in writing. In 1926 he told his mother that he was one of the few people he knew who had lived a heroic life. Admitting that this was a boastful thing to say, he pointed out that year after year, in the face of hostility and criticism, he had "been steadfast in my devotion to the high, passionate, and beautiful things of this world." This rather pompous boast was reiterated in 1927, and by 1929 he was boasting that by the time he was fifty-five or sixty he would have produced fifteen or twenty books, if he lived that long. The next year he told his mother that the critics were saying wonderful things about the characters in *Look Homeward, Angel*, but at this point he was being defensive about the criticisms from his family and the people of Asheville.

About the same time Wolfe told John Wheelock, an editor

at Scribner's, that no one else had one-fourth of his power and richness, and that his baseness was better than the nobility of his critics. He admitted that he was guilty of "colossal egotism" but defended it as the inevitable by-product of the creative process. Two years later he mentioned to Fred Wolfe that autographed copies of the first edition of *Angel* were bringing twenty-five dollars. In 1933 he wrote to Robert Raynolds that some of his work was so good he almost had to cry about it, although when he was working on something he was more likely to curse God, and men; and he confided to Belinda Jelliffe that what he most wanted was fame and high esteem. Wolfe always admitted that his two strongest drives were for fame and love, but he assumed that this was true for all men. For Tom, the need for fame seemed to be the stronger need of the two, which may be another way of saying that his self-love was intense. Shortly before that time he wrote in his notebooks, "Faust's own problem . . . is mine. . . . He wants to know everything, to be a god—and he is caught in the terrible net of human incapacity."[10]

It is hard to explain some of Wolfe's behavior except by the theory of intense narcissism. His dependency, and his need to receive constant reassurance of his mother's inapparent love, remained with him throughout most of his life. Why else would he consider it his mother's obligation to continue to support him when he was twenty-five years old, and already had a master's degree, and had proven himself capable of being a college instructor? His brothers had supported themselves without family aid from the age of about sixteen. Moreover, whenever a friend failed to display what Wolfe considered sufficient admiration of him, Tom would break off the relationship. In *The Web and the Rock*, George Webber breaks away from his roommate, Jerry Alsop, because Jerry does not appreciate his writing. Part of the reason for Tom's break with Max Perkins stemmed from Tom's

---

10. *Notebooks*, p. 259.

feeling that Max was treating him as just another writer, though of course other factors complicated that situation.

In *You Can't Go Home Again*, Wolfe depicts George Webber as convinced that in writing his book he had done something never done before. He shows George avidly reading all of the reviews, searching for words of praise, and feeling crushed when he is criticized. George is delighted when he begins to receive fan letters and invitations to attend parties or give talks. (Actually Wolfe later came to despise these activities.) When the people of Lybia Hill (Asheville) criticize George, he wallows in a morass of self-pity. When Webber learns that his second book is a success, he is delighted just as Wolfe was delighted when Sinclair Lewis went out of his way to list him as one of the promising authors of his generation. Indeed Tom later made the effort to spend a week with Lewis who was in England at the time. When the Germans made him into something of a literary hero Wolfe was extravagant in his praise of the German people, although later he became disillusioned by the Nazi political movement.

Dependency and Counter-dependency

One of Wolfe's most striking personality traits was his excessive dependency. This trait must have originated in the marked overprotectiveness showered upon him in his early childhood by his parents and siblings. As the last of Julia's seven living children he was held in a state of prolonged infancy by his mother's protracted nursing, by her dressing him as if he were a small child, and by her keeping him with her as much as possible until the move to the Old Kentucky Home, and to some extent for some years thereafter. When he was twenty she was still denying him adult privileges with the excuse, "Why you're my baby!" Tom's father was also rather protective, and turned to this youngest child for the filial responses which he almost certainly knew were to be the last he was likely to receive. He enjoyed Tom's visits, and was exceptionally paternal toward the boy until his adolescence. Mabel, who was approaching womanhood when Tom was a boy, also adopted a very maternal attitude toward her youngest brother, although it was at times mixed with a streak of sadistic punitiveness. There is no question that she enjoyed playing mother to Tom, and possibly it gave her some satisfaction to feel that she was a better mother figure than Julia. To the end of Tom's life Mabel referred to him as a boy. Ben's devotion to this younger brother was exceptionally strong, and he became, quite early, something of a father-surrogate for Tom, protecting him from some of Julia's more neglectful behavior, and providing him with privileges and support. Finally Margaret Roberts, Tom's teacher at the North State Fitting School, unquestionably showed especially strong maternal feelings for Wolfe, and except for the seven-year period following publication of *Look Homeward, Angel*, continued to fill a maternal role for him.

All of this overprotection from five parent figures produced in Wolfe a more than average need for support, which he later struggled to throw off, though never successfully. Consequently his relationships with other persons in his adult life were also unusually dependent. He seemed especially helpless and, therefore, vulnerable, a quality which elicited a nurturant-protective response from others. This response was particularly true of Aline Bernstein, his mistress, and Max Perkins, his editor, both of whom Tom turned to as parent figures to help him with even the simplest problems such as laundry, or money. During Wolfe's love affair with Aline Bernstein—who was eighteen years older than he—his dependency became evident in his letters, written mostly in the periods when he was in Europe and she in America. He did not have to plead for money, since she provided it quite generously, and he was more dependent upon her signs of love and affection. Unfortunately some of the letters to Mrs. Bernstein have not been published. Those which do appear in print tend to be the more impersonal ones, in which Tom reports his travel experiences; but even in these one can sense that the relationship was not so much one of equals, or of lover and mistress, as of mother and son. After the break with Aline Bernstein, Wolfe became very dependent upon his editor, Max Perkins. Since Tom met with him almost daily for both personal and literary reasons, the relationship was admittedly one of support of Tom's dependency needs, which Max was pleased to gratify. Perkins became a father figure to a very dependent son, and this relationship lasted until about 1936, when Tom's need to demonstrate his literary and personal maturity became strong, largely because of the gibes of critics about his literary dependence on Perkins. Following this relationship, Wolfe turned to his agent, Elizabeth Nowell, who took over most of Perkins's functions though as intimate a personal relationship did not develop. Nevertheless, Miss Nowell served not only as Tom's literary agent, but also as his manuscript editor, and personal manager. Tom seemed to find the management of most personal chores unbearable, and wanted someone else to take care of all of life's problems. These desires are quite evident in Wolfe's letters, and are also reported fully in his novels.

Countering Tom's strong dependency was a need to move toward independence, which sometimes took the form of overreaction, or counter-dependency. Wolfe himself identified his early novels as the search of a young man for the meaning of life, and his desire to remove the bonds which tied him so tightly to his family. His first efforts to break away from the ties to home, with their resulting loneliness, are the major theme of *Look Homeward, Angel*, and this theme is carried on in *Of Time and the River*, which takes Wolfe's biography up to the time when he was twenty-five. In subsequent years, when he developed a dependency first on Aline Bernstein and then on Max Perkins, he became disturbed by the binding quality of these relationships, and struggled to break away from them. The problem was that Wolfe always had to struggle. He could not just break away, but had to overdo the process in a soul-searching and personality-destroying process of attack and counter-reply from the puzzled former patron. Having gone through a phase of profound and effusive over-gratitude for the support and affection Aline and Max had given him, he would then proceed into a phase of bitter criticism and abuse, most of it unjustified. His dependency needs were so strong that efforts to break away were very traumatic for him. (This is why it should be labelled counter-dependency, rather than just movement toward independence.) Tom's letters and novels abound in manifestations of this tendency. Most of *The Web and the Rock* seems to be consumed with the vituperative outburst against Esther (Aline), and *You Can't Go Home Again* includes much justification of Tom's rejection of Max, usually for rather insufficient reasons, such as his alleged disloyalty to Tom, or his attempts to censor Tom's work, or similar inaccurate criticisms. Similarly, the letters approach the edge of paranoia in their inappropriate and vituperative cries of rage. When Tom broke with Perkins and returned to Asheville, looking for comfort, he learned to his dismay that "you can't go home again." That is, he learned that he could not expect to reestablish the dependency relationships of his childhood. This discovery shook him and left him feeling frightened and alone.

To what degree was Julia Wolfe responsible for Tom's excessive, lifelong dependency? Although it is evident that she shared this responsibility, to some extent, with W. O., Mabel, Ben, and Margaret Roberts, and even with Aline Bernstein and Max Perkins, it seems psychologically defensible to assert that the foundation for most of Tom's more pervasive traits of character and personality was acquired during his early formative years, when the basic personality was molded. And Julia's overprotectiveness in these early years can probably be taken to have been instrumental in bringing about the dependency, and subsequent counter-dependency, which characterized all of Tom's life, and expressed his essentially narcissistic approach to life.

6

HIS SISTER MABEL, AND HIS SEXUAL TENDENCIES

WOLFE HAD TWO SISTERS, EFFIE AND MABEL. EFFIE WAS fourteen years older than he, and married when he was eight. Tom did not see much of her and did not care a great deal for her. She was the Victorian of the family, very proper, rather prim, and perhaps distant. She married a fairly unsuccessful man and had seven children. Tom Wolfe, Mabel, and their mother, Julia, all seemed to consider Effie as somewhat self-centered. She probably had very little influence on her famous younger brother. Tom's relationship with Mabel was entirely different. Although she was ten years older than Tom, she influenced him significantly. Tom describes Mabel as generous, warm-hearted, self-pitying, a person who would do everything she could for anyone who needed help, but very much wanted to be appreciated. Her three most pronounced traits were her deep devotion to her father, a certain sadistic hostility that would at times break through her usual warmth and generosity, and a tendency to become overwrought and hysterical under pressure. Although her memoirs, *Thomas Wolfe and His Family* tell us much about Mabel, the fact that she was an avid social climber concerned with her reputation led her to omit or gloss over anything unfavorable. For example, she mentions W. O.'s drinking only casually, and says nothing at all about her father's or her brothers' promiscuity. Nor does she refer at all to Tom's celebrated mistress, Aline Bernstein. As a result the most valuable source of information about Tom's relationship with Mabel is not her own book but rather Tom's letters and his first two novels, in which she figures prominently as Helen Gant.

Mabel was big-boned, tall, thin, animated, and rather attractive in her youth; pictures taken in her maturity show a woman who seemed to exude purposefulness and warmth. After completing high school she embarked on what she had hoped would be a singing career. Although she had wanted to become a concert singer, she did not progress beyond Chautauqua programs, movie houses, and hotel orchestras. She and a friend travelled together for several years to these engagements, but this venture in no way changed her proper behavior and outlook. She remained a nice small-town girl, and after a few years settled down in Asheville to care for her father and to marry Ralph Wheaton, a moderately successful salesman for the National Cash Register Company. Wheaton managed several of the Company's agencies, but principally the Asheville one.

Mabel started to take care of her father when she was a little girl, and at sixteen became his housekeeper, and at the same time helped her mother prepare the noon meal at the Old Kentucky Home. There was a strong bond of affection, and similarity, between Mabel and W. O. Wolfe, and the rivalry between Julia and Mabel for W. O.'s affection was open and bitter. W. O. made little secret of his preference for Mabel, and she obviously enjoyed and used this appreciation. Fred was also very fond of her, and would consistently defend her in the course of the family arguments. To Fred she was quite obviously the ideal of American womanhood. Although Mabel knew for many years that her father was dying of cancer she could never bring herself to believe it, and would experience hysterical spells and deep depression very often, but especially whenever W. O. had to go to Baltimore for radiation treatments. During these spells she would rage at the rest of the family for being so inconsiderate of her father, or even at the doctor for not taking care of him properly. She particularly blamed her mother for W. O.'s illness, just as she had accused Julia of contributing to Ben's death by not taking good care of him during his final illness.

Mabel craved excitement, and was very extroverted. She would defend people whom others criticized, particularly if they were criticized for drinking, or sexual activity. Thus, she befriended several women who were thought to have loose relationships with men, including her brothers, and she would defend her father's drinking and whoring. She herself drank considerably, but secretly. However she became very angry when Tom got drunk several times, and upbraided him bitterly. Possibly she felt that as the baby of the family he was too young for such behavior.

Mabel's relationship with Tom was that of both mother and rival. When he was little she played at mothering him, and when Julia moved out and Mabel took over W. O.'s household she definitely saw herself as a mother substitute for Tom whenever he visited his father's house. She deliberately vied with Julia for Tom's affection and made hostile comparisons as to which one fed and generally treated Tom better. Given the daughter's personality and the mother's, it is likely that Mabel had little difficulty in winning that particular contest. By the time Tom approached puberty he definitely preferred Mabel to Julia in many ways. Both in his letters and books he was to pay warm tribute to her skills in mothering him. At the same time, in spite of this warm bond, there was a strong feeling of rivalry toward Tom on Mabel's part—a resentment that Mabel never felt toward her brother Fred. This resentment became especially apparent when she would find Tom reading rather than working at selling newspapers, at which times she would scream at him in a rage. When he was in the prepubescent stage they spent a lot of time roughhousing, and Mabel alternated between playing with him somewhat seductively and then becoming sadistic, slapping him around until he burst into deep sobs. Then Mabel would be overwhelmed with remorse and try to cajole him back to good humour with a display of oversolicitude and affection, fixing him something fine to eat, or sending him to the store for ice cream which the two of them would eat together. It is not difficult to see why Mabel resented Tom's place as the baby of the family and as his mother's favorite. The contrast between her own situation and his was very marked—she had to work very hard, and received little appreciation for doing so, whereas Tom was required to do very little, and yet was much loved. So, although she felt genuinely fond of Tom and even maternal toward him, she at the same time resented him and harbored strong feelings of hostility, which occasionally broke through her more controlled behavior.

In Tom's writing there is a recurring phrase—"dark Helen in his blood"—which appears to refer to a deep, and probably sexual, passion, although he also used the phrase to refer to the South, and to Germany. But most often it is used to describe his feelings toward several of the women with whom he had sexual relationships. This phrase was most likely a confabulation of the themes of Helen of Troy and Helen Gant (Mabel) in his novels. Wolfe did admit to some incestuous fantasies and dreams in several letters, and we may assume that these probably related to Mabel, since this phrase is used in the description of one of these fantasies. In one manuscript he mentions a dream in which Eugene goes into the arms of a Helen-like woman, who then turns into a snakeheaded Medusa. Certainly this is classical symbolism for the Oedipal and possible castration fears that may have prompted these incest fantasies. It would seem likely that a prepubescent boy would experience some unconscious sexual feelings toward a mother substitute like Mabel, who seductively frolicked with him. That Tom had slept with his mother until he was nine, and occasionally thereafter, and that the males in his family openly flaunted their sexual promiscuity may well have exacerbated these dreams and fantasies.

Mabel's jealousy of Tom mounted when he was given the chance to go away to college; but in spite of the strain that this put on their relationship, Tom continued to write to her with great warmth and frankness. In 1925 he wrote her from Europe, just after she had undergone a serious operation, sending best wishes for recovery and good health and confiding his unhappiness over his unrequited love for Ann, whom he had met through Kenneth Raisbeck. Pouring out his heart, he asked Mabel's permission to call her "My Dear," and confessed that she was one of the few women to whom he could turn, just as his father had been able to turn to her. Admitting that he was badly hurt, he begged her not to laugh at him, for he was a man now—love was making a man of him.

About the same time he also wrote to Ann and described Mabel in a passage which shows how deeply he admired her: "Since she was ten years old she was the only person who could manage my father; he was bigger than I am, and quick as a cat; occasionally he drank terrifically. During the last eight years of his life, he was dying palpably—a huge, magnificent machine going to pieces: she gave her strength to him. She has lived in a constant state of nervous irritation and excitability: she is fierce, tender, angry, biting, caressing, by turns. Her voice breaks in sheer desperation. She is 5 feet 11 tall, and thin as a rail. She blazes with restless energy. Strong commonplace people drink her vitality like wine: they never forget her, and they return to her. I have never known her to be 'brave' about anything. I have seen her weep, fret, and despair; I have seen her face death two or three times. She would die if she had nothimg to spend herself on: nothing to weep, fret, despair about. She wants to be told she is generous, good, thoughtful. She likes adulation. But when one suffers a hurt, her voice is low and gentle: she has large wonderful hands, and all the pain goes out under their touch.

The simple and terrific fact is that with all her fuming, fretting, weeping, her love of adulation, I have never seen her do a selfish thing. I mean it is simply not a part of her. I say it is a *terrific* fact: it is. There's nothing beyond it. She has more human greatness in her than any woman I've ever known. I suppose, honestly, that's why I sometimes get tired of the women I meet —particularly women who are carefully calculated."

In 1926 Tom sent Mabel a long letter on the evils of the frenzied real estate manipulations that were going on in Asheville. Julia was actively involved, and Tom, who showed more prescience than most, warned Mabel and Fred not to succumb to the lure of quick riches for he feared that this speculative bubble would eventually burst. He urged them to forget the "rotten poison" of lust for riches that had never been anything but a source of bitterness, recrimination, and suspicion in the family. He also took this opportunity—he was twenty-six at the time—to say that he had received more family support than his siblings. This is probably not true; W. O. Wolfe had left each of his children $5,000, with the residual to go to Julia. However, because of his heavy medical expenses, his estate amounted to only about $11,000 or $12,000. Fred Wolfe and Mabel's husband, Ralph Wheaton, his executors, worked out an agreement whereby the two daughters each received $5,000, and the balance went to Frank. Tom and Fred each signed statements that they had received their "share," but this really referred to the money paid toward their college tuition. Actually Mabel received, and perhaps deserved, more in cash than had been spent on Tom, but he recognized that his college training had been an invaluable asset to him, and consistently maintained that he had been treated fairly. Mabel, on the other hand, constantly alleged that Tom had been given special privileges.

From this time on, Tom repeatedly pleaded with Mabel, as he

did with Julia and Fred, that the family unite and show love and affection for each other, instead of bitterness. But this proved difficult. In 1927 he reminded Mabel that because he had been different from the others she thought him "queer" and a "freak," but begged her to realize that any hostility or bitterness which he might have shown toward her during his years at college or at Harvard had by this time subsided. But in 1929 he wrote to Max Perkins that he had visited with his family for a week, and that the family "got one another crazy." He saw this as an unfortunate situation for which no one in particular was to blame.

By 1933 the Depression made things very difficult for the Wheatons; Ralph was sick and had lost his job, and Mabel was running a roominghouse in Washington. During this period Tom visited her and also wrote her not to be bitter, because bitterness could kill those upon whom it feeds. (Later, in 1938, he implied that she had every reason to be bitter against the whole capitalistic system.) He also told her that she, at least, was spared one trial of life which he had had to bear—that of loneliness. He said his loneliness began when he was about eight years old, which places it at around the period when Julia took him away from the rest of the family. It was at this time that Tom became an avid reader, probably escaping from his loneliness by immersing himself in books. And it was precisely his habit of doing this that so enraged Mabel who was kept busy with her many responsibilities.

Because Tom had no wife or children of his own, he seemed to feel more need for Mabel's affection and good will than she did for his. In the early years Mabel expended most of her energy taking care of her father, and later she had a husband to care for. After her father's death, and when it became apparent that she was to be childless, she seems to have had more time to devote to Tom. In 1936 Tom wrote Mrs. Roberts about the difficult time Mabel had had during the previous few years. He commented with pride on the way she was always able to pull herself together, and, indeed, to keep the whole family together, adding that in spite of her railings and tirades she was always willing to give anyone in need the shirt off her back. In these traits she was very much like W. O.

Shortly before he died, Tom wrote Mabel two very supportive and encouraging letters. She had been quite ill, as had her husband, and her world seemed to be falling apart. These letters, in March and May of 1938, conveyed his hope that she would quickly recover her health, and reassured her that he would do everything he could to support the family in recent litigation which a local bank had brought against Julia and her heirs. He begged Mabel to let them become reconciled about any past differences and apologized for any unkind things he might have said about any of his family in *Look Homeward, Angel*. Then he suggested that she forget all the "blarney" about her being so self-sacrificing. Everyone admitted that she had made sacrifices for her father, but he pointed out that she did it because she wanted and needed to. Similarly, he said it wasn't true that he had been the lucky one in getting away from home; that she had stayed at home because she wanted to, and that he had, in fact, left home because he had discovered that there was no place for him there. He went on to decry the "money ugliness" which had come between the members of the family, and said that he felt he had gotten his share and no more or less. He added that there was not a grain of business sense in the entire family—a statement which conflicted with the comments he sometimes made about Julia in his more beneficent moments. He confessed to Mabel that he was weary and had gotten no rest during the previous summer when he had visited with his family. Asheville he described as a ruined and defeated town, filled with ruined and defeated people, and he encouraged Mabel, who had returned there in 1936, to get away from it.

Apparently Mabel was concerned that people were spreading

some sort of scandal about her (she had always worried about being childless) and he told her she should ignore any gossip, because she was bigger than all of the others in Asheville. He urged her not to apologize for herself, or to brood about W. O.'s death. Again he reiterated that the old pre-1929 world would never return. He foresaw an exciting path in the future and would help her find it.

By one of those strange ironies of fate, Mabel was to be the last person to figure significantly in Tom's life. After Tom became ill with pneumonia in the West, Fred went to Seattle to be with him while he was in the hospital. At the end of about a month Fred had to return to work, so Mabel left her own sick husband and went out to Seattle to be with Tom. It was she who first heard the diagnosis that he was probably incurably ill with either cerebral tuberculosis or a tumor. Since Tom wanted desperately to be out of the hospital, she arranged to rent a lovely apartment for his convalescence; however they only occupied it for a day because a specialist had ordered Mabel to take Tom to Baltimore immediately for a brain operation at the Johns Hopkins Hospital. Tom and Mabel spent what was probably his last happy day in this apartment, and then she and a relative, who was a nurse, accompanied him East by train. Julia met them in Chicago, bringing along fruit for Tom to eat. By this time he was suffering periods of mental confusion, and almost continuous severe headaches. Nevertheless, Mabel would not accept the diagnosis that one physician after another gave after examining Tom. Indeed, she was unable to make the phone call to Julia to tell her about it, and the physician had to take over in the midst of the call. Her desperate effort to get the doctors to tell her that Tom would live was reminiscent of her unwillingness to believe that W. O. was dying. Meanwhile, Tom put his trust in Mabel and the doctors with childlike dependency. Their last days together almost recapitulated the earliest days when Tom was a little boy, and Mabel his big sister and mother surrogate. When he died she was hysterical with grief.

Wolfe's Oral Sexual Tendencies

What influences did Mabel have on her brother's personality? It seems almost certain that she shaped much of his image of his sexual ideal. The women with whom he formed sexual relationships of some durability were remarkably similar to Mabel, both physically, and to some extent in personality. All were considerably older than he. Aline Bernstein is the most striking example, for she was forty-three years old when they met and Tom only twenty-five. Moreover, Tom strongly favored women who were good cooks, and stated that the sight of a woman cooking a meal for her husband was the most satisfying sight in the world. Mabel fitted this category too, as well as being a very maternal person, encouraging Tom's tendency toward dependency, and, to a considerable extent, toward narcissism.

Mabel's inconstancy—a certain fickleness and sporadic quality in her affection for Tom—seems to have made him suspicious of many of the women he met in later life. In her friendly periods Mabel was warm and responsive and rather earthy, not unwilling to call sex by its name and to recognize it as a significant part of life. Tom certainly felt this way himself, and typically chose women who shared that feeling. But Mabel also tended to draw limits; and it seems reasonable to see in his feelings for Mabel some evidences of the Oedipal conflict which Tom experienced; a boy may feel sexual interest toward his sister, but he can't do anything about it because of the incest taboo. Since Julia Wolfe also was inconsistent in her treatment of Tom—being unconsciously seductive at some times and very proper at others—Mabel's similar inconsistency probably reinforced Tom's split-imago conflicts. Mabel's behavior must have contributed heavily to Tom's feelings of insecurity. On the one hand loving and warm, she could also be very critical and cruelly reject Tom. In these moods she accused Tom of being a typical Westall—synonymous with being niggardly, dominating, and queer—rather than one of the charmed circle of Wolfes. While her use of such epithets as "freak" and "queer" probably did not carry the connotation of homosexuality, they were clearly derogatory, as was her mimicking of his gestures. This kind of response from a mother-figure is not likely to help build a wholesome personality in a child. Mabel's criticism hurt Tom deeply, and continued to rankle, even in his adult life. He later pointed out that when a child is constantly criticized and told he is selfish, he begins to want to get away from the person who treats him so unsympathetically, and is driven to isolate himself from others as well, which finally condemns him to loneliness.

Wolfe's attitude toward sex comprised a confused combination of an immature preoccupation with oral activities—which he often equated with sex—and a restless, almost uncontrollable search for heterosexual libido objects, which prompted him to act in the manner of the typical Don Juan. Aside from the more diffuse signs of oral sexuality, such as his stuttering, drinking, chain smoking, excessive coffee drinking, intense verbal productivity, compulsive writing, and voracious eating (mentioned in almost all of his books and in many of his letters), he frequently referred to the sex act itself in terms of an oral experience. He usually compared the different parts of the female body to various foods, and often spoke of "feasting" on his mate. Aline was quite aware of this preoccupation, but tolerated it uneasily, while Ann, the Boston girl (in Europe), appeared somewhat disgusted by it. The food references were a ritualistic part of his lovemaking, but he went way beyond an "I love you so much I could eat you" attitude; he would actually describe preparing different parts of his inamorata's body as if they were various foods being selected at a market and then lovingly cooked and consumed in an orgiastic feast.

This preoccupation with eating, especially as a part of the sex act, can probably be traced to Tom's early relationship with Mabel when she would tease and slap him in a kind of love play and then, when she had reduced him to tears, would comfort him with petting and gifts of food that she lovingly prepared for him. As mentioned earlier, Julia's prolonged nursing may have laid the foundation for Tom's strong interest in food, while W. O.'s emphasis on the importance of food, and his insistence on Tom's eating large quantities of it, probably reinforced this feeling. Later, the rivalry between Julia and Mabel over their talent as cooks, and their efforts to please Tom with good food, continued the pattern. As an adult Tom usually ate only one meal a day, but it was a gargantuan one which made up for the meals he had missed. He compared the cooking of different countries at some length in his books and letters and in his pocket notebooks, and knew the restaurants where good food could be found. However, as far as the sexual connotation of food is concerned, it is probable that Mabel was the person most responsible for his confusion of food acquisition and sexuality.

7

OTHER WOMEN IN HIS LIFE

Margaret Roberts

MRS. MARGARET ROBERTS WAS WOLFE'S TEACHER DURING his high school years. Her husband had been the principal of the Orange Street School which Tom and his siblings had attended, but then he and Mrs. Roberts decided to start a small private school to be known as the North State Fitting School. While the sons of the more affluent Asheville people were naturally invited to enroll, another rather unique method of recruiting students was used as well. Before quitting the public school, Mr. Roberts summoned all of the children to the auditorium and, as Tom described it in *Look Homeward, Angel*, told them to write a short essay on the topic "The Song of the Lark." Ostensibly this was an essay competition for which a prize was to be awarded, but in fact the essays were used to identify promising students who were then invited to enroll in the new school. It is reported that Tom's essay was far better than most, and that Mrs. Roberts told her husband, "We must have that boy." Later a legend grew that even then she described him as a genius. The Roberts asked the Wolfes to enroll Tom, and eventually W. O. and Julia agreed; Julia was probably pleased at the idea that Tom would be associating with the better boys of Asheville. The

Roberts were so pleased with Tom, their star pupil, that they strongly encouraged the Wolfes to let him remain for a fifth year so that they could give him additional preparation for college. W. O. Wolfe refused, however, and insisted that Tom must go to college, and specifically to the University of North Carolina, rather than to Virginia, Tom's first choice, or to Princeton, his second choice.

The experience at the Roberts's school profoundly shaped Wolfe's career. Mr. Roberts taught the classics, and his sister taught mathematics and German. Tom took these courses without any great degree of enthusiasm, but with considerable success. Mrs. Roberts taught literature, writing, and history, and it was with her that Tom found his metier. He had already read everything in the public library of Asheville, but now the Roberts opened up to him the treasure trove of their books which he fell upon eagerly. Mrs. Roberts was an excellent teacher and steered Tom's undisciplined mind through the English classics, particularly poetry, which was to become his main interest and pleasure. On numerous occasions Tom called Margaret Roberts "the mother of my spirit," conveying beautifully and accurately what she meant to him. She had complete faith in his creative ability as a writer, and also acted as his mentor; nor was her guidance ever faulty. He later described her as one of the three great teachers he had had, the other two being professors of English and philosophy at North Carolina. Tom excelled in every academic activity at the school, graduating at the top of his class, and winning practically all of the prizes given. By this time he had decided that he wanted to become a writer, and there is no question but that his inspiration had come from Mrs. Roberts. Mrs. Roberts also took care of Tom's physical needs while he attended the school. She was deeply concerned about his health, and saw that he got some exercise and enough sleep, and did not read all of the time; she made sure that he received decent meals, and that he kept himself neater than was his custom. For several winter periods Tom boarded at the Roberts's school, and it is apparent that Margaret Roberts became a real mother surrogate to him, without any of the drawbacks that marred Tom's relationship with Mabel or his mother.

In his personal notes Wolfe mentioned a dream of sleeping with one's teacher's wife, suggesting that he may have had sexual fantasies and wishes toward Mrs. Roberts.[1] It would certainly have been natural if he had, for she was not only the mother of his spirit, but mothered him physically as well, and even kissed him (as is mentioned in the novels). But probably these fantasies were much like the typical incest fantasies of most boys who are uninhibited enough to be aware of such inner feelings. Throughout most of his subsequent life, except for a seven-year period of estrangement, Wolfe and Mrs. Roberts corresponded regularly, and it was to her that he would confide his literary ideas and ambitions. Sometimes he sought her advice on other matters as well. Mrs. Roberts did not approve of his affair with Aline Bernstein, and Tom wrote her several letters in which he defended his relationship with Aline.

The strain which developed between Margaret Roberts and Tom Wolfe stemmed from *Look Homeward, Angel*, published in 1930. Margaret eagerly anticipated publication of the book, primarily as a fulfillment of her confidence in her pupil's ability, and Tom sent her an early, inscribed copy. Although he had nothing but good to say about her in the book, her husband, depicted as Mr. Leonard, was described as rather dull and pedantic, strong on discipline and learning for learning's sake, but not an inspired teacher. Mrs. Roberts was deeply hurt, for she held her husband in high regard. She wrote to Wolfe that he had hurt his friends and "crucified his family." Tom wrote back a long letter trying to explain that he had meant no harm, and repeated the praise of the major reviewers in an attempt to reassure her of the

---

1. *Notebooks*, p. 584.

book's literary merit. It was some years later, in 1936, that Mrs. Roberts wrote Tom that she had forgiven him and assured him of her maternal love.[2] Tom then resumed his correspondence with her, almost as if there had been no break, and wrote her a number of long, warm letters during the last two years of his life. On his visit to Asheville in 1937 they met again to their mutual pleasure.

In his letters to Mrs. Roberts, Tom sometimes discussed the problems of his family, or gave her advice on the education of her children, but mostly he wrote about his literary activities and ambitions. It was apparent that in Margaret Roberts he continued to find the intellectual peer and tutor with whom he could commune freely and meaningfully. Only twice did critical comments about Mrs. Roberts enter his correspondence. In 1936 he wrote to his mother that he was afraid Margaret was reluctant to forget the past (*Angel*) and to resume their friendship. And in 1929 he wrote to Mabel that he was afraid Mrs. Roberts was something of a snob, because of her club work, and her very obvious pushing to assure that her daughter would attend a socially elite school. But these were minor criticisms, expressed with regret rather than with malice or anger. In general, Wolfe's devotion to Margaret Roberts was all but absolute, and he drew from her the intellectual support which no other woman but Aline Bernstein was ever able to give him. Had all the women in Tom's life come up to the example set by Mrs. Roberts, he would have been a much less maladjusted person.

Clara Paul

During the summer when he was sixteen, Tom experienced his first intense crush on a girl, immortalized in *Look Homeward, Angel* as the affair with Laura James. Her real name was Clara Paul, and she had brought her young brother to stay at the Old

---

2. *Letters*, p. 517; see also Turnbull, pp. 264-65.

Kentucky Home for a few weeks of convalescence. She was twenty-one years old, engaged, and planning to be married shortly. Both Mabel and Julia made it quite clear in their memoirs that everyone in the family, including Tom, was well aware of her engagement. Nevertheless, Tom fell hopelessly in love with Clara, as he confessed to Mrs. Roberts many years later (1924). Tom accompanied Clara and her brother on various sight-seeing trips and picnics around the countryside, with Clara taking care of the expenses. The Wolfes encouraged Tom to go along to help take care of Clara's brother, because they were quite pleased with Clara's friendly attitude toward all of them. Later Mabel mentioned to Julia that "her baby had fallen in love," but Julia made light of the matter, and Clara herself wrote to her sister that her landlady's son had a crush on her, but seemed hardly older than her young brother, and she felt sorry for him.[3]

Although the family and Clara treated the whole thing as a case of puppy love, Tom was very serious about it; perhaps he hoped that his charm or love for Clara would cause her to change her mind about her forthcoming marriage. As he described it in *Angel* it was an affair, but Turnbull doubts that there was any sexual involvement. Clara was married several weeks after leaving Asheville, as planned, although in *Angel* Tom treated her leaving as a jilting. He did not get over his feelings for her for over a year, and the following summer he went to work in Norfolk, partly because Clara lived there. He looked up her house, but never got up the nerve to make his presence known. In the fall of 1918 Clara died in the flu epidemic.

Tom romanticized Clara, and at the same time developed strong sexual feelings toward her, feelings somewhat unique for him. In most of his relationships with women he suffered the split-imago phenomenon, seeing them either as madonnas or madames.

---

3. Turnbull, p. 327.

Had the affair not been a hopeless one from the start, it is possible that it might have culminated in a mature love and marriage, such as Wolfe was never to experience. But that it was hopeless was significant: Tom chose to fall in love with a woman who was older and engaged to be married, thereby successfully evading the possibility of any permanent commitment.

Boston Girl

Wolfe's first experiences of sexual intercourse apparently occurred with prostitutes whom he was taken to visit in Durham by older college associates. He made it quite clear in his letters and writings and his pocket notebooks that he engaged in a very active sex life, and Miss Nowell described him as oversexed. In 1929 he wrote to an Asheville editor that he had had intercourse in ten different countries, and in *The Web and the Rock* George Webber claims to have slept with two hundred whores. Wolfe told one girl that he had slept with hundreds of women.[4] His writings described early sexual overtures made to him by the Negro women in Asheville, and he wrote numerous accounts of his visits to whores, in places all the way from cheap pine shacks in Norfolk, to the plushest bordellos of Paris. He also wrote of fantasies of sexual seduction by beautiful and wealthy women for whom he might have performed some favor, such as returning a lost pocketbook. After he became famous he was considered irresistable by women, and many, according to his biographers, eagerly slept with him; he in turn accepted their gifts willingly, but with little sense of obligation.

By the time he was a graduate student at Harvard, he was frequently having affairs with girls, and in 1923 he commented to his mother that he was always falling in love, but that it never lasted more than a week or two. But he also proudly reported

---

4. *Letters*, p. 299.

that he was working hard, and had not visited a girl for weeks. In his letters to his friends, such as Kenneth Raisbeck, he portrayed himself as quite a libertine. On one occasion he reported having been apprehended by the campus police for his sexual activity with a girl, treating the affair with the jocularity of a young rake. However, one letter, to an unknown girl in Boston, does reveal something of the intrapsychic conflict that he experienced in some of these situations. The letter began with a romanticized version of their relationship in which he described himself as overwhelmed by adoration for her beauty and feminity. He then accused her of having spoiled this mood by quickly asking where the liquor was, making it clear to him that she was used to spending nights with boys with whom she traded personal favors for booze. Wolfe felt this to be a personal blow, and an insult to his intelligence, but he got the liquor and went to bed with her. He started to love her, but at the same time saw in her all the qualities of the bored seductress and flippant "digger." He was left with ambivalent feelings. He would continue to think of her tenderly and sadly, as something beautiful and lovely; but, he also wrote that he could see life leaving its dirty thumbmarks on her, commenting that although she was good and fine, he would give her back to the vicious slimy sea. This letter might be considered a youthful outburst of fatuous prose. But it does reveal a confused youth suffering from a confabulation of the sublime woman with the earthy whore. Was she the immaculate and ethereal goddess, or the vulgar prostitute who, in jaded despair, sold her body for a little money or liquor? He never discovered that neither picture was a very accurate one of the majority of women. He could admire girls like Olin Dows' sister, a woman of refinement, and he could look with contempt upon all of the whores he visited, or saw from the Pullman sleeper in his many nightly train rides through little towns. But he couldn't find a woman whom he could love and respect, while also enjoying a physical relationship with her. Two or three times he did approach this sort of relationship, but even then some important quality was always missing. In this sense he never reached the stage of adult genital sexuality typical of the normally adjusted male. Most women remained for him primarily objects of sexual gratification.

Ann

As already mentioned, Wolfe developed a deep love for the American girl he met in Paris, identified in *Of Time and the River* as Ann. She and a friend, Elinor, both from wealthy Boston families, were travelling together after Elinor left her husband, and set up a Bohemian menage in Paris with Kenneth Raisbeck. Tom encountered Kenneth by chance, and, for the month of January, 1925, the four became inseparable companions, taking part in Paris night life and taking trips to other cities in France. Ann was the younger of the two girls, described as five years older than Tom, rather heavy, sullen, and brooding, except when she smiled, at which times he saw her as beautiful. Tom fell deeply in love with her, and thought at first that she returned his feelings. Eventually he discovered that Ann was in love with Raisbeck who by this time had made it clear that he was an overt homosexual, and so could not reciprocate Ann's affection. Tom was very bitter about this situation, and in despair broke up the relationship with all three.

Tom had little contact with the girls thereafter, but he wrote about his love so realistically in *River* that it is one of the most moving episodes in the book. He also wrote to Mabel about the situation confessing that he was hopelessly, madly, and desperately in love with Ann, who couldn't possibly reciprocate his love. He wished that he could break through this feeling, but all he could feel just then was that his heart would burst. Yet he recognized that he would get over the affair the way other "passionate, proud fools" do, and it would make a man of him. Assuring Mabel that Ann was a great, good, and wonderful person, he explained that he had said goodbye to her pretending that he was the sort of person to whom such things meant very little. He also admitted that he had never had the faintest intention of marrying her, or anyone. This statement may have been simply a form of bravado or pose, or he may have unwittingly revealed again the conflict between his desire to love, and inability to reconcile love and lust.

Wolfe's Oedipal problem is vividly illustrated in his relationship to Ann. In *River* Wolfe describes an evening, late in their association in Paris, when Ann and Eugene are left alone together in her room after dinner, sitting before a warm fire. Eugene, lying on the floor, feels a welling up of love for Ann, and then falls asleep. Shortly thereafter he awakes to hear her repeating his name; he becomes passionately aroused, and starts to make love to her. Ann, however, remains quite passive, and Eugene finds himself unable to consumate his desire. He does not know what holds him back; he has never wanted any woman so much before in his life "and at the same time he felt a horrible profanity in his touch, as if he were violating a Vestal virgin, trying to rape a nun." He is unable to understand these "senseless feelings of guilt and profanation." Asking himself whether they stem from his consciousness of her "exclusiveness" and her fine old Boston background, he finally concludes that this is so, and sums up the source of the trouble in two words, "*New England.*" Then he makes a desperate attempt to seduce her. His lovemaking is a remarkable mixture of love and contempt: "Oh, Goddamn you! . . . I love you! . . . Oh, you big, dumb, beautiful Boston bitch . . . By God, I'll do it!—Oh, you sweet, dumb, lovely, trollop of a Back Bay—Ann! . . . Oh, by God, I'll thaw you out, I'll melt your ice, my girl—by God, I'll open you." Suddenly Eugene is seized with horror as he thinks he sees fear in Ann's face. He pours out his apologies, but Ann responds by asking his forgiveness for having led him on. After much browbeating by Eugene she finally admits that she really loves Starwick. Ann's confession sends Eugene into a furious and jealous rage.

Lest we be inclined to make the assumption that this is the fictional fantasy of a clever novelist, we need only turn to Wolfe's letters to find corroboration. He wrote several letters to the real Ann during the next few months, and all of them support rather fully the details described in this episode of *River*. Tom wavers between pledging unswerving love and admiration for her, and writing long and boring lectures about the essential frigidity of all New England women. He accuses Ann of misrepresenting his feelings for her, and at one point, rather insultingly writes, "you must know that you exerted very little physical attraction for me. . . . Physically I was repelled as I am repelled by most Boston women. On the one occasion that I remember touching you with any affection, I had the terrible internal shame . . . that I have had only once before—when, as a child, I saw two very cold reserved people, a man and his wife [Wolfe's parents?] . . . go into each other's arms." He then discusses an older New England couple, almost certainly his Uncle Henry and Aunt Laura Westall (he identified the man as an older man whom he thought he loved) and explains that when he thought about their sexual relationship "the old horror of that dead cold Northern flesh came on me again. For the first time, I dared to think of this man in bed with his wife; and unutterable shame for him came on me again." He was apparently trying to tell Ann that he believed most New Englanders (including Ann herself) incapable of expressing physical love.

Wolfe goes on to accuse Ann of abusing him and degrading his friendship, a classic example of the anxiety aroused by the Freudian primal scene. Neurotically Wolfe never outgrew this anxiety, and projected the blame for his rejection of certain girls whose maternal qualities he admired, onto the girls themselves, accusing them of the frigidity which was almost certainly his own psychosexual impotence in the presence of idealized maternal women.

A School Principal

Tom's love affair with Aline Bernstein (see chapter 8), which continued with varying degrees of intensity from 1925 to 1930, was to be the most enduring and significant one of his life. But after his breakup with Aline, he became involved with someone else for a period of several months. He described this young woman, a school principal, in a letter he wrote to his mother in June, 1931. After explaining that he had gotten everything settled with Aline, and was now at peace with everyone, and "free and heartwhole," he portrayed his new girlfriend as a very beautiful woman who had a Ph.D. and was a school teacher in a Long Island community. He was attracted because she earned almost $5,000 a year—an excellent salary in those days—and had an apartment in Manhattan with a beautiful view of the East River. She came from the West and had common sense and character, having grown up in a resourceful and successful family. He wished he could have introduced her to his mother, but had not yet met her when his mother visited him a short time before.

In spite of Tom's initial enthusiasm, the relationship typically deteriorated after a few months. Tom describes the situation in the letter he wrote to the young woman when it was all over, telling her how much he admired and loved her—that he could not hope to reproduce the state of joy he had felt in the dignity and independence which each of them was able to experience in knowing each other. He explains that as a child he was cautioned to fear the subtlety and duplicity of women. Although he had known hundreds of women, he no longer felt promiscuous, but instead felt a great sense of fidelity to her. Referring to a recent change in their relationship, he admits that he was upset to learn that she no longer cared for their sexual relationship, but wanted only companionship, and used sex as a way of holding his interest. This hurt him because the sexual relationship was indivisible, for him, from their friendship. When they had first gone to bed he was sure that she had wanted it, and for him she was like "the best butter and eggs and honey that was ever made, as lovely and desirable as any woman on the earth." (Again one notices the food analogy in his love imagery.)

In his letter to her, Tom also contrasted her very favorably with the typical Southern girl, whom he had come to find repulsive for "her drawly voice, her coquettish airs, her apologies for working." He had come to believe that all Southern girls were "foul, dull, stupid, nasty." (This supports an earlier comment he had made to a girlfriend at Harvard that he found Northern girls so much more attractive than Southern ones, primarily for their straightforwardness and sense of independence—masculine, rather than feminine traits.) He liked the school principal for not asking much of him, he tells her, but when she started to hint at marriage, and to say that their relationship could be a fully satisfying one only if it included a sense of commitment, he found he could not bring himself to such a step. He mentions that she admitted that she might have used him to forget a former lover. It is possible, he adds, that he, too, might have used the relationship to get over "the insanity of love [for Aline] which obsessed me for several years," and from which he was just fully emerging. Nevertheless he tells her he found comfort, companionship, and peace with this girl; it was soul-satisfying. He ends his letter saying, "You are one of the finest and most desirable young women I have ever seen. . . . Do you understand from this . . . remarkable, honest, and *wholely serious* letter—that I know your value as a person, your great worth and beauty? Do you understand that I could never misprize or undervalue such a person as you —that if I could not offer you everything in me, it is because everything in me once went into something, someone, else, and if it ever returns like that, it will take time? . . . I think it will never come that way again. . . ."

In this relationship all of the characteristics of Wolfe's narcissism and stunted psychosexual development reappear—the comparison of sex with the ingestion of food, the requirement that the woman be independent and mature, and that she not make any demands of him. Whenever women expected him to give much of himself in a relationship, his interest in them quickly chilled. He was, of course, hurt that she ceased to find him a desirable sexual partner, but that is hardly a sign of narcissism, since few lovers can contemplate such a thought without dissatisfaction. Wolfe rationalized his failure to give himself completely to her on the grounds that he had spent all of the love he had on Aline, and would never again be able to know the kind of love he had felt for her. Such a rationalization is frequently used when a person finds himself unable to feel love as deeply as he wants to. Of course, many people who have loved deeply are able to fall just as deeply in love again.

Taken as an isolated incident, this broken love affair might not seem particularly significant; but in the context of Wolfe's whole life style of relating to women, it is another convincing example of his frustrating sexual immaturity. Tom admired competent, resourceful women, like Julia, Mabel, Margaret Roberts, and Aline, but he had trouble combining that admiration with an enduring sexual love and assuming some responsibilities in the relationship. One desirable aspect developed in his relationship with the principal: he experienced the sense of sexual fulfillment as a part of a broader sense of total significance and self-worth. With this woman Wolfe found that sex was not mere lust, as it was with so many women. For a short time at least, Tom found himself capable of fusing sex, love, respect, and self-respect into a happy well-adjusted blend. Thus he was showing some signs of growing out of the primarily narcissistic psychosexual state in which he had been trapped until now. Unfortunately, given the girl's problems and his own, this maturing selfhood was not destined to survive for long.

Thea Voelker

In the summer of 1936, when Wolfe was in Berlin, he was asked to pose for a portrait for a Berlin newspaper; the artist was a thirty-year-old beautiful Nordic divorcée named Thea Voelker. Although Tom disliked the portrait she sketched, he was immediately enchanted by the artist. He had insulted her work, but arranged with his German publisher to hold a party and to invite her as a guest. Then he proceeded to pay attention to no other guest but Thea, and to leave the party early with her. Thus began a brief and stormy affair which involved a deep love on Thea's part but a not-so-profound love on Wolfe's part. They became almost inseparable for some time, and finally Tom arranged for them to spend an idyllic period in the Austrian Tyrol village of Alpbach. It was not easy to arrange, for as a German citizen, Thea had difficulty obtaining permission to travel, even to Austria. Wolfe spent most of the time drinking with the farmers of Alpbach, who were delighted with him. He spent his money lavishly on wine for all because he had to use up his German royalties in Germany and Austria. Thea did not approve of Tom's drinking, and they quarrelled bitterly, but they made love just as vigorously. Finally the idyll ended, but not without Tom's, perhaps symbolically, climbing nearby Galtenberg mountain alone, on the morning after a terrible drinking spree. Mountain climbing is interpreted by Freudians as tantamount to seducing a woman, but for a man who grew up in the shadow of Mount Mitchell, that may be a forced interpretation. It could as easily be interpreted as demonstrating superiority and masculinity by an act of great daring. Tom typically did not climb for sport, but from the beginning of the stay in Alpbach he seemed to have had an obsession to "conquer the height."

Tom and Thea separated, patched up their affair, and separated again. Wolfe described their relationship rather poignantly in *You Can't Go Home Again.* Miss Nowell said that he promised Thea he would take her back to America and marry her. To do so would have been difficult, for only Jewish citizens were permitted to leave Germany at that time. Moreover, there were important differences between them. Thea was somewhat religious, while Tom often said that he had lost his faith in God at fifteen. During their time together, Tom seems to have suffered one of his depressions. Thea wrote Perkins that Tom was fearful that he would lose his literary skill, and had gone through a period of frenzy and anxiety.[5] Yet Tom was, according to all accounts, almost deliriously pleased at the adulation that the Germans showered upon him, and told many people that he loved Germany almost as much as his own country. One might conclude that Tom experienced one of his typical manic-depressive phases.

In any case, Tom's intentions to marry Thea did not last long. Back home, in the fall of 1936, he wrote her two somewhat preoccupied letters, which were dictated to a secretary. He thanked her for sending him a book of portraits for his birthday, and then described how hard he was working. Thea wrote several letters to him in English, which show a great deal of interest on her part. Tom's letters were entertaining, but not love letters. He ended the first one with "Meanwhile, with all my sincerest and most affectionate greetings, with all good wishes to you for happiness and success in all you do, I am, ever sincerely, Your friend." Certainly there was a quality of adieu about this closing. The second letter, written at Christmas, was quite noncommittal. He told Thea how hard he was working, and wished her a happy

5. Turnbull, p. 340.

Christmas. It ended "And now good-bye, good luck, and may Christmas bring all happiness and good cheer to you." This sounds like Ave et Vale! Tom's impassioned love for the Nordic goddess had cooled rather quickly after his return to New York.

The same could not be said for Thea. When Tom died, she wrote Max Perkins a letter, in broken English, expressing the deepest tenderness for Tom, indicating that he had been for her the greatest and most inspired love of her life. Her devotion to Tom was rather selfless; in him she recognized the genius of a Beethoven, and she was content to love him and do for him, without expecting much repayment for this devotion. She mentioned to Perkins Tom's great fear of death, and described his agitation about his work: "crashes from one violent state into the other, possessed devils, meeting deadly; or tormented, trembling, vibrating creature that helpless makes responsible the outer world for his pain; destroying, raging man who with cold amusement—but always with the own torment—ruined other persons." Thea loved him deeply, and felt that she could never love any other man with the same peak of exhilaration and devotion. According to Turnbull, Thea later married a German soldier who was killed in the war, and eventually committed suicide.

What distinguished Wolfe's affair with Thea from his relationships with other women? To begin with, unlike most of the other women he was drawn to, Thea was younger than Tom. It is also surprising that he was not completely put off by her religiosity, since Tom was usually disdainful and critical of those who displayed any signs of piety. Like some of Tom's other loves, she was physically beautiful, independent, and professionally competent. But above all she admired him and made it clear that she was in awe of his genius, as were many of her compatriots. Tom could not resist such praise and appreciation. Perhaps equally important to Tom was her complete willingness to nurture his dependency feelings—to mother him. Since she was a typical European woman, much of her nurturant attitude could probably be taken for granted, but Thea's letter to Max Perkins makes it clear that she felt particularly devoted to Tom, and would have happily gratified his ever-present narcissistic needs.

Elizabeth Nowell

The relationship between Wolfe and Elizabeth Nowell was mostly that of author to his literary agent. Miss Nowell, a reader for Scribner's Magazine, opened her own literary agency in 1935, and Wolfe was her major client. Tom continued to negotiate the contracts for his books directly with Scribner's, and later, Harpers, but Miss Nowell managed the sale of his short stories. Most of these stories were early versions of material that he later wove into his books. Miss Nowell was to devote much of the rest of her life to promoting his works. Indeed her services to him went beyond that of literary agent, since she also edited his works. Wolfe trusted her implicitly, and allowed her to make recommendations about length, content, and even style, undoubtedly encouraged by the fact that her judgment almost always proved correct, for she sold many manuscripts for him. In many ways she took over the functions formerly performed by Max Perkins, and by her comradely handling of Tom's sensitive feelings was usually able to persuade Tom to make the revisions that were needed to make his manuscripts publishable. Only once did he turn on her and query whether she might be secretly representing Scribner's interests rather than his own, but this was apparently no more than a momentary upsurge of the paranoid feelings that were beginning to color Tom's relationship with everyone in the late thirties.

Miss Nowell is described by Kennedy as an attractive and generous woman with a ready wit and a tendency to good natured raillery. She "held her own" very well in a man's world, and Kennedy notes that she seldom allowed her essential warmth and sensitivity to emerge.[6] She and Tom rapidly developed a good

---

6. Kennedy, p. 255.

rapport based on mutual respect and affection. Because she was neither deferent nor dependent, she was able to build a lasting friendship with Tom. Up to the time of his death Tom addressed her in correspondence as Miss Nowell, and Turnbull says that they typically addressed each other in person as "Wolfe" and "Nowell." Certainly their relationship was of the kind that develops between two colleagues who share common concerns, though eventually Miss Nowell was to become Wolfe's most trusted friend. During the last year of his life he could be reached only through her, since even his family did not have his address for several months.

Turnbull mentions that Miss Nowell was a breezy, talky, tartly smiling young woman from an old New England family, a blend of tomboy heartiness and sentimental, mothering warmth. (She sounds like the perfect companion for Thomas Wolfe.) Sometimes they addressed each other as "Hey, sweetheart," or "Listen, you big bastard." Tom became so dependent on her that when a girl threatened to bring a paternity suit against him, he told her to see Miss Nowell about it, because she took care of everything for him.

On his Western trip it was mostly to Miss Nowell that he wrote his letters, which were largely newsy accounts of his trip, or discussions of possible writing plans for the future. It is apparent that during this period she was the one person to whom he felt close enough to confide. Moreover he trusted her to make important decisions about what material was ready to be published, and in what manner.

Tom seldom revealed his feelings toward Elizabeth Nowell publicly, but in 1934 he wrote to Robert Raynolds that she had excellent judgment and ability, and that her editing had improved a story of his. In 1935 he described her as "absolutely honest and reliable . . . genuinely interested in your work."[7] Only once did he let down the barriers to Miss Nowell herself, unless

---

7. Ibid., p. 258.

there were other letters which she chose not to include among his published *Letters*. (She did edit some of the letters, and omitted others whose publication, she feared, might injure the persons mentioned in them.) In a New Year's letter written in December, 1937, Tom made a joke about his feeling for her, commenting "that is no agent, that is my friend." He ended this particular letter by saying "Anyway, dear Agent, I send you my love and with all my heart my wishes for nothing but the best for both of us next year."

Two years earlier, when Tom was leaving for Europe, Miss Nowell wrote confessing to him that perhaps she suffered from some kind of Yankee repression, but adds "goddamn it you must know about it whether I show it by sitting up all night working with you or by raving around like most of these other fool women."[8] She remarks that she thought he had more talent and poetry and sincerity and greatness in his little finger than all the other writers put together, and she says that she received a tremendous inspiration from working with him. She was embarrassed at writing in such adulatory tones, but says that she has tears in her eyes, while writing, and that she would show her admiration by "working like hell" on everything while he was away. Wolfe must have been overwhelmed with pleasure and satisfaction at these signs of Miss Nowell's appreciation and respect for his work.

The depth of Elizabeth Nowell's dedication to Wolfe can be measured by the fact that she continued her editorial work on his writings long after his death. She worked closely with Edward Aswell in editing Tom's three posthumous novels, and later took on the onerous work of editing Wolfe's *Letters*, a task which required more than six years. Finally she undertook to write the first major biography of Wolfe, though she was dying of cancer. Although Kennedy and Turnbull later wrote ex-

---

8. Ibid., p. 256.

cellent scholarly biographies that were somewhat more factual than Miss Nowell's, her book had a unique quality. Only someone who had known and loved Wolfe could have drawn the kind of portrait she presented—an honest but loving account of someone she had known personally and with whom she had worked closely.

Miss Nowell subsequently married, and there is nothing at all to suggest that her relationship with Wolfe was in any way a sexual one. That she was his devoted admirer is beyond question; she also was willing to serve as his protector, and to minister to his dependency, as well as his literary, needs. It is possible that in his dealings with Elizabeth Nowell Tom was unconsciously reminded of his brother, Ben. She had the same sort of gruff manner that concealed genuine fondness and warmth, and the same willingness to have Wolfe depend on her for help with many of his problems. Perhaps it was these qualities that attracted Thomas Wolfe and fostered their close friendship.

8

ALINE BERNSTEIN AND WOLFE'S ATTITUDES TOWARD WOMEN AND SEX

THOMAS WOLFE AND ALINE BERNSTEIN BOTH DETAILED their turbulent love affair in their published works. Tom dedicated *Look Homeward, Angel* to Aline and recorded his first sight of her in the last chapter of *Of Time and the River*. A very large portion of *The Web and the Rock*, and a somewhat smaller part of *You Can't Go Home Again* are devoted to the affair. Aline Bernstein recounted her side of the affair in her novel *The Journey Down*, and the short story, "Eugene" (in her book *Three Blue Suits*), described a typical day during the period when the affair was at its height. Their correspondence was published in part, although Miss Nowell unfortunately did not include many of the letters to Mrs. Bernstein in her edition of Wolfe's *Letters*, because at the time Aline Bernstein indicated that she herself hoped to publish Wolfe's letters to her. Subsequent to her death, however, Nowell, Kennedy, and Turnbull included much of this material in their biographies, so that some significant portions of it are available.

Tom and Mrs. Bernstein met on the *Olympic* returning from Europe in the late summer of 1925. His romantic report of his first glimpse of her (at the end of *River*) may be a somewhat fictionalized account, although he may, as he said, have seen her board the ship at Cherbourg. They were actually introduced to each other by a friend on the second night before reaching New York. Tom was really no stranger to Mrs. Bernstein, for she had with her the manuscript of his play *Welcome to Our City*, which she was reading in her capacity as a director of an experimental art theater.

Mrs. Bernstein was eighteen years older than Tom, but she was an energetic, vivacious, creative person, who although married to a very wealthy and successful stockbroker in New York, carried on a highly successful career of her own as a theatrical stage and costume designer. She was the daughter of an actor, and earlier in her life had studied painting, but tended to find the world of the theater more interesting than the more isolated life of a painter. Extremely extroverted, she was characterized as jolly and entertaining, and always the center of an active, artistic group. Certainly her personality and life style were in marked contrast to those of the very shy, almost reclusive Wolfe. At first Tom found Aline's friends a bit frightening, and later, probably because of his failure as a dramatist, threatening. Eventually he found them disgusting, and referred to them disparagingly as lesbians, perverts, and degenerates of the theater, or as exploitative members of the business world. Aline Bernstein had two almost grown children, but she and her husband had long since reached an agreement which permitted her to have her professional life, and also an unrestricted personal and sexual life. The Bernsteins' marriage probably was a compromise of their incompatible interests, based mainly on terms of living convenience. Though they did not share many interests, Mr. Bernstein accepted, even if he did not understand, his wife's artistic friends. Early in the Wolfe-Bernstein relationship a somewhat troublemaking acquaintance of Aline's remarked to Tom that "[Aline] likes young men; I'm sorry, but that's what they say about her."[1]

1. *The Web and the Rock*, chap. 36.

In fact, Aline had previous lovers, including one famous painter, and this barbed reference to Aline's past later became the source of a great deal of trouble between them, since it fanned his concern about her fancied infidelities to him.

On board ship Wolfe immediately became deeply interested in Aline and, according to her, tagged around after her for the remaining day of their voyage to New York. That she was half Jewish, and always identified closely with Jewish life and customs, seems not to have bothered him at first, but later this, too, became a source of friction because Tom was profoundly anti-Semitic. His biographers and most literary critics have tried to minimize the extent of Wolfe's anti-Semitism, offering as evidence remarks from former acquaintances that suggest that Wolfe was only superficially anti-Semitic; but actually his books, letters, and personal diaries, like the recorded comments of his mother, reveal him to have been not only deeply anti-Semitic, but also hostile to practically every ethnic group, particularly Negroes, and at various times the French, the Germans, and the English. He had all of the prejudices typical of a provincial boy from the South during the early part of the century. Very late in life he was to take umbrage at the suggestion, reported to him by Mrs. Sherwood Anderson, that friends in North Carolina had remarked that Wolfe was Jewish. On hearing this Tom delivered an oration which implied that the very notion impugned him—and even more seriously, his relatives—and could wreck their personal and financial futures. So violent were his remarks that the Andersons and others present pointed out that they revealed a deeply anti-Semitic attitude on his part. This only made Tom more angry and led to the breakdown of the relationship between Wolfe and the Andersons.

According to Turnbull the friendship with Aline first became close on the last night aboard ship, but then Tom and Aline did not see each other for some weeks after disembarking.[2] Tom

---

2. Turnbull, pp. 95, 102.

made a trip to Asheville and was disappointed not to find a letter from Aline upon his return to New York. He promptly wrote her a very pompous note saying that if she were interested, he would be glad to see her again. Aline called him the next day and suggested that he meet her that night at the theater where she worked. Tom met her, and was on the one hand favorably impressed by her importance in this setting, and on the other somewhat unfavorably impressed by the theater crowd. Several other meetings took place, but their love affair really began on his twenty-fifth birthday, October 3, 1925, when they met for lunch and then spent much of the rest of the day together. Tom, typically, got quite drunk, and Aline took him home in a taxi. He was furious, and thought the affair was over, but the next morning she called him, and suggested ways of curing his hang-over. There then began two years of an intensely deep and affectionate relationship, which for both of them was to prove, by their own frequent admission, the most satisfying period of their lives. A few months later Mrs. Bernstein rented a large upper-floor loft, presumably as a workspace for herself, but actually as living quarters for Tom, and as a place where they could be together in privacy. Tom paid part of the rent. She visited him every day, and cooked delicious meals, and except when she was at the theater they would happily spend most of their time together. It is reported by Pollock and Cargill that Tom, at that time, would pace up and down the faculty room at New York University, happily saying that he was in love. According to Nowell, Tom once asked Aline to marry him. Two years later Tom and Aline moved to a large second-floor apartment which provided them with more habitable quarters, including a kitchenette and a bath, the first he had been able to call his own.

Aline seems to have convinced Wolfe that his style of writing was not appropriate for dramatic productions, and urged him to attempt the type of autobiographical fiction for which he later became famous. To enable him to devote more time to his writing, she financed his living, on and off, for the next five to seven years, although he continued to teach at the University, rather sporadically, until about 1930. Aline also subsidized several of his trips to Europe, again to broaden his writing opportunities. They spent several summers together in Europe, and he often remained there for longer periods, convinced that he wrote better in Europe—which was only partially true.

How long could a relationship between two such different people be expected to last? Their ecstatic love endured for about two years, reaching its peak during the summer of 1926, part of which they spent in the English lake country. Here Tom actually started to put *Look Homeward, Angel* together, although he had accumulated notes and portions of themes for over a year. At one point, after a happy day of motoring with Aline and some of her theater friends through the beautiful countryside, Tom tearfully begged Aline never to leave him. She promised that she never would. Ironically, it was he who was later to leave her.

Tom spent that fall in Europe, writing, and travelling extensively but made a point of cabling Aline that he was hard at work and remaining chaste. He returned at the year's end, and they resumed their relationship with great relish, but not without his having noted in his diary on shipboard, "What rut of life with the Jew now? Is this a beginning or a final ending? Get the book done."[3] Obviously Tom was already beginning to feel ambivalent about the relationship. By 1928 he was having sexual relations with other women whom he would bring to the apartment when Aline was away. As he later confided to Max Perkins, though his feelings of love for Aline remained strong, he had lost much of his sexual interest in her. In the summer of 1927 she was beginning to sense his restlessness, and was hurt when he spent three weeks with Olin Dows at Rhinebeck and did not get in touch with her. She wrote and suggested that they go to

---

3. *Notebooks*, p. 96.

Europe again. Tom quickly accepted the offer, and they were back together in Europe for the summer. Tom returned home somewhat later than Aline, and while in Paris visited a sumptuous bordello, described in *Of Time and the River*.

During the following academic year Tom taught night classes and finally finished *Look Homeward, Angel*. Then he, or more correctly, Aline started trying to interest a publisher in it. The manuscript was reviewed by several publishers whose editors were her friends, but was rejected on the grounds that it was too long, or, in some cases, because it was too autobiographical. The tension of again becoming a professional failure was almost unbearable for Tom, who turned to liquor for courage—even to teach his classes. He also started quarrelling bitterly with Aline, projecting his frustration onto her. He began to show signs of quite unjustified jealousy, and would phone her in the middle of the night to see whether she were alone or had a lover with her. Aline, too, became more demanding, but the more she asked him to be faithful, the more strongly he felt the need to break away. He was happy to have her cook wonderful meals, and to supply him with constant reassurance and praise for his work, but he also wanted to continue his life style of compulsively possessing hundreds of women all over the world until he was middle-aged. Then, so he planned, he would settle down in domestic tranquility with a wife who, if one reads his letters carefully, would serve primarily as a housekeeper and cook. Here he was recapitulating the life style of his father with remarkable fidelity.

In June of 1928 Tom openly asked Aline for his freedom; they both went to Europe that summer, but did not see each other there at all. However, they corresponded constantly, and Tom began to realize how much he missed Aline, and he wrote her tender, endearing love letters; everything he visited, even the Beethoven house in Bonn, reminded him of her (she was slightly deaf). By the time Tom returned to America he had spent six days following a drunken brawl at the Oktoberfest in a Munich hospital doing some soul-searching. More important, by that time he had received word from Max Perkins that Scribner's was interested in publishing his book. When he returned, Aline, who had been desperately lonely for him, was at the pier, and they resumed their relationship. Tom had decided, as a result of his own loneliness, that he wanted to take up where they had left off, and Aline was overjoyed to do so.

At this point there began what Turnbull calls the "Indian Summer of their love." It was a pretty one-sided affair, with Aline doing all of the giving, and Tom all of the taking. She was grateful for the few hours of the day that he was willing to devote to her. Only occasionally would Tom respond with love and affection, so that Aline did complain of lack of attention from time to time, and Tom considered this nagging. He had dedicated the book to Aline, and gave her the manuscript and the first copy in October, 1929, with a tender inscription acknowledging their friendship, and the material and spiritual support, love, and faith she had given him. This period in their relationship was not a very happy one, however, because Aline could not help showing the grief she felt over his lack of deep commitment to her. As a result there were many days when she was not the cheerful, gay, almost manic little cherub he had loved, and instead he would note that the "small flower-face wept bitterly." He would beg her to stop crying, believing that there was no way of recapturing the passion he had once felt for her, and which she still seemed to feel for him.

Wolfe went to Europe again in 1930, and told Aline not to write to him. When a mutual friend got in touch with him during his travels, he became convinced, in his paranoid way, that she was spying on him for Aline, and would not even accept or open Aline's letters. When Scott Fitzgerald spent some time with him, he developed the same delusion and thought, as well, that it was part of a conspiracy to keep him from his writing. Then

Aline cabled and threatened to commit suicide; this caused Tom to feel both guilty and hostile. Actually, Tom went through a period of intense depression which reached near psychotic proportions during this European trip; this reaction was brought on in part by some unfavorable criticisms of the English edition of *Look Homeward, Angel*, but especially by his concern over Aline's reaction to his desire to break off their relationship. When Aline cabled threatening suicide, Tom cabled her, and begged her not to write to him. However, when he returned from Europe he let her visit him, and cook for him once a week, and she would send him letters pleading for a reconciliation, or rather a return to their former love. She kept assuring him of her great faith in his creative abilities, and cooked him exotic and sumptuous meals; Tom, in turn, accused her of infidelity with the "corrupt and poisonous vermin of the theater." Tom's ambivalence was, as usual, tremendous. He could not break away completely, but he was totally unwilling to go back to the old relationship. It is a tribute to Aline's devotion that she endured three or four years in this state. Wolfe was having many relationships with other women, including the school principal mentioned in the previous chapter, and he even sporadically talked of the possibility of finding a wife and settling down.

An almost final break came in an especially cruel incident which occurred in early 1932 while Julia Wolfe was visiting Tom. (Aline had met Mrs. Wolfe previously at Mabel's roominghouse in Washington, and there had been no sparks.) On this occasion Aline appeared at Tom's apartment while Tom and Julia were having breakfast. Tom had just learned that his agent, Madeline Boyd, had accepted advance royalties for the German edition of *Look Homeward, Angel*, without forwarding his share to him. He was in a violent rage, and unfairly blamed Aline, because she had originally introduced Tom to Mrs. Boyd's husband, which had led to the eventual acceptance of *Angel* by Scribner's. Tom ordered Aline to leave and never return, but she refused to go without a kiss, an act which must have enraged Julia, who promptly pushed Aline out of the door, locked it, and then when she saw Aline standing outside of the apartment building, motioned her to go away. Tom sided with his mother, which reveals how far he was from being truly adult. The next day he read Julia parts of an entreating letter from Aline in which she wrote that she had had $500 for Tom when she came to see him but that in her misery after their quarrel she had thrown one of the $100 bills off the Brooklyn Bridge. Julia commented cynically that all Jews grabbed for a nickel and that she doubted very much that Aline had thrown the money away. At this point Tom made some feeble efforts to defend Aline, but that was all. His lack of manliness and failure to stand up to his mother in defense of the woman who, by his own admission, had meant more to him than anyone else, and who still cared deeply for him, reveals the depth of his immaturity. Miss Nowell stated in her book that Tom remained an adolescent until he was thirty-seven. It would be more appropriate to say that to the end of his life Wolfe never outgrew his psychosexual immaturity.

Another act of immaturity and hostility occurred a little later, when Tom wrote—though never mailed—a note to Aline's son on the back of one of her letters. In it, he demanded that if the son had any shred of pride and decency left in him he should see to it that his mother stop disgracing herself and her family by doing her utmost to wreck the life of someone twenty-five years [*sic*] younger than she. Tom once wrote a similar note to her husband, but also never mailed that one.

Apparently blinded by his own neurotic desperation, Tom seemed incapable of realizing how profound Aline's grief was. She attempted to commit suicide at least twice and possibly three times during this period. All three biographers placed a first attempt in 1931, but in the preface to his 1968 edition Kennedy indicates that after the death of Edward Aswell (who administered Wolfe's estate after Perkins died), he was permitted to review correspondence between Wolfe and Aline which made it clear that her hospitalization in 1931 had not been prompted by a suicide attempt, but by attacks of dizziness and fainting spells combined with shock at the news that Wolfe had returned from Europe but had not called her.[4] However, she had certainly threatened to attempt suicide shortly before that. Kennedy says in Wolfe's *Notebooks* that she attempted suicide by an overdose of sleeping pills taken at her summer home in Armonk in 1934, that she had to be hospitalized as a result, and that Wolfe visited her in the hospital.[5] She also spent some time in a sanatorium in California at that point. A later suicide attempt is reported by Turnbull to have occurred in July of 1935, in the presence of both Wolfe and Perkins. Aline arranged to be at a certain bar that she knew they frequented. Wolfe rushed over to her, and later all three went to Scribner's to talk, since Aline still hoped for some sort of reconciliation. At one point after Wolfe and Perkins had momentarily left the room, the two men returned to find her apparently swallowing a bottle of sleeping pills, which Wolfe knocked out of her hand. However, a careful check by a physician revealed that she had not swallowed any of them.[6]

Tom's indifference to Aline's suffering could not be attributed to lack of knowledge of her sensitivity. He knew that she had been in psychoanalysis for a period of two years while they were still together, for he would ask her to tell him everything she had said during the psychoanalysis, just as he later begged her to describe all of her most trivial childhood memories so that he could write about her more knowingly. His story "The Good Child's River" is based almost entirely on what she told him of her childhood, while several parts of *The Web and the Rock* are based on incidents in the life of her father.[7] Furthermore, Tom knew that

---

4. Kennedy, preface to 1968 ed.
5. *Notebooks*, p. 654.
6. Turnbull, p. 218.
7. *From Death to Morning*, p. 169.

Aline was undergoing psychiatric treatment after their affair deteriorated and that it was upon her psychiatrist's recommendation that she started writing her own memoirs, *Three Blue Suits*, and *The Journey Down*. Neither of these books pleased him. About the former he wrote her that she had been unfair to him, depicting him as an exploitative lover who abandoned his mistress as soon as he found another source of income. In fact, that is almost exactly what happened.

Aline, however, was not entirely fair to Tom, for she did not mention his poverty when she met him, the marked difference in their ages, or that she was Jewish, all problems which Tom now considered serious. Of course, as she replied to him in a letter, these things had not seemed to worry him when he was finding their affair so satisfying; why had they later become such impedimenta to their relationship? Perhaps Aline should have known better than to have an affair with a man little more than half her age; but the relationship obviously served important needs for her. Probably Tom was at fault in rejecting a woman who was devoted to and loved him deeply; but he, too, had his neuroses to deal with, and his inability to handle them adequately is one of the great tragedies in his life.

Despite all of this, Aline was able to regain her equanimity, and when Tom took a new apartment in September, 1935, it was she who arranged to have it furnished, even deciding against venetian blinds because she knew he was mechanically inept. Thereafter they saw each other infrequently, but corresponded from time to time, particularly when each would achieve some milestone in his or her artistic career and the other would write congratulations. These letters were in general cordial. In 1935 Tom, after receiving congratulations from Aline on *River*, could write, "When I got your letter I wept with joy and pride. . . . My heart is full of affection and loyalty for you—it has always been . . . I know your value, know the princely ore of which you're made." And he had sent her a copy of *River*, with the passages describing her marked with the notation "My Dear." But each could also write the other critical letters. Aline criticized the story "The Web and the Earth" as too verbose, although Perkins considered it Tom's most perfect piece of writing and said "Not one word of it should be changed." And Tom wrote Aline a letter in 1935 (never mailed) in which he referred to her life in the theater as "a lie of life, false, cynical, scornful, drunk with imagined power, and rotten to the core. And through that rottenness . . . there will run forever the memory of your loveliness—your flower face and your jolly and dynamic little figure on my steps at noon—the food, the cooking, and the love. . . ." Such ambivalence is hard to understand, except as it may appear at the core of the narcissism of the very young, or in the immaturity of those who have never passed, or perhaps even reached, emotional adolescence. Such was Thomas Wolfe.

Tom's Need for Aline

What psychological characteristics made Aline Bernstein so appealing to Wolfe? Most important her motherliness, her concern with his welfare, led her to modify her life as much as was feasible to provide sustenance for Tom's needs. She gave him lodging, and more important for him, provided him with excellent food. (If there was ever a man whose heart was reached by way of his stomach, it was Wolfe.) Aline catered to all of Tom's obvious and overt dependency needs. Moreover, she gave him financial support, and saw that he dressed more appropriately. Turnbull says Wolfe called Aline "My grey-haired, wide-hipped, timeless mother." Perhaps Tom was attracted by Aline's generosity. W. O. Wolfe had taught all of his children to love food, and Tom's happiest childhood memories went back to W. O.'s bountiful generosity; Aline replicated these situations, and Tom responded with much satisfaction.

For a while, Aline provided sexual satisfaction, too. As a

deeply satisfying experience this phase lasted for only about two years, although several times over the next three years they did experience physical fulfillment. It is likely that as Aline came to seem more like Tom's sister, Mabel, both in behavior and to some extent in age and appearance, she also awakened the incest taboo in Tom's libidinal life; this force negated a strong genital response, although oral responses remained quite tolerable—eating, drinking, kissing, and hugging to the breast were still acceptable.

Aline supported other dependency needs of Tom's. She introduced him to influencial people, helped get his book into the hands of a receptive publisher, and fought some of his professional battles for him. In addition, she helped him to make decisions, which were always very hard for him. Not one to hesitate, or to question her own judgment, she was the antithesis of the hesitant, indecisive Wolfe, who could wait months to decide which publisher to sign a contract with, would not pay his bills, pack his suitcase, or answer his mail without encouragement and support. Much of this nurturance Tom greatly appreciated, but as he felt more secure, and was recognized as something of a success in the world of writers, Aline's over-nurturant behavior may have begun to seem suffocating, resembling Julia's excessive mothering, which he had spent years struggling to escape.

Another important satisfaction that Wolfe derived from Aline, was the ego-support based on her strong and frequently expressed belief that Tom was a talented person, even a genius—praise Tom could not resist. At times Wolfe seemed confident that he eventually would be recognized as a writer of genius, although his actual insecurity was revealed by the frequent boastfulness which led him to tell Julia Wolfe, Margaret Roberts, and Aline that they would some day be famous because he had "entombed" them in his books. When Tom and Aline first became lovers, he derived much satisfaction because he had such a distinguished mistress. While he envied Aline her success, for a time at least he basked in it. She was on a first-name basis with all of the important literati and artists of New York, and although he felt that they regarded him as the peasant who was Aline's current protegé, it was gratifying to have his peers at the University, and his North Carolina friends, know about his beautiful, wealthy, and distinguished mistress. Undoubtedly Tom was also impressed by Aline's competence. He had no use for silly, coy or inadequate females. As is clear from his letter to the high school principal (see page 149), he liked women who were self-assured and capable. Aline's high standards and her contempt for shoddy performance accorded with his own respect for fine craftsmanship.

Aline's personality was helpful to Tom because her cheerful, buoyant nature provided a perfect foil for his somewhat morose one; she enjoyed life and found it so gay that she imparted some of her own joie de vivre to those around her. Perhaps in this respect Aline was like W. O. Wolfe in his earlier years, and significantly different from Julia with her whiney, petulant, mouth-pursing and stingy demeanor. In this respect Aline also resembled Mabel Wolfe although in later years Aline also displayed the hysteria and depression that afflicted Mabel when life became difficult.

Moreover, they shared many interests, among them a love of poetry. Tom's interest in poetry was first awakened by his English teacher, Margaret Roberts. A voracious reader during his early years, Tom found himself reading less as he devoted more and more time to his writing. Eventually he confined his reading almost entirely to poetry, which he and Aline read together. He reread the Greek and Roman classics, which he first read at Roberts's Fitting School and Chapel Hill, and also the poetry of the Old Testament. Indeed, he often said that his favorite book was Ecclesiastes. Perhaps some of his interest in the Old Testament stemmed from his desire to find a meaning to life. Nor should one overlook the influence of his father's oratorical style, which was not unlike that of the prophetic books of the Bible which W. O. often recited in Tom's childhood.

Tom and Aline also shared a belief in the mystical. Aline's psychoanalyst was a student of Jung, and both Tom and Aline found fascinating the theme of the collective unconscious of the race. In *The Journey Down* Aline reports a visit to a tea leaf reader, and the influences of dead relatives and unidentifiable "forces." Tom was basically an emotional, rather than a reasoning person, one who could write about the visits of ghosts, as he did in several of his books, and was willing to believe in the occult, just as his mother did.

Aline's Need for Tom

It is difficult to explain why the talented, popular, and effervescent Aline Bernstein clung so tenaciously to the moody Wolfe, even when he was insulting and cruel in his attempts to rid himself of her. Simply to repeat the comment that "She liked young men" is not enough of an answer, even if one knew why she might have been especially attracted to younger men. Certainly there were others who would have been more willing to share her life than Wolfe was after 1930.

Turnbull mentions that Aline was described by her sister as a person who always "got her way"; that if she pursued her object tenaciously enough she always won out after some struggle.[8] This may have been true; Aline was a rather dominant person, in what psychologists label a passive-aggressive way—not too obvious about it but persistent in holding her ground until her opposition was worn down. But simply the will to dominate a situation would hardly account for the masochistic, self-defeating, and humiliating tactics by which she subjugated herself to Tom

8. Turnbull, p. 168.

for a period of several years. However it might be a partial explanation for why she so deeply needed to hold Tom's unrequited love. Tom himself attributed her difficulties to the menopause. It is likely that Aline experienced her climacteric just before or during her affair with Tom (ages forty-three to fifty), but to attribute the whole complex situation to this single cause is to oversimplify. More probably her stage of life is a partial explanation of her dynamics at this time. Her need to be considered a desirable woman would have been at a testing point, currently referred to as the period of middle-aged crisis. (She admitted that she has not slept with her husband for many years.) But Tom's humiliating and even degrading attitude toward her, and his frank turning to other women for sexual satisfaction as early as 1928 must have been a punishing, rather than a reassuring experience for Aline. But it is true that in the earlier period of their love Tom made her feel youthful and beautiful since he was an ardent, though probably not a particularly romantic, lover.

That Aline needed to turn to someone for a fairly enduring and sustaining love seems probable. Not only did she and her husband no longer have a sexual relationship, but although he was said to be most considerate of her, he lived in a different psychological life-space from hers; he found his satisfactions in Wall Street, and Aline found hers on Broadway and in Greenwich Village. The psychological distance was much greater than the geographical. Tom, on the other hand, was deeply interested in art and literature, and when they first met he was an aspiring dramatist, which related closely to her own field, and that of her father. One need not necessarily draw Oedipal implications from the fact that both Tom and Aline's father were interested in the theater; the simple parallel of the interests is sufficient. But Tom was, after all, young enough to be her son, and Freudians could point out that that is precisely the point; the woman who is unsatisfied in the love relationship with her husband often does turn to her son. But there may have been various reasons why Aline Bernstein's own son was not approachable as a lover or symbolic lover, not the least of which would be the incest taboo. He may not, for instance, have shared her interest in art and the theater. But Tom, like Aline, loved art, poetry, literature, and drama, and for both of them it was not just a hobby, but a vigorously pursued vocation; Tom, indeed, cared for little else, except food and sex, and Aline's interests were almost the same, except that she also loved to be with people.

Related to their shared interest in art is the fact that Aline was absolutely convinced that Wolfe was a person of great genius; she never deviated from this opinion despite all their quarrels. She would say that he was emotionally disturbed, even insane with jealousy, but she always reasserted her continuing belief in his genius. To Aline this was a very important quality indeed, and in being his mistress and sharing his creative life, she was herself fulfilling her own very great creative needs. Tom was not exactly a project for Aline, but he certainly provided her with a person to whom she could devote her great energy, so that she was not only living a deeply fulfilled life, but also a vicariously creative one. She financed his living, prepared his food, bought his copybooks for him, and discussed his creative ideas with him. Moreover, she had the literary contacts which could bring about the fruition of this genius. In this sense, helping Tom vicariously fulfilled her own literary aspirations. Later, when their relationship had virtually ended, she herself turned to writing, and produced several autobiographical works as a result of this effort. While they were lovers, she also poured out her life history to Tom, partly because he asked her to and partly, it would seem, out of the same need that prompted her to go to a psychoanalyst. But the outcome of these self-revelations differed significantly in each case. By telling her analyst about herself she could obtain self-understanding, but by telling Tom about her life she could, perhaps, obtain immortality, which would, indeed, be a more permanent form of self-actualization.

Aline may have realized her deep unhappiness at the time she began her relationship with Tom. Her history of psychoanalytic and psychiatric treatments may have been in part the result of her troubled relationship with Tom, but when she began the psychoanalysis her love affair with Tom was actually at its most gratifying stage. She was, however, a woman whose maternal needs were no longer gratified through her grown children, who were probably attempting to lead independent lives. Consequently, she directed her interests toward the young people of the arts and the theater; in *The Web and the Rock* Wolfe described the comradly, even motherly, relationship that she had with the young actors. Tom's great dependency needs were the perfect foil for a woman who strongly needed to mother a young man. And this mother-son relationship tended to perpetuate itself long after their affair was over. She was still furnishing his apartment in 1935, and Miss Nowell reported that when he was taken desperately ill in 1938 Tom telephoned Aline long distance to let her know that he was very ill, and thought he was dying. Aline, however, did not believe him, for he had called her too often in the past when he was merely in search of a little sympathy because of his legal troubles or hostile book reviews, so this time she ignored the ominous tone of the conversation.

In summary, the need to find a young man to mother, the need for a lover who would reassure her of her womanhood, and the need to sponsor Wolfe's marked artistic talent and promise combined to make Tom irresistible to Aline Bernstein, and led her to cling tenaciously to him even at the price of cruel rejection and deep humiliation.

The Break with Aline

Perhaps the negative trait most frequently mentioned by Tom's biographers was his jealousy, and Wolfe himself, as well as Aline, focused on this in their attempts to find an explanation for his need to break away. Tom referred to his jealousy as a dreadful "madness" which would seize him, as though it were a sort of uncontrollable or hereditary drive. That it had neurotic origins is confirmed by the fact that it was without substance in reality. Every evidence indicates that Aline was quite faithful to Wolfe, and that she loved him deeply. In discussing his jealousy, in regard to sex, two aspects should be mentioned. The first relates to the jealous fear that Aline might be involving herself with other young men. We know that he suffered from this fear frequently, and often called her, even in the middle of the night, to determine whether she was engaged in what he called her "bawdy missions." Over and over she reassured him that she was his "faithful Scheherezade," but it seemed to do no good. To the psychologist, such jealousy would be interpreted as a projection of Wolfe's guilt for his own infidelities which had become quite regular. There was a strongly paranoid quality about his suspicion of Aline's possible infidelity. Then, too, his fear of her imagined infidelity may have come from the knowledge that most of the women with whom Tom had sexual relations tended to be quite promiscuous persons, often prostitutes. He may have been almost incapable of conceiving of sexual fidelity, for he had not observed it in his father or brothers (except Fred), nor in the women he consorted with. Julia and his sister Effie were monogamous women, but his split-imago thinking would have seen them as madonnas not as sexual mates.

Still another facet of this jealousy was that with Tom's strong need for love and appreciation, he wanted to have all of Aline's time and attention to himself. Consequently he was resentful when she spent time with her friends, her family, or her business associates, evidently interpreting this as a sign that she preferred them to him. Perhaps her refusal to devote herself completely to him reactivated for Tom some of the feelings he had had as a child when Julia Wolfe divided her time between him and the boardinghouse.

One must also consider the possibility that Tom was jealous of Aline's professional competence and success. She was, after all, widely recognized in her field, and Tom, at the time of their affair, was merely her unknown protegé. Furthermore, the sphere in which she was successful—the world of drama—was precisely the one in which Tom reluctantly had to admit his own defeat. It is not a part of our cultural structure for the male to easily accept the fact that his female companion is professionally more successful than he. While this does sometimes happen, it is only rarely that a successful relationship can be maintained on this basis. That Tom would find such a situation tolerable for any length of time was highly unlikely given his own background. Much of the friction between W. O. and Julia arose because of her superior education and greater social and financial aspirations, and finally she proved financially more successful than her husband. This reversal of roles in the case of his parents may well have made Tom particularly sensitive to Aline's success in her field, as well as to the disparity in their social and financial positions.

Two other justifications that Tom advanced for breaking off his relationship with Aline were that she was much older than he, and that she was Jewish. These were only superficial explanations, however. If we analyze the dynamics of this situation we find that at the beginning of their affair neither matter seemed to cause Tom much concern. Actually Tom used Aline's Jewishness as a sort of ego support for himself. This intelligent, sensitive, insecure, and ambitious young man must have found it difficult, many times, to maintain his self-respect in his relationship with a woman who was so competent professionally, and who seemed so successful. One of the few ways in which Tom could feel superior to Aline was to flaunt the fact that he was not Jewish and that she was. It was probably precisely at those times when he felt most vulnerable and insecure that he would address her as, "my gray-haired Jew." By attempting to demean her, he could feel more important. It was his unconscious effort to protect his ego against too great a devaluation. Then, when their affair began to pall and he found it so difficult to renounce their relationship, he seized on her Jewishness as a rationalization for the break. It was a convenient reason, but not a basic one. He used their age difference against her in the same way. Had he had a stronger ego and keener insight into his own behavior, he could have handled the termination of his affair with Aline more kindly and effectively.

With his typical suspiciousness, Wolfe came to question Aline's sincerity. How could she still be a fine person if she was a part of "the sickness of the theater" as he called it? He picked up a certain artifice in the behavior of some of the actors, and saw it as insincerity. And he wondered why Aline was not, like himself, repelled by this. He caricatured the mincing manners of some of the homosexual actors, and found them revolting, but Aline treated homosexuals as if they were a normal part of the group. Tom interpreted this as showing either that she accepted perversion or that she was hypocritical, neither of which he could tolerate. Since he could not be as broadminded as Aline, he questioned her sincerity.

What may have bothered Tom most was Aline's possessiveness. The tighter she tried to hold him, the more urgently he felt the need to break this bond. In this situation we see a perfect reification of his relationship with Julia Wolfe. The basic theme of *Angel* was Tom's effort to cut this umbilical cord, and as soon as he sensed it being tied again, he felt compelled to break away. Had Aline not been so maternal, Tom would probably not have liked her as well, but might have stayed with her longer. His basic ambivalence between his dependency needs upon a mother, and his counter-dependency needs, was one which is typical of many young males of our time; the phenomenon of Momism has probably driven more young men to psychotherapy than any other, and it certainly drove Thomas Wolfe both toward, and later away from, Aline Bernstein.

Finally there is the matter of Tom's marked promiscuity. His sexual interest could not remain fixed on one libidinal object for very long and he was quite the opposite of a monogamous male in every sense of the word. In so far as Aline took over many of the Julia-Mabel mother responsibilities, she may, indeed, have become the object of his incest taboo. It might well be that he simply became frightened by the incestuous quality of the relationship with her, and so became impotent and sexually disinterested in her. That he did become sexually disinterested is an established fact, based both on his own report, and on his actions. In *The Web and the Rock* Wolfe described the "dark regiment of Jewish women in their lavish beauty [who were] . . . the living rack on which the trembling backs of all their Christian lovers had been broken . . . they were more lost than all the men whom they had drowned within the sea-gulf of their passion . . . whose lives had been nailed upon their lust, and whose wrung loins hung dry and lifeless like a withered stalk from the living wall of their desire . . . the guts got sick, numb, and nauseously queasy, and the loins which once had leaped and quivered with a music of joy and life, under the poisonous and constricting fury grew sterile, sour, and dry." Thus Wolfe described the curdling of the greatest love and passion he had ever known. The themes of impotence, and need to get revenge for projected guilt feelings are obvious. That this was a man frightened by the perceived voracious and overwhelming appetite of the feared female seems undeniable. There is a grandly paranoidal quality about this description. Taken seriously, it would justify any kind of desertion or retribution. Tom's feeling for Aline was a childlike, self-gratifying sort of love, and therefore his sexual interest was not able to endure.

Wolfe's Sexual Attitudes

One aspect of Wolfe's attitudes toward sex, the oral sexual responsiveness, was discussed in chapter 6 dealing with his relationship to his sister, Mabel. The other phase, his "galloping promiscuity" was most evident in his inability to remain sexually faithful to Aline Bernstein for more than two years. It may be helpful at this point to summarize Thomas Wolfe's attitude toward women and toward sex. As a consequence of his relationships with Julia and Mabel, Tom came to expect women to be fickle—warmly responsive at one moment, and rejecting at another—so that one could never count on their love. He thought that women often plagued men with nagging demands about minor matters, and thus interfered with a man's concentration on his work. Women were possessive, wanting one to love only them, and never to leave them. They were ambitious, prodding men to produce more and more, and critical when the results weren't all they had expected them to be; this ambition often involved making money. Women pretended to be virtuous, but actually lied and tricked men. They were also emotional creatures who often wept in order to get one's sympathy. Sexually, they either tempted men with their sensual delights, or were frigid. In general, women were good only for sex, or for preparing food. This negative attitude toward women is illustrated by an incident described by Pollock and Cargill, who quote Wolfe as telling a woman instructor at New York University that "All women are bitches."[9] Actually she was a friendly and pleasant person; however Wolfe was drunk at the time, and so presumably less inhibited.

By contrast, Tom thought of men as strong, sure sources of affection, more concerned with people and their needs than with making money. Men were generous and willing to share their worldly goods with others. They were loyal, and would comfort, console and advise one another. And although men expected one to be able to do something productive, they were patient,

---

9. Thomas C. Pollock and Oscar Cargill, *Thomas Wolfe at Washington Square* (New York: New York University Press, 1954), p. 77.

generally uncritical, and willing to help one attain his goals. Many men were sensitive to the finer things of life—to art, drama, and poetry.

As to sex, Tom had learned from his parents that men have strong appetites which need to be satisfied. In fact, one couldn't really count himself a man unless he had frequent sexual relations with women. By contrast, good women found sex repulsive; they wished to keep themselves pure and fine. On the other hand, easy, cheap, or depraved women were interested in sex; some were willing to "sell their bodies" for a price. In general these women lived in the poorer sections of town and were physically rather repulsive creatures, so that having intercourse with them seemed shameful and bestial, though "necessary." Some of this attitude is revealed in Tom's description of George Webber's feelings toward the "pregnant hags in slumtown" in *The Web and the Rock*: "How had man been begotten? Why they had got him between brutish snores at some random waking of their lust in the midwatches of the night! They had got him in a dirty corner back behind a door in the hideous unprivacy of these rickety wooden houses, begotten him standing in a fearful secrecy between apprehensive whisperings to make haste, lest some of the children hear! . . . He had been begotten in some casual and forgotten moment which they had snatched out of their lives of filth, poverty, weariness, and labor, even as a beast will tear at chunks of meat; begotten in the crude, sudden straddling gripe of half-rape on the impulsion of a casual opportunity of lust; . . . He had been begotten without love, without beauty, tenderness, magic, or any nobleness of spirit, by the idiot, blind hunger of lust so vile that it knew no loathing for filth, stench, foulness, haggish ugliness, and asked for nothing better than a bag of guts in which to empty out the accumulations of its brutish energies."

In satisfying his sex drive Wolfe was not able to accept overt homosexuality. His strong reaction against it may have been due to the attitudes he learned as a child in a small, conservative Southern town; it is possible, too, that he found himself attracted to men and panicked when this happened, fearing that this meant that he too was a homosexual. As a consequence he overreacted, being unnecessarily critical of Aline's friends and attacking Kenneth Raisbeck. Wolfe also could not accept autoerotism; he made several references to it as "our wild hunger for ourselves," and "twiddling desire between palid fingers," and he used the word *Narcissus* in referring to the early love life of the young male. Since Tom was scornful of both masturbation and homosexuality, and could not tolerate the idea of sex with a good woman, he was left with the problem of how to find sexual satisfaction. His solution was one of wandering forever in his Don Juan existence, hopelessly searching for fulfilling sexual relationships with satisfying women.

With such attitudes, it becomes understandable why Thomas Wolfe had difficulty relating to women. He met Aline at a very stressful period in his life; for the first time, he was living independently of his family. Since he was living in New York, away from his primary family group, he could not easily turn to them for support or affection. His father and Ben had died, so that there was no father figure to whom he could turn. During this period he was also struggling to find his identity as a creative artist; his playwriting was not going well, but he did not know how to change to achieve success. Under these circumstances Aline had much to offer him. She could ease his financial problems, give him reassurance about his personal worth, and help him discover his true talents. However, after *Angel* was published and Wolfe acclaimed as a promising young writer, he had less need for her financially, emotionally, and artistically. Finally, after he came to know Max Perkins, who could satisfy most of those same needs even better than Aline could, Tom had very little need for her.

PART III

DIAGNOSIS AND PROGNOSIS

9

DIAGNOSIS

Wolfe's Pathological Defenses

TO THE PSYCHOLOGIST, THOMAS WOLFE'S LETTERS, DIARIES, and books indicate that he utilized defense mechanisms characteristic of the normal range of adaptive responses to feelings of threat or conflict, but that he apparently employed these techniques to a degree bordering on the maladaptive. These symptoms include a strong need for catharsis, obsessive and compulsive behaviors, a tendency toward extremes of affective states bordering on the depressed and the manic, and a tendency toward suspiciousness that approaches paranoia. Generally his biographers and literary critics skirt the issue of his adjustment, either because they lack enough technical knowledge to write with confidence in this area, or because they believe that Wolfe's personality is not relevant to the quality of his writing, or, perhaps, because they are reluctant to denigrate a greatly admired literary figure. Bernard DeVoto states flatly in his 1936 review of *Story of a Novel*, however, that Eugene Gant (Wolfe) is a borderline manic-depressive exhibiting the classic alternations of fury and despair, accompanied by signs of obsessional neurosis and compulsions.[1] This comment infuriated Wolfe who made

1. "Genius Is Not Enough," pp. 3-4, 14-15.

frequent hostile references to it. In 1957 Malcolm Cowley wrote that many physicians would say that Tom's alternating moods of exuberance and despair indicate that in the last years of his life he was the victim of a manic-depressive psychosis, and that he also developed paranoid symptoms, with ideas of reference and delusions of persecution and grandeur. Cowley cites Wolfe's "severance" letter written to Perkins as the most obvious example, saying that "in places it was a crazy man's letter."[2] Beach, Braswell, and Frohock, in theoretical articles, express similar views, though somewhat less extreme than Cowley's.[3] And both Kennedy and Turnbull, in their biographies, refer to psychotic episodes, particularly of depression, but sometimes of euphoria, or of suspiciousness.

That these tendencies existed, and were at times quite marked, is the thesis of this chapter. However to use the word psychotic in regard to Wolfe requires that one accept the position that his behavior crossed the borderline between the controllable and the uncontrollable, that he was unable to adapt sufficiently well to his life's needs and obligations to be responsible for himself, and that his awareness of the difference between reality and unreality was so impaired that he could not manage his affairs in a safe and effective manner. Such allegations do not seem to be justified, so that Wolfe must be considered as having reached only borderline levels of the conditions mentioned. He never did anything dangerous to himself or harmful to others; he was reasonably able to support himself after he began to publish; and while he frequently lost friends as a result of his withdrawal or his hostile behavior, he also continued to make new friends, and to hold on to at least a few people, besides his family, who remained loyal to him.

---

2. "Thomas Wolfe," *Atlantic* 200 (1957): 202-12.

3. Joseph W. Beach, *American Fiction, 1920-1940* (New York: The Macmillan Co., 1941), chap. 9. Braswell, "Wolfe Lectures," pp. 11-22. Frohock, "Of Time and Neurosis," pp. 349-60.

His Need For Catharsis

Wolfe experienced—and recognized the value of finding—catharsis for his emotions in his excessive verbal outpouring: in his tendency to harangue people on the one hand, and in the prolixity of his writing on the other. His most obvious recognition of this tendency is to be found in the note to the publisher's reader which accompanied *Angel*.[4] In it he mentioned that some of the book was written for catharsis, and having served its purpose could be cut with propriety. Tom wrote to J. G. Stikeleather that "a writer writes a book in order to forget it." In a similar vein, he mentioned to Julian Meade that writing was not an escape from, but an approach to reality, and on this basis he defended the autobiographical character of his work, just as he did on many other occasions when criticized for this quality. In 1935 he wrote to his mother that the value of autobiographical writing was that it permitted an author to explore his mind, and that if an author explores his own experiences fully, he will find out what the whole earth is about. Frohock quoted a statement of Wolfe's that at times when he wrote, it felt as if a black cloud had discharged itself inside him.

Kennedy discusses Wolfe's dredging from his memory an unbelievable profusion of material, and compares *Angel* with a psychoanalysis, in which Wolfe was consciously attempting to produce total or complete introspection.[5] (The book was written at the time when Aline Bernstein was undergoing her psychoanalysis, and Wolfe was apparently much impressed with the process of deep introspection. He was also impressed with stream of consciousness writing, which influenced both his need to write and his manner of writing.) Kennedy states that Wolfe wrote *The Story of a Novel* to expiate his guilt for having required so much assistance from Perkins in the writing of *River*;

---

4. *Letters*, pp. 129ff.
5. Kennedy, pp. 62, 64, 114-17.

and Nowell mentions that when Tom couldn't write he became nervous, surly, and brooding, and suffered from the fear that he was going mad.[6]

Also cathartic was Tom's frequent resort to writing long letters, sometimes very angry ones, which he then either intentionally or unintentionally did not mail, but sometimes carried around in his pockets for days or weeks, reading and rereading them. Similarly, many accounts of the talking "binges" which Tom and the other Wolfes engaged in exist. Terry mentions that when Tom and Julia got together on her infrequent visits to New York they couldn't stop the flood of memories, and that on her first visit when Terry was present the three of them talked most of the night.[7] In her book, Mabel described similar talking jags on the occasions when Tom visited her in Washington. Often Julia was also present, since they made Mabel's Washington home their rendezvous during the period when Tom felt he was exiled from Asheville. One of his more unusual cathartic activities was Tom's squeal, a sort of primitive, manic, cry of exultation or exhilaration which he would emit when happy or excited, as when he was telling stories with his family, or when contemplating a huge repast that he was about to eat. These squeals are mentioned in several books, and in *The Web and the Rock* he interprets George Webber's loss of his ability to squeal as a sign of diminishing enthusiasm in his relationship with Esther (Aline).

Occasionally Tom expressed the fear that he might dry up, to cease to be productive. Many authors experience this fear, particularly after their first book or two, but Tom's reaction was usually the opposite of this because he was constantly aware of the vast store of material. He would often gloat about how many words he had written in a given day, and was reported to have

6. Kennedy, p. 336; Nowell, p. 80.
7. *Letters to His Mother*, introduction.

been seen walking along the streets of Brooklyn in the middle of the night chanting in obvious exultation, "I've written ten thousand words today!" However, in *You Can't Go Home Again* Webber expresses the fear that he might dry up after he reaches forty. But more often Tom voiced the feeling that he would never be able to write down all of the things he felt the need to write. In addition to providing Tom with some catharsis for his feelings, his writing may also have been an effort to recapture his lost childhood, for which he seemed to be continuously searching. Through writing about it, he could project himself back into the period, and to some degree experience the satisfactions of his childhood.

Compulsive and Obsessive Behavior

Wolfe showed a great many of the classic compulsive and obsessive behaviors found in anxiety neuroses or in manic-depressive conditions. One of his earliest compulsive behaviors was his stammer, which developed in childhood. Fred Wolfe had a more severe stammer, and Mabel also showed this symptom at times, but not as severely as Fred's. His stammer appeared most frequently when Tom was very excited or agitated; he commented on his being a poor public speaker because of this tendency, but regarding his Purdue speech, he joked that he "could certainly stammer three hundred dollars worth." Actually his stammer mostly manifested itself when he was with strangers, or beginning to make a speech, but it usually left him quickly unless he became excited, or felt a need to say more than he could say in the time available.

Tom's compulsive writing was his most prominent trait; even discounting his tendency to exaggerate his productivity, he still wrote prodigious quantities, resulting in some of the difficulty in getting his plays, as well as his books, published. When he submitted a manuscript it was generally four or five times the length of the final, edited version. However, when asked to cut certain sections or passages he ended up by lengthening them. He seldom actually revised material, but was more likely to rewrite it totally, usually producing a rewrite longer than the original. At the time Perkins took the manuscript for *River* away from Wolfe, Tom had written a million words, and was adding to it at the rate of 50,000 words a month! Kennedy comments that Tom was more of a storyteller than a writer, and that he did his writing in the form of long stories much like his mother's lengthy anecdotes.[8]

Wolfe's compulsion to work is understandable, since both his parents, and particularly his mother, seemed to feel the same need. He often felt that he worked because he was really lazy, and had to overcome this unworthy trait in himself. In *Angel* he comments that whenever Eugene Gant felt like lying in bed he would hear his father's voice calling "Get up, boy." This compulsion would seem to be a very logical outgrowth of a situation in which a boy was required to start work at the age of eight, not because the money was needed, but so that he would learn the value of work.

Similarly, Wolfe was unable to complete many tasks. It took him four or five years, on the average, to write a book, and then he was always convinced that it was not finished, and that he needed more time to work on it. He wrote apologetic letters to Perkins explaining that he felt that there was so much more that ought to be said in a book, while Perkins was trying to get the book down to manageable proportions.

One of the compulsive tendencies that Tom acquired from his mother was the habit of collecting useless junk, though he was never as bad about this as Julia, whose room at the Old Kentucky Home was said to be filled with string, papers, bottles, and all the odd things she could collect. Tom would do this for a while, and then about every year or so, as he was getting ready to move

---

8. Kennedy, p. 2.

to a new residence, he would go through the junk and discard most of it, except for his papers, which he never destroyed. He even kept receipts and sales slips for years. However, Tom never discarded cut manuscript; he saved it in large packing cases which he kept in his apartment, and frequently, according to Edward Aswell, pulled out some of the rejected writing and revised it for use in a later book.[9]

Tom's memory, which he seems to have acquired from Julia, was also compulsively detailed; he remembered almost everything, and continually drove himself to remember in even greater detail. Perkins said that Tom felt he had to say everything, eat every food, read every book, see every sight, and meet every person there was. This accounted for some of his urge to wander all over the world; he had to discover everything there was to be seen or experienced.[10] The desire to see everything possible, plus his manicky excitement, caused Tom to roam the streets, and to wander from country to country so that he could say that he had been everywhere. In the story "Only the Dead Know Brooklyn" in *From Death to Morning*, he recounts Eugene's searching out of remote sections of the area like Red Hook or Flatbush, much to the wonderment of the natives. But Cowley contends that his compulsion to see and do everything caused him to deny himself all of the usual satisfactions of the average man, such as a wife and family, or a home and a car. An example of this need to know about everything was Tom's concern to hear every detail of Aline's previous life; he would ask her to remember the smallest trivialities, as well as the greater experiences, such as what it felt like to bear a child, or to be a man's mistress.

Some other more ritualistic compulsions are recounted in Wolfe's various books. In *Angel*, Eugene, as a young man, after getting sexually involved with an older married woman at his

---

9. Note in *The Hills Beyond.*
10. Perkins, "Thomas Wolfe," pp. 269-77.

mother's boardinghouse, engages in ritualistic prayer, muttering a set formula sixteen times each night while he holds his breath, to expiate his guilt, even though he has already rejected any formal religion. Earlier in his life, Eugene (and probably Tom) had said his prayers in rhymes of four, and if he failed to get a proper sequence and count, he would have to start the whole ritual over again. One of the rituals he practiced consisted of trying to twist his hand a certain way as a means of finding the lost dimension and stepping through the door to a secret world. Describing George Webber, Wolfe mentions that for a period of ten years he had a spell for almost everything he did. For example, he held his breath while walking along a certain block, and on Sundays he always did the second thing he thought of, rather than the first. These compulsions eventually governed everything Webber did: the way in which he proceeded along a street; the places at which he had to stop and look; or the way he climbed a tree. On certain days he would have a compulsion to single out a specific part of each person's face to look at; one day it would be noses, another day teeth, and so on. During the period when Webber was waiting for a manuscript to be returned he went through a whole series of daily compulsions, such as getting out of bed on a certain side, changing his brand of cigarettes, holding his breath, or counting his steps. Tom himself had great difficulty in making decisions, and was even unable to decide whether or not to enter the Scribner's building for his momentous first meeting with Perkins.

Perhaps his most dominant obsession was with time—with the idea that time was slipping away from him, and that there was insufficient time left to accomplish all he had set out to do in life. This was probably related to his concern with death—one of his other major preoccupations—as well as to his compulsions to complete so much writing, and to encounter all of life's experiences in the time allotted to him. The obsession with time was ubiquitous in Tom's work: the time in *Of Time and the River* was the same which was still pressing him when he came to realize that "you can't go home again." (Frohock felt that death and time were Wolfe's two great obsessions.) In *The Web and the Rock* Webber is afraid that he will miss the opportune moment when the secret of life will finally be revealed to him. In *You Can't Go Home Again* Webber is troubled because he is not sure whether time is his enemy, or his friend. If it is his friend, it is that because it is allowing him the chance to get all his thoughts onto paper. Only in his later life did some of these compulsions leave Wolfe. In *You Can't Go Home Again*, he comments that Webber arrived at a point where he no longer felt a need to look at each person in a crowd, but was able to generalize certain characteristics about groups of people. Moreover, Tom himself was apparently no longer so insecure about the quality of his writing, having become more assured during those last years.

One might question whether the compulsions Wolfe described in his novels were ones in which he himself was caught, or whether they simply demonstrated careful observation of the behavior of others. But the fact that compulsions are described in each of the four novels, from *Look Homeward, Angel* through *You Can't Go Home Again*, strongly suggests that they were indeed methods of adjustment used by Wolfe himself. This conclusion is supported by the fact that these compulsions are described in the same way, and are of the same type in each novel. Further supporting evidence is the fact that Wolfe's compulsive need to read everything, see everything, and experience everything, as well as his need to write compulsively, are well documented in his letters, his notebooks, and in articles about him written by those who knew him. The ubiquitous lists found in his notebooks also support this conclusion. So we are probably safe in assuming that Wolfe practiced other compulsive behavior as well.

A compulsion is an effort by the person to gain control of a situation which is causing him anxiety, and in which he feels helpless. The compulsive person learns very early an overly strong need to conform to his parents' orders and to handle his assigned tasks very carefully. Unconsciously he feels that if he is very careful, he will carry out his task correctly, and will earn his parents' praise; whereas if he does not do this, he will be criticized, and worse yet, will be unloved. Thus he develops various systems to ward off this calamity. He may count things carefully, or he may work out a special order for handling a situation, or he may learn to say magic formulas, or use any of a number of other types of compulsions. All of this may not sound very different from the orderliness of a normal person: actually it differs from it only in the fact that the system is unusual and doesn't seem logically related to the task, and in that the person feels excessive anxiety if he does not carry it out according to plan. A good example of this is Wolfe's description of how George Webber touched each cement block on a wall as he passed by it, and touch each of the end blocks twice. Moreover, if he failed to do this correctly, he could not relax until he went back and did it over again.

It is apparent that many incidents in Wolfe's childhood caused him to feel helpless, and so made him susceptible to developing compulsions. A basic element in this was his mother's overprotectiveness and her refusal to let Tom try to do the things that other boys did, and so learn the skills he needed in order to feel competent. Mabel compounded this by her unpredictable reactions to Tom—he never knew whether she was going to be loving or critical. His curls, and his lack of masculine skills at self-defense added to his feeling of helplessness when other boys at school teased him, or tried to take his lunch from him. Not until he was about twelve and had grown tall and thin did he begin to feel less helpless physically. And psychologically he still felt helpless because he had learned such a dependent style of life. Under these circumstances, when he felt he had so little control over what was happening to him, it is easy to understand why he tried to find some way of gaining control. Since both of his parents were somewhat compulsive—W. O. with his rituals for handling daily life, and Julia with her compulsive memory for details and her hoarding needs—it was to be expected that Tom would learn to employ this type of behavior.

Another aspect of compulsive behavior is important in relation to Tom's ambivalent feelings toward parent figures. According to psychoanalytic theory, compulsive behavior typically occurs in relation to the child's training about right and wrong, good and bad, cleanliness and dirtiness. In our culture such issues are apt to occur first in connection with toilet training. Achievement of this skill is a difficult task for a little child, and he is most likely to manage it with a minimum of stress if his parents are patient, and their requirements of him are realistic. If, however, his parents are quite strict with and punish him, he will feel hostile toward them. Even if they aren't very critical, if he has had an especially close relationship with his mother before this period, he may interpret her new requirements of him as harsh, and feel that he is unloved because her behavior contrasts so sharply with her earlier uncritical affection. The adult who develops compulsive symptoms is thought to carry within himself unresolved infantile conflicts over angry self-assertion and the need to remain dependent. He vacillates between love and hate toward parent figures. There is some evidence that Wolfe may have undergone fairly rigorous toilet training. In one passage of *Angel*, Wolfe described Eugene Gant as a young school boy, needing to go to the bathroom but too embarrassed to raise his hand to ask the teacher for permission. In a later passage Wolfe described Eugene, on a trip to the hot springs with his mother, as fascinated with the idea of ridding himself of all "corruption" at the baths. Certainly as an adult Tom showed much evidence of strongly ambivalent feelings toward parent figures—particularly women—first needing to love them and depend on them, and then needing to hate them and trying to break away from them.

Manic Depressive Behavior

Wolfe went through most of his life suffering from periods of extreme emotional intensity which bordered on the pathological. As he became older the mood became more intense, and the tendency to shift back and forth in mood became more rapid, so that the intervals between shifts were of shorter duration. These periods of mood deviation, whether toward the euphoric or the depressed, are identifiable since he was not one to conceal his feelings, and a considerable portion of the contents of his letters and notebooks concerns his state of mind, whether good or bad. His depressions and elations were usually caused by events which occurred in his life situation, and these can be classified into five main types (to be discussed below).

Wolfe was aware of his lability of mood, and of his fear of insanity. (He referred to this fear frequently, though it is not clear whether this is what he had in mind when he spoke of "the curse in our family," since this phrase may merely have been a reference to an eczema condition, or to the tendency toward alcoholism.) Tom was quite specific about his fear of insanity, and mentioned it on many occasions. His first reference to it seems to have been in a letter to his mother in 1923, about six months after his father's death, when he wrote, "I think I am inevitable. I believe nothing can stop me now but insanity, disease, or death." In March of 1925 he wrote to Mabel, "I'm afraid that I'm a bit mad—I mean actually off. I think I have been since the first week after I came to France, when the play was stolen. But I'm not afraid of it. . . . Lately the fear of my madness has lost what terror it possessed, and has been tinged with a beautiful quality." This was after Tom's unsuccessful effort to begin a love affair with

Ann, and his quarrel with Kenneth Raisbeck. In May of 1929, during the period when *Angel* was being edited, he wrote to Mabel: "I am the one remaining American who knows nothing about driving a car and who has no desire to own one. Is this another sign of my 'queerness?' Well, I sometimes feel like the only sane person on a stroll through a madhouse; all the maniacs are nudging one another and saying: 'See that guy? He's crazy. . . .' Don't be afraid of going crazy—I've been there several times and it's not at all bad. If people get too much for you take a long ride on a train."

In 1930, after Tom had more or less broken off with Aline, he wrote from Germany to Henry Volkening, who had taught at New York University: "As for the incredible passion that possessed me when I was twenty-five years old and that brought me to madness and, I think, almost to destruction [his affair with Aline]—that is over: that fire can never be kindled again." But the next month he wrote to Max Perkins that he was going "through periods of the most horrible depression, weariness of spirit, loneliness and despair. . . ." And again a few months later he wrote to Volkening, "I am tired of madness and agony. . . ." His notebooks also reiterate these concerns about possible insanity.

In 1935, while Tom was waiting for *River* to appear, after a period of intense personal self-driving to finish the book, he wrote in his personal notes, "the artist at work may be a kind of maniac."[11] Kennedy thought that Tom was rather proud of his driftings near to the borderline of insanity. That same spring Tom wrote to Max from London, "I will confess to *you* that there were times there [on this recent trip to Paris] when I really was horribly afraid I was going mad—all the unity and control of personality seemed to have escaped from me. . . ." Then after some unfavorable reviews of *River* had appeared, in 1936 he

---

11. *Notebooks*, p. 666.

wrote to Julian Meade saying that the writer "must be prepared to hear himself described as a manic-depressive, a pathological item of the specialist in criminal psychology, a half-wit, or the grandson of Wordsworth's idiot boy, the bird that fouls its nest, a defiler of the temple of religion, a political reactionary, or a dangerous red, or a traitor to his country." Finally, Tom's sister Mabel reported in her memoirs that in 1937 when he made the summer visit to the cabin at Oteen, North Carolina—after his quarrel with Scribner's and Perkins had become rather bitter—his doctors had told him that if he didn't slow down and get some rest, he would have a nervous breakdown.

It is not at all difficult to identify the different periods of elation or depression in Tom's life by means of his letters and notebooks, and if one follows the report of the mood of the protagonists through the four main novels, which cover the period from birth to the age of thirty-six. In order to make these stages more apparent, they are presented here in the form of a chart giving the year of his life, the major events likely to produce psychological shifts of affect, the tendency at a given time to lean more toward the euphoric or the depressed end of the emotional spectrum, and the psychological character of the precipitating event which marked the beginning of each period of mood-swing. These events can be classified into five main types: the first two produced elevated affect, or the tendency to manic behavior; the latter three tended to produce depressions. These five categories are:

1. A new experience of being loved or accepted; the gratification of Tom's love-needs, (producing an elevated affective state).
2. Having a play or book produced or published, thus gratifying his life-urge for fame or professional recognition (an elevating event).
3. Separation from a loved one, either by death, or termination of a relationship (a depression-producing event).

4. Rejecting or strong criticism of a play or book, thus frustrating Tom's drive for fame or professional recognition (a depressing event).
5. Finding himself in a strange, loveless, and somewhat frightening new environment (generally a rather depressing event for Wolfe).

All of these events are presented in chronological sequence on chart 3 and their interrelationship is quite obvious. Study of the chart suggests that it is inappropriate to conceive of Tom's mood-swings as stemming from hormonally-determined events which occurred at regular intervals, as is often presumed to be the case with the classic manic-depressive. In Tom's case these swings tend to follow the pattern characteristic of reactive depression, when circumstances trigger off the latent tendency toward euphoria or depression. Tom's major mood-swings appear to have followed major events in his life which were of such a character that they could be labelled critical events and determinants of his emotions. In order to locate the description of these events in the novels, one must remember the periods of Wolfe's life that are covered by each book: 1900-1920—*Look Homeward, Angel*; 1920-1925—*Of Time and the River*; 1925-1928—*The Web and the Rock*; 1928-1936—*You Can't Go Home Again*. These book titles have also been included on chart 3.

An account of all of the numerous references and allusions to affective states in Wolfe's books and letters would make tedious reading, but several are presented here to convey their intensity and flavor and to attest to their authenticity. Consider the *Letters*, for instance: in 1924 he wrote to his mother, "I don't know how to conserve nervous energy; I burn it extravagantly." Several months later he wrote her "Within me somewhere terrific energy is generated—I must always be going—either attacking a book or my play furiously, or teaching furiously, or racing around, as fast as I can go, even in the sun. I take things with too

CHART 3

Wolfe's Periods of Elation and Depression and the Concurrent Events in His Life

Year	Event	Novel	Depressed or Manic	Love Denied	Love Unavailable	Fame Denied	Love Gratified	Fame Gratified
1906	Moves to Old Kentucky Home	Look Homeward Angel		*				
1912	Enters North State Fitting School						*	
1916	Enters University of North Carolina				*			
1917	Romance with C. Paul; accepted in fraternities; starts editorial work							*
1918	Ben dies			*				
1919	Play produced; campus successes							*
1920	Goes to Harvard				*			
1921	Play not very successful at Harvard	Of Time and the River				*		
1922	Father dies			*				
1923	Play rejected by New York Theater Guild					*		
1924	Moves to New York to teach at New York University				*			
1925	Raisbeck quarrel; meets Aline Bernstein	The Web and the Rock					*	

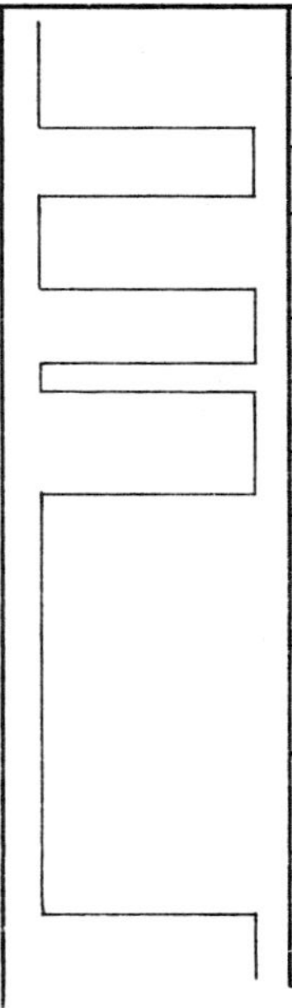

CHART 3 —*Continued*

Year	Event	Novel	Depressed or Manic	Love Denied	Love Unavailable	Fame Denied	Love Gratified	Fame Gratified
1926-27	Travels in Europe often with Aline	**The Web and the Rock**					*	
1928	Rift with Aline; Oktoberfest			*				
1929	Meets Max Perkins; publication of **Look Homeward, Angel**						*	*
1930	Family, *et al.*, critical of **Angel;** goes abroad to escape from Aline Bernstein	**You Can't Go Home Again**		*	*	*		
1931	Has difficulty writing second book					*		
1932	Final break with Aline; difficulty writing			*		*		
1933	Begins **Of Time and the River**							*
1934	Works closely with Perkins; stories published						*	*
1935	**River** successful; fame in Europe							*
1936	Criticism of **Story of a Novel;** lawsuits frequent; fight with Perkins			*		*		
1937	Visits Asheville			*				
1938	Signs contract with Harpers; final illness				*			*

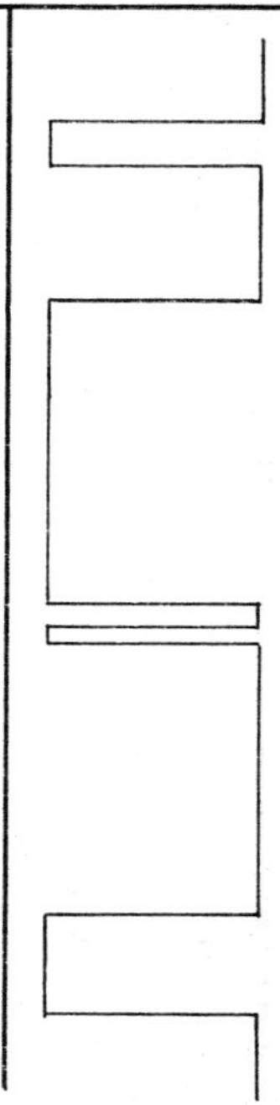

great intensity; I can never do things by halves. As a result . . . I have become desperately tired—not bodily, but mentally. . . ." In 1931 he wrote her "I have been much depressed by the news of the sudden and terrible death of a man [Kenneth Raisbeck] I knew at Harvard, who was one of my best friends there."

In 1935 Tom wrote to Max: "In Paris I couldn't sleep at all —I walked the streets from night to morning and was in the worst shape I have ever been in in my life. All the pent-up strain and tension of the last few months seemed to explode, . . ." and then he went on to describe the hallucination mentioned below. This was the period when he was convinced that *River* would prove to be a failure, and Max had sent him to Europe in an attempt to distract him from his anxieties.

In *The Story of a Novel* he wrote in 1935, "It may be objected . . . that in such research as I have here attempted to describe there is a quality of intemperate excess, and almost insane hunger to devour the entire body of human experience . . . I readily admit the validity of this criticism." Later in the same book he wrote: "At the end of the day of savage labor, my mind was still blazing with its effort, could by no opiate of reading, poetry, music, alcohol, or any other pleasure be put to rest. I was unable to sleep, unable to subdue the tumult of these creative energies, and as a result of this condition, for three years I prowled the streets. . . ."

In 1937 he wrote to Sherwood Anderson about "my death-defying duel with the universe—just the business of living which I make so damned hard. . . ." Other illustrations abound of his reports of his depressed states, and some of these are discussed later in relation to his paranoidal tendencies.

Of the many references to manic or depressed states to which Eugene Gant or George Webber were subject, we will cite just one from each of the four books. In *Look Homeward, Angel*, in describing Eugene's experiences at the State University, Wolfe wrote "At other times he slouched by, depressed by an unaccountable burden of weariness and dejection. He lost count of the hours—he had no sense of time—no regular periods for sleep, work, or recreation, although he attended his classes faithfully, and ate with fair regularity. . . ." In *Of Time and the River* he wrote: "Then he would come down off the hills into the town again, go home, and prowl and mutter around the house. . . . His family saw the light of madness in his eyes, and in his disconnected movements, and heard it in his incoherent speech." In *The Web and the Rock*, which has many such references, he wrote about George: "He had come away to forget her [Esther]: He did nothing but remember her. He got sick with the pain and the thought of her. . . . His limbs grew numb and weak, his heart was feverish and beat with a smothering thud, his guts were nauseous and queasy, and his throat burned him. . . . He could not digest the food he ate, and he vomited several times a day. At night, after prowling about feverishly through the London streets until three or four o'clock in the morning, he would go to bed and fall into a diseased coma in which events and people of his past life were mixed with the present. . . ." This is a classic description of an agitated depression.

In *You Can't Go Home Again* one of the best descriptions of a deep depression relates to the period when George Webber was living in Brooklyn and writing his second book. Wolfe wrote: "Loneliness, far from being a rare and curious circumstance, is and always has been the central and inevitable experience of every man. . . . To live alone as George was living, . . . he finds that there are times when anything . . . the most trivial incidents, the most casual words, can in an instant strip him of his armor, palsy his hand, constrict his heart with frozen horror, and fill his bowels with the grey substance of shuddering impotence and desolation. . . . Sometimes it would be nothing but a shadow passing on the sun. . . . Whatever it was, at such a time all joy and singing would go instantly out of day, Webber's heart would drop out of him like a leaden plummet. . . . Then he would feel like one who walked among the dead. . . . These hideous doubts, despairs, and dark confusions of the soul would come and go. . . ."

Wolfe also experienced some other symptoms in the form of hallucinations. In the periods of his deeper depressions he would become, as he wrote in 1933 to Alfred Dashiell of *Scribner's Magazine*, "so beset with demons, nightmares, delusions, and bewilderments" that he would lash out at everyone. He found it difficult to tell "how much bloody anguish I have sweat and suffered when I have exorcised these monstrous phantoms and seen clearly into what kind of folly and madness they have led me." And he wrote to Belinda Jelliffe, a New York friend who had also come from North Carolina, that while he may have been "tormented and pursued by all sorts of demons, phantoms, monsters and delusions" of his own creation, he had gotten out of his work the certitude and truth that had escaped him elsewhere.

It cannot be said with any certainty whether the final scene in *Look Homeward, Angel* in which Eugene Gant meets his brother Ben's ghost and carries on a prolonged discussion, was an hallucination, a dream, or a purely fictional device. Eugene is depicted by Wolfe as being puzzled. Eugene says that he must be imagining the situation, and later when the ghost of Ben denies that he is dead, Eugene asks which of them is really the ghost. A much more certain hallucination is recorded by Tom in a letter to Perkins in 1935 when he reported that once in Paris he felt the horrible dissociative experience of seeming to disintegrate into at least six people, with the other shapes of himself moving out from him, and then moving back into him. And he swore to Perkins that he was not dreaming. He had been going through a frenzied period of reactive depression at the time.

Tom also dreamed a lot, and his dreams were usually not pleasant. Though few of them have been published, the several that have show the signs of a very anxious and tormented psyche. In one nightmare Wolfe reportedly dreamed that he had neglected his classes for a year, and suddenly felt almost insurmountable guilt because of this, and anxiety over the mountains of uncorrected themes which he ought to be working on, instead of travelling in Europe and doing his own writing.[12] Another "vivid and horrible" nightmare is reported in *You Can't Go Home Again.* George Webber dreams that he is running and stumbling over the heath of a foreign land, fleeing in terror from a sense of nameless shame for having committed a crime for which there is no name, making him an irreconcilable putrescence fleeing from a vast naked eye; then the dream shifts to his native town, but none of his former associates recognize him, and he is obliterated from their lives.

What was the source of Tom's manic and depressive reactions? First, his father set him an example of this sort of behavior. W. O. was a very labile person, who had periods of elation and depression, with the depression becoming more persistent in his later years. Thus, Tom could have acquired this type of response either through genetics or learning, or a combination of the two. Tom's periods of elation occurred when things were going well. The depressive reactions were probably the consequence of two major factors. The first relates to his early childhood and the fact that he had, as discussed in chapter 5, a mother who demanded excessive productivity of him. At first Julia (and W. O.) loved Tom extravagantly, and praised him indulgently for his childish efforts. One example of this is Mabel's account of how, when W. O. took the infant, Tom, into the backyard one day, Tom is said to have mooed at the cow. W. O. was delighted with this behavior and proudly told the whole family about it. The fact that it became a family legend is significant. Then, too, there is Julia's discussion of how lavishly Tom was praised for his ability to read the little books his parents and siblings had read to him; actually he had simply memorized the words, as children often do. This early praise gave Tom an unrealistic idea of his

---

12. *Story of a Novel*, pp. 68, 69.

capabilities and achievements. Related to this is the fact that Tom apparently used W. O. as his ego-ideal. He developed an ideal which seemed to be based on an infantile, enormously exaggerated picture of what W. O. was like. To Tom everything about his father seemed larger than life.

Following this early period of love and indulgence, his parents, and especially his mother, were quite critical and expected a high level of performance and rigid conformity to their standards of conduct. As the last child, and specifically as the last son, Tom was expected to fulfill the Wolfe family's desire for success and social recognition. Tom introjected many of these standards and learned to evaluate his behavior as his parents would evaluate it, so that he, personally, came to expect a good deal of himself. When someone tries to model himself after an ego-ideal like Tom's of W. O., and when he has unrealistic ideas about his capabilities, the result is an adult who cannot possibly achieve at a level appropriate to his fantasy of what he should be. The consequence is inevitable experiences of failure, producing guilt feelings and consequent judgment of the self as unworthy, inferior and unlovable. Examination of chart 3 reveals that each time Tom judged himself a failure as an author, or each time he was threatened with loss of love, he became depressed.

The second factor contributing to Wolfe's depressive tendencies was that in his effort to be very productive at work, Tom excluded from his life many other sorts of activities that could have made him feel more successful and could also have helped him to have more normal social relationships. Consequently, when he became depressed, he had nothing else in life to give him a sense of satisfaction and so help him pull himself out of his depression. Actually Tom's reactions to periods of stress seem to follow a pattern somewhat as follows: first he tended to use compulsive responses, including excessive drinking, and as one might predict, these were not effective in solving his problems. Then Tom would travel, in an effort to escape from the situation; this, too, was usually not very effective. Sometimes he would redouble his efforts and begin a period of frantic activity. Finally, when none of this helped, he would become depressed.

Paranoidal Tendencies

For all of his adult life Wolfe was subject to feelings ranging from the suspicious to the clearly paranoidal. This is not surprising, since both his parents and most of his siblings showed this behavior trait to quite a pronounced degree. W. O. Wolfe gave almost daily displays of suspicion in his diatribes against Julia, or almost anyone else whom he might see as in some way impairing his interests. Granted that some of this speech was more dramatic than malicious, W. O. nevertheless implied that he was constantly subjected to insufferable agonies at the hands of innumerable foes who were grinding his soul into the depths of degradation and despair. He forever saw himself stretched on the rack suffering excruciating tortures because of the malice of some human, or even unearthly, forces which were pitted against him. Julia's suspiciousness was of a quieter sort, but perhaps more deeply seated in a profound sense of endless injustices committed against her. She carried with her at all times the Westall tendency to anticipate the worst from all but Westalls, and she was forever on the alert to outwit the foe. She loved litigation, and set up situations in advance in such a way that it would be possible for her to take her foes to court; moreover, she always won. The same pervasive suspiciousness and hostility seems to have affected all of the children, except perhaps Effie and Fred, who tended to be more trusting and outgoing. Frank, Mabel, Ben, and Tom could, at times, be very kindly, but whenever they felt the least bit slighted or injured their anger rose quickly, and they were hypersensitive and suspicious of injury. Similarly they tended to fear the unknown, and this made them the victims of deep ethnic prejudices, so that they were always anticipating slights from Negroes, Jews, Irish, or any other group. In this regard they had the defensiveness and suspiciousness of the poor white, combined with the cautiousness and withdrawal tendencies of the Southern mountaineer.

Tom's paranoidal attitudes are most apparent in his letters, although his novels and diaries certainly abound with evidences of the same symptom. Of two hundred and sixteen published letters to his mother, twenty-one contain passages which are at least hypersuspicious, and sometimes much more nearly paranoidal. Of four hundred and twenty other published letters, fifty-one have the same character. Some of them, particularly those sent to Max Perkins in the last two years of Tom's life, are deeply paranoidal. Several fill page after page with recriminations, self-defensive statements, and bitter criticisms of Max, impugning his motives. (These kinds of letters are familiar to administrators of mental hospitals who never let their patients actually mail them because of their vituperative and critical nature, usually unjustified.) The things which Wolfe seemed to become most angry about and which caused him to feel persecuted included the following:

1. An apparent sign of lack of love or fondness, as in the failure to reply to his letters, or even to send him the money he requested.
2. An over-eagerness to hold on to him, as was true of Aline Bernstein, when he was trying to break away.
3. A failure to recognize his merit as a writer, or any attempt to criticize his works.
4. Matters having to do with money, particularly his mother's or siblings' acquisitiveness, which he called their "money madness."
5. Business letters which took a legalistic position or attempted to hold him to the terms of a contract or agree-

ment which he had made, but which he subsequently considered an infringement upon a friendly relationship.

A delusion which developed later in his life, was Tom's totally unfounded idea that the world was engaged in a conspiracy to keep him from his work: critics, lawyers, and even women's clubs were all part of this conspiracy; it really approached the delusional level in the last two years of his life, so that he secreted himself from the world, and even from his family, and could be reached only through Miss Nowell. Similarly Tom developed the delusion that Max Perkins, unquestionably his dear friend, enjoyed seeing him in misery, when in fact Max was suffering almost as much as Wolfe because of their inexplicable falling out. Tom was emotional and intemperate; often his wording was much stronger than his intended meaning, and he was forever apologizing for losing his temper and saying or writing some very bitter remark about which he later felt great remorse. Even when one takes into account this exaggeration in his letters, he was nevertheless often very hostile and overly suspicious. Perhaps the quality and color of the letters can best be revealed by short excerpts presented in chronological order:

Date	*To*	
1920	Mother	"I have chosen—or God has chosen—a lonely road for my travel . . . and even the best of you . . . may have sympathy, but little understanding."
1921	Mother	". . . whatever taunts may be thrown at me, if any, of selfishness, pride, conceit, snobbishness, or what not, strike against as tough a hide as a sensitive fellow can call to his defense."
1921	Mother	"I have waited from day to day for some answer to my special delivery let-

		ter. . . . If the time has come for me to go out on my own, so be it, but please try not to treat me with the indifference while I am alone and far away. . . . You didn't want me at home, you said nothing about my returning. . . ."
1923	Mother	"[Life] is savage, cruel, kind, noble, passionate, selfish, generous, stupid, ugly, beautiful, painful, joyous . . . it's all these I want to know, and, by God, I shall, though they crucify me for it."
1924	Mother	"the world is at me with its long fingers, and must have its payment. . . ." "I love North Carolina. . . . But what has it to feed my spirit, my mind? . . . After all, haven't you all worshipped the long bank roll too much?"
1925	Ann	"I am a very suspicious person . . . It began to dawn on me that I was being asked to go along as a kind of stimulant and travelling companion to Kenneth."
1926	Professor Watt	"I feel . . . that my own destiny has been matched [by my mother] against that of a piece of black earth in Carolina, and a piece of sand in Florida, and that the land always wins."
1926	Mother	"Money in our family has been a deadly poison . . . it has been a breeder of suspicion, of jealousy, of falsehood among brother and sister."
1926	Mother	". . . in every family there's always a stranger, always an outsider. In our family Ben was the stranger until his death—I suppose I'm the other one."

1927	Mother	"I think of my . . . childhood . . . as a man thinks of a dream full of pain, ugliness, misunderstanding, and terror. . . . Strangers we are born alone into a strange world."
1927	Mother	"It has taken me 27 years to rise above the bitterness and hatred of my childhood."
1928	Mother	"in spite of an ugly and rancorous feeling towards me which may exist in the family . . . I want to see you all . . . no matter how much pain and ugliness I may have to remember."
1930	Perkins	"Why have things got to be made so unfair and hard for me? . . . It makes me vomit!"
1930	Wheelock	"Some of the reviews . . . have said things that [were] . . . dirty, unfair, distorted, and full of mockery. . . . There is no life in this world worth living, there is no air worth breathing, there is nothing but agony and the drawing of the breath in nausea and labor, until I get the best of this tumult and sickness inside me. . . . people have charged me and my work with bombast, rant, and noisiness."
1930	Dashiell	". . . when you see some bastard who tells you lies about Europe, and worse lies about America . . . spit in his face —no, piss on him instead, for the carcass of such a lying degenerate must not be dignified by spittle from the lips of an honest man. . . . I tell you I had rather have ten years more of life there [in

		America] . . . than a hundred years of shitty ex-patriotism."
1930	Perkins	". . . if you hear scurrilous and slanderous stories about me . . . spread by any of the ten million envenomed and reptilian ———s who walk the streets of this earth full of hate, malice, and poison, put them down as lies . . . . in the end, if anyone gets betrayed or deserted it will be me."
1930	Perkins	"For God's sake, don't think I am mad with suspicion and distrust. . . . By God, these are real things and true things, and these people [columnists] are liars and cheap swindlers . . . . when I meet these people my heart turns rotten, and my guts are sick and nauseous."
1931	Volkening	"The literary business in America has become so horrible that it is sometimes possible to write only between fits of vomiting. . . . I . . . say keep away from . . . writers."
1931	Perkins	"But do you really think that after what I have seen during the past eighteen months, I would cling very desperately to this stinking remnant of a rotten fish, or any longer feel any sense of deference or responsibility to swine who make you sign books to their profit even while you break bread with them who try to degrade your life to a dirty, vulgar, grinning, servile, competitive little monkey's life? . . . As I under-

		stand it, I am not bound now to Scribner's or to any publisher by any sort of contract . . . neither have I taken money that is not my own." [he had accepted royalty advances]
1933	Mother	"It took me fifteen years of being alone to make a life for myself, and now that life is my own . . . no outsider is going to violate it. The privacy and obscurity of my own life is something I will defend with all I have and I will not allow people to thrust themselves into my life. . . ."
1935	Perkins	"Scribners last month carried *three printed attacks* on me" [actually three mild reviews in *Scribner's Magazine*].
1936	Mother	[A nine-page paranoid discussion of the lawsuit he was bringing against an Irish boy for misappropriating some of his manuscripts.]
1936	Perkins	[Six pages of debate over the royalty to be paid him on *The Story of a Novel* ending with] ". . . but I do say that you cannot command the loyalty and devotion of a man on the one hand and then take a business advantage on the other."
1936	Greenfield	[A lengthy and bitter criticism of Bernard DeVoto, never mailed.]
1937	Perkins	"How dare you give anyone my address!" [Telegram].
1937	Perkins	"Are you—the man I trusted and reverenced above all else in the world—trying, for some mad reason I can not

		even guess, to destroy me?" [long letter filled with material in similar vein].
1936, 1937	Perkins	[Twenty-two page letter announcing his severance with Scribner's and Perkins; a passage is quoted in chapter 4.]
1937	Fred	"But the last year or two, it has sometimes seemed to me that there is a general plot abroad not to keep people like myself out of work but to keep them from doing the work they already have."
1937	Robert Linscott	[Long angry letter because Houghton Mifflin asked him to sign a waiver of legal responsibility for the safety of his manuscript while it was in their offices; the letter was never mailed.]
1937	Fred	"I don't think I'm going to be helped much by any of you, and I no longer expect it, but if you can't help, for God's sake, when I am fighting for a living, don't rush in and shoot off your mouth about matters you know nothing of" [never mailed].
1938	Arthur Mann	[Four printed pages of discussion of his anger toward the Irish boy, against whom he had just won a lawsuit] ". . . it is better to be gyped, than to go through life with your fangs bared in a snarl . . . . You learn some pretty sad things about people—one is, how many people there are who say they are your friends [who] cannot be depended on when a question of profit is involved."

1938	Mabel	"From my own point of view . . . the profession of law . . . ought to be abolished. . . . [The lawyer] is a kind of parasite with a recognized established position. . . . The lawyer works both ways, either as a representative of dishonest and unscrupulous people . . . or as a representative of honest people who have to defend themselves. In both cases, obviously, it is the lawyer who wins out . . . the good lawyer . . . too, is a member of the whole bad system."
1938	Elizabeth Nowell	"Max [Perkins] still tells people that he is my friend, and then he runs me down . . . the people who say they love you are often the ones who do the most to injure you . . . now Perkins, under this mask of friendship, is doing the same thing . . . . it's almost as if *unconsciously*, by some kind of *wishful* desire, he wants me to come to grief, as a kind of sop to his pride, and his unyielding conviction that he is right in everything—the tragic flaw in his character."

If one turns to Wolfe's major novels, one finds an abundance of descriptions of the paranoidal reactions of his autobiographical protagonists Eugene Gant and George Webber. In *Look Homeward, Angel* by the time Gant had entered the North State Fitting School, frequent disillusion—so Wolfe tells us—had fostered a strain of bitter suspicion in the young man. His siblings were quite envious of his especially privileged schooling, and their jealousy expressed itself in barbed stings. During his summer experience at Norfolk Eugene saw himself as a stranger in the crowds of hostile and critical people, particularly the girls. He felt like a man who had been relocated, and whose earlier life was a ghostly memory; he felt that strangers were laughing at him, but he attributed this to their envy of him, and their fear of him because he was different. When he returned to the university after Ben's death, he sometimes thought that he heard other young men talking about him in their rooms and saying that Eugene Gant was crazy. While he felt that he was in truth the conqueror of the world, he was sure that the others were ridiculing him behind his back, and their scorn made him bitter: "He inherited his father's conviction at times that the world was gathered in an immense conspiracy against him." Yet Eugene saw himself as "Jesus-of-Nazareth Gant," "Marshall Gant" and "Ace Gant." During this period he would often rush away at night and visit other little towns around Pulpit Hill, introducing himself by fictitious names like Ben Jonson, or William Blake, or telling strangers that he was a carpenter and the "Son of Man." If Eugene Gant's experiences and behavior are reflections of what Wolfe actually felt and did at that stage of his life, one can only conclude that Wolfe at that time displayed the classic symptoms of paranoidal delusions.

In *The Web and the Rock* George Webber's behavior toward Esther Jacks (Aline Bernstein) was often admittedly quite paranoid. On the occasion of his first luncheon with her, on his twenty-fifth birthday, he drank too much and had to be taken home by her. When he realized what was happening he was filled with a murderous fury, which made him want to smash and splinter everything. And eventually his paranoid preoccupation with Esther's alleged infidelity led Webber to quarrel with her constantly. He ordered her out of his apartment, accused her of robbing him, and cried out that she had driven him mad and wrecked his life. But in his more lucid periods he could admit to himself that he cursed Esther because he hated himself. He realized that something had gone wrong within himself; he could not work any more, he felt his creativity being impaired, and he projected the blame for this onto Esther. Half of *The Web and the Rock*, rather than merely an account of a great love affair, is actually a classic description of a paranoid reaction to a sexually frightening situation by an overwhelmed man who fears both sexual and creative impotence.

The paranoid person typically is one who, during childhood, has not been able to develop basic trust in people, because he has not been adequately protected from excessive tension and anxiety during his early years. Consequently, when as an adult he is in a crisis situation, he is unable to turn to others for help, but rather goes off to try to work out the problem by himself. He is also a person who has not had sufficient practice at role-playing as he is growing up, and so is unable to consider points of view other than his own in trying to interpret a situation. Consequently, when he finds himself in a threatening situation he tends to persevere on one interpretation of it. In addition, he has learned to escape blame himself by placing the blame on others. Thus his interpretation of the situation leads him to deny guilt or responsibility himself and to assume that someone else is causing his misery. At the same time, the very conditions which prevented his having enough experience at role-playing have usually been responsible for his spending a great deal of time alone, so that he has had fewer opportunities than the average person for social correction of his misperceptions of events. Thomas Wolfe experienced just such conditions. As a child he lived in a household permeated with tension because of the hostility between his parents. In this household, he had little practice in assuming any role but that of the baby of the family. His relative social isolation meant that he had few friends, and consequently, little opportunity to check his conclusions about the meaning of events with anyone else. Moreover, his parents and older siblings set him an example of paranoid reactions to circumstances. Both parents exhibited a compensatory behavior of a sense of unusual self-worth, which at times verged on ideas of grandeur. Both parents pushed Tom in the same direction, and with both Margaret Roberts and Aline Bernstein expressing unqualified conviction about his great literary promise, it is easy to see the source of Wolfe's notion that he was a genius. When these feelings about himself were not always supported by those around him Wolfe tended to feel persecuted, and to want to retaliate against his persecutor. This would initiate a vicious cycle of behavior, which frequently lead into the paranoid syndrome. Tom's tendency always to live alone, and his almost total naiveté about the world and the way people really react toward the intellectual and withdrawn person, did little to alleviate the tendency toward producing paranoia. Finally, his strong narcissism and the feeling that he deserved the best—which became evident at least from the time when he planned to go away to college—would not easily tolerate frustration, but could readily lead into depression, and eventually to paranoidal thinking and behavior.

The person who, as an adult, experiences paranoid persecutory reactions, has, in his early life, been dominated by an expectation of punitive treatment and has learned to be ready to meet this treatment with counterattack. Such a child has been excessively punished for wrongdoing and has introjected his parents' critical attitudes. These attitudes produce strong anxiety feelings, which the child tries to handle by projecting them outside himself and then experiencing them as coming from a persecutor, against whom he vigorously tries to defend himself. When the adult is placed under severe stress, he regresses to this infantile pattern of reaction. He experiences himself as persecuted, and his projected hostilities are interpreted as coming from someone outside himself who is trying to torture or kill him. Such an adult might be placed under stress by any of several types of situations, such as the realization that he has done something wrong, and therefore deserves punishment; or he might feel threatened by possible loss of love from someone very important to him. In either of these two examples, he would feel hostile, and at the same time would anticipate punishment for his hostility feelings. Having learned to handle his feelings by denial and projection, he would disown his feelings, and experience them as the feelings of someone outside himself. We see numerous examples of this in Wolfe's behavior toward both Aline Bernstein and Maxwell Perkins, when he accused them of deserting him, betraying him, and making his life miserable in various ways. This pattern of denial and projection did not solve his problems, of course, and so was not an effective solution. Instead it puzzled and hurt his former patrons, and seriously affected his relationships with them.

Summary

Diagnostically Wolfe is seen as a deeply neurotic man who suffered from insufficient gratification of his strong life urges for love and fame. As a result he exhibited many signs of general depression with some agitated depression and occasional euphoria. While it would not be appropriate to call him a victim of a manic-depressive psychosis, he certainly can be classified as a psychoneurotic with severe labile and cyclical emotional features. In addition, he exhibited many evidences of paranoidal behavior; again, this was probably subpsychotic in intensity most of the time, although even Wolfe himself spoke of having been "mad" on a number of occasions. Certainly he was also a very compulsive individual. But his overall problems of adjustment did not keep him from being a very creative person, and may, in fact, have contributed to his creative drive. The problems did, however, produce much internal strife while he was in the process of creating his works.

10

PROGNOSIS

CONSTRUCTING A PROGNOSIS IS ALWAYS A SPECULATIVE MATter, and in this case one might question its value in view of the impossibility of checking its validity against subsequent reality. Nevertheless, given the wealth of self-revelation Tom Wolfe offers in his books, notebooks, and letters, one cannot help but be fascinated by the personality of this complex, troubled, and talented man, and it is hard to resist the temptation to speculate about what would have happened to him had he lived longer.

Recognition should be given to the significance of Tom's basic need for love and fame, the former being found especially in an exaggerated dependency upon support and nurturance from another person. Wolfe felt that the only way he could achieve fame was through his writing; but he never knew whether each book would be well received, and so he remained anxious and worried throughout the entire writing process. Although Wolfe's first book, *Look Homeward, Angel*, brought him a considerable amount of international fame, it also provoked rejection by his family and his former friends in Asheville. So that while it temporarily satisfied his desire for fame, it at the same time frustrated his need for love, which had never been fully satisfied except in his very early childhood.

After Tom experienced the loneliness of Harvard and the early New York years, he found in Aline Bernstein many of the qualities of the accepting, nurturing mother, and related to her dependently for several years. However, having become overly sensitive to Julia Wolfe's possessiveness, Tom felt a need to break off the relationship with Aline when she began to replicate this possessiveness. He then turned to Max Perkins, who was an accepting, supporting father figure for him for the next five to six years. Again, when Max began to dominate too much, and also seemed less able to give Tom some of the emotional support he craved, Tom felt the need to break off this relationship. But in the case of both Aline and Max, Tom could not break away entirely and returned to them intermittently.

Tom kept trying to recapture the nurturance he had experienced in the early years of his life in Asheville, but in his last major book, *You Can't Go Home Again*, he indicated that he had finally discovered that one cannot return to the lost past in order to find satisfaction, but must look to the future. This may have constituted some progress in the achievement of emotional maturity. Whether he had also learned to function independently is another question, however.

Elizabeth Nowell thought that Tom showed greater maturity during the last year of his life, and would have been a considerably more mature person had he lived, but the facts do not support this conclusion. Although Wolfe was a much more sophisticated person than he had been when he left Asheville, and although he had acquired some social compassion, his personality was still fundamentally the same. His talk of returning to live with his mother, and the attempt to return to Asheville, do not indicate maturity as much as regression, probably brought on by the breakdown of his dependent relationship with Max Perkins. And during 1937 he lapsed into one of the most severe depressions of his life. At this time his lawsuits were at their height, and he was in the process of breaking off his relationship with Scribner's. Moreover, he was suffering from some unfavorable criticism, and his letters of this period were the most paranoid of his life. Even though he tried to attain a more regular life style in the spring of 1938, he still complained of his inability to sleep. And in June of 1938 he wrote Miss Nowell one of his most paranoid letters about Max Perkins. Probably the only real change that occurred in Wolfe in the period of 1937-38 was that—having found a new publisher who paid him handsome advance royalties—he felt more secure about his professional work and was able to devote more of his attention to less personal concerns. He showed a greater interest in larger issues and was more optimistic about the future of America than most of his contemporaries. But personally he remained quite immature: his basic narcissism had not diminished much, nor had his depressive and paranoid tendencies.

If Wolfe had not died in 1938, but had lived another thirty years or so, what kind of person would he have been? We can be fairly sure that the two needs which were so strong through his first thirty-seven years would have remained dominant in his life style. But what would have happened in regard to the satisfaction of his need for fame? Certainly he would have continued to write. But would this writing have brought him fame? Critics varied in their comments about *You Can't Go Home Again.* Some considered it his most mature book, and the first one that was not primarily preoccupied with his own emotions. But others found it disappointing because it lacked the lyrical prose that had made *Angel* an outstanding book. Would his creative ability have continued to flourish? Turnbull, after carefully reviewing the pros and cons, said that he believed the answer was no. He felt that Wolfe had come full cycle, and that he was still, in the last book, writing primarily about his own inner self.[1] The auto-

---

1. Turnbull, pp. 345-46.

biography was just about finished, and in *You Can't Go Home Again* it had ceased to hold the reader's interest in the same way that *Angel* and *River* had done. Most critics considered Wolfe's last books inferior to the first two, although there is, of course, some disagreement on this point. Artistically the later books may have been superior, and their sale was strong, indicating much popular interest; but over the years they have failed to command the attention that the two earlier books do. Had he lived, Wolfe would, of course, have polished and reworked the manuscripts of the last two books before their publication, and if this had been done they might have been considered superior to the first two books.

There are few writers whose later works continue to show all of the quality of their earlier, great works. Turnbull points out that most of the best work of Hemingway, Faulkner and Fitzgerald, for instance, was their early work. Wolfe had probably said most of what he had to say by 1938. Furthermore, Tom had the middle-age crisis to look forward to, when younger men with new ideas would tend to displace him. Typically this is a period of some fairly marked depression, and Tom had already shown a strong tendency in that direction. If his work had begun to deteriorate in quality, he would have been subjected to more severe criticism, and he was particularly vulnerable to this. He would almost certainly have made even more use of the defensive symptoms which he displayed throughout his life, only they would have been more exaggerated. Compulsions, depression, and paranoid ideation would have been quite likely.

If Tom had had any other medium for attaining a sense of success he might have been able to counter the frustration he would have experienced from diminished literary success. But he had no hobbies except for travel, and this often brought on symptoms of depression because it heightened his sense of loneliness. With his main raison d'être—his literary career—no longer able to yield full satisfaction he would certainly have felt frustrated. He might have turned to teaching, but he lacked a

Ph.D. degree, and this might have proved an obstacle to advancing in that profession. Moreover, he had resigned from his teaching job at New York University as soon as he no longer needed the income because he found teaching difficult and did not enjoy it. He might have obtained a position as a writer-in-residence at a university, but unless he was producing work which satisfied him, he would probably have considered this a prostitution of his abilities, and would have been unwilling to continue under those conditions. Moreover, his eccentric personal habits, lack of ability to keep appointments, and tendency toward alcoholism, would not have endeared him to the typical university administration.

Under such circumstances of diminishing professional success, some people can turn to those around them for emotional support and can substitute a satisfaction of the love need for satisfaction of the hunger for fame. But could this have happened for Wolfe? He had demonstrated on many occasions, and particularly with Aline Bernstein and Max Perkins, that he could not maintain a close personal relationship successfully for a significant period of time. Might he have married successfully? This seems quite unlikely; both Cowley and Turnbull imply that Wolfe was incapable of dividing his loyalty between his work and a wife.[2] It is, however, more likely that he was unable to relate to women well enough to build a good marriage. On five or six occasions he wrote of his intention to settle down and marry, possibly when he reached the age of thirty-five. But his conception of a wife, as revealed in those letters, was of a housekeeper rather than of a marriage partner. The example of marriage which his parents had set for him was a very poor one, and his attitude toward women was largely negative. He perceived them

---

2. Cowley, "Thomas Wolfe," Turnbull, pp. 231-32. Wolfe told James Mandel, a student who typed manuscripts for him, that he would probably marry at age seventy-three (see also Pollock and Cargill, *Thomas Wolfe*, p. 94).

as dominating, demanding, possessive, and deceitful. A wife would have expected Tom to pay attention to her, and she probably would not have tolerated the promiscuity which seemed so necessary for him in order to retain his sense of sexual adequacy. A wife might have expected him to be more careful about his appearance, and might have restricted his tendency to drink and while away the night in conversation. This sort of inhibition of his lifelong proclivities would have been irksome to Wolfe. For any marriage with Tom to have succeeded his wife would probably have had to be extremely nurturant. She would have had to expect little from him in return, and would have had to be grateful for the crumbs of affection he was willing to give her, as Aline Bernstein was after their affair had cooled. Also, as his symptoms increased she would have needed to have a good understanding of their psychological significance, in order to be able to tolerate them. The likelihood of Wolfe's finding such a wife seems pretty remote, even had he really been inclined to try to do so.

If not a wife, then who else might have given Wolfe the emotional support he would have needed? An editor? Edward Aswell, Tom's posthumous editor, was Tom's own age, and in the ten months during which they knew each other, they seemed to get along well together. Aswell respected and admired Tom greatly. But it is unlikely that he could have remained as completely accepting if they had had to work together as author and editor. Probably his responsibilities as an editor would have come into conflict with Tom's need to be simultaneously supported and given great freedom. The other males to whom Tom had previously turned for support of his dependency need had been older, as in the case of his brother, Ben, and his editor Max Perkins. How would he have reacted to an editor his own age? Tom had a considerable amount of difficulty in avoiding friction with his brother, Fred, who was only six years older, and yet Fred seems to have been a very tolerant person. It seems unlikely that Tom and any other editor could have had the sort of symbiotic relationship which existed for a while between Tom and Max Perkins. But without that sort of relationship, the situation would probably not have been very satisfactory. If Tom's books had declined in popularity, and sales had dropped, an editor could not easily have remained uncritical. One might predict that Wolfe would have kept changing editors, blaming each successive one for his difficulties, as he had blamed Perkins, and would have gone on trying to find an editor who really understood him. But his reputation for having difficulties with his editors was widespread, and he would have had trouble finding companies willing to take him on without imposing fairly severe strictures on his work. That Tom could have tolerated this is not likely.

Could Tom have turned to an agent for emotional support? Elizabeth Nowell was devoted to him and tended to combine the roles of editor and mother in her dealings with Tom. However, if she had been unable to continue selling Tom's work as well as she had done in the thirties, he might have blamed her for what were really his own literary failures. It is hard to predict how such a relationship might have fared. It would, however, be expecting a great deal of an agent to provide the emotional support which Wolfe would have needed.

Could Tom have turned to his family for support? His efforts to do so on other occasions had not met with much success. At the time of Tom's death, Julia Wolfe was already seventy-eight years old, and lived for only seven more years. She remained quite active and alert until her death, but after 1945 Tom would not have been able to turn to her, and if he had lived to be seventy, he would have needed someone else to relate to for the remaining twenty-five years of his life. Mabel and Fred would have been possible sources of support. Mabel died in 1958, and she might well have offered Tom some of the support he would have needed, until he was fifty-eight. Fred Wolfe survived the entire period, and the relationship with Fred had been a rather good one in the later years of Tom's life. But Fred married in 1943, and this might have altered the situation somewhat. Both Fred and Mabel would have been the most likely persons for Tom to have turned to, and such a relationship might have worked out satisfactorily, although neither of them was entirely uncritical of Tom, and each had his or her own spouse to claim first place in his attention. We must conclude, then, that Tom would have continued to search for someone to give him the emotional support he needed, and that this search would probably not have been very successful. The effect would have been to make life increasingly unsatisfactory for Tom, with neither his need for fame, nor his need for love being very adequately gratified.

Wolfe could probably have been helped to handle the problems which would have mounted with the onset of middle age if he could have accepted some form of psychotherapy. He had promised Aline Bernstein that he would undergo psychoanalysis. But it is unlikely that he would ever have been willing to undertake any sort of psychological treatment. Tom made three or four references to psychologists, psychiatrists, Freud, and psychoanalysis in his letters and writing, but all of them were critical. He held psychology and psychiatry in low regard. Since he typically obtained catharsis for his feelings of stress through his prolific writing, this and his profuse talking with acquaintances would have siphoned off some of the tensions, but would not have effected any significant degree of self-insight. Probably the effect of this self-analysis would only have been to reduce the likelihood of his seeking professional help. His training had caused him to be contemptuous of medical help and unusually slow about seeking it, and he preferred to ignore the existence of medical problems and to deny them, even when he had them called to his attention. So he would not have been likely to seek help for any considerably less obvious problems, lying mainly in the area of his personality, rather than in tangible bodily malfunctions. Considering his attitude toward the payment of medical and dental fees, it is likely that he would have considered the cost of psychotherapy unreasonable and outrageous.

The prognosis for Wolfe must, then, be unfavorable. His personality problems would have been likely to become more, not less, acute, and since he was already showing borderline symptoms of manic-depressive and paranoid conditions, it is hard to believe that these conditions would not have become intensified if he had lived several decades longer. The fate which was to overtake Fitzgerald and Hemingway is not likely to have spared Thomas Wolfe. He probably died around the height of his literary career, when his personal and emotional adjustment were already tending to show signs of strain which could have led to eventual distress and even disintegration of ego strength. His life seems to have been a tragic one, and it seems unlikely that it would have become any less so had he lived longer.

The image of the heroic figure, cut off in the prime of his life, is in many ways more appealing than that of the slowly deteriorating victim of ageing and eventual decay of the flesh. Wolfe felt that Ben's death was a tragedy, because he was young, with his life unfulfilled, whereas the death of his father was not a tragedy, since W. O. Wolfe had lived a full and fairly satisfying life. The death of Thomas Wolfe came somewhere between these two extremes, and perhaps had in it neither the elements of tragedy to be found in unfulfilled ambitions, nor the other sad image of deterioration, possible senility, and decay of vitality. Perhaps, then, death, with which Thomas Wolfe was so preoccupied in all of his writings, was in his case the proud brother who came to take him at a time when he had reached the apogee of his successes in life.

SELECTED REFERENCES

These references discuss the psychological characteristics of Thomas Wolfe. Excellent complete reference lists appear in Leslie Field, ed., *Thomas Wolfe: Three Decades of Criticism* (New York: New York University Press, 1968), and Richard Kennedy's *The Window of Memory: The Literary Career of Thomas Wolfe* (Chapel Hill: University of North Carolina Press, 1962). Articles reprinted in Field, ed., *Three Decades of Criticism*, Hugh C. Holman, ed., *The World of Thomas Wolfe* (New York: Charles Scribner's Sons, 1962) and Richard Walser, ed., *The Enigma of Thomas Wolfe* (Cambridge: Harvard University Press, 1953) are indicated by the short title following the entry.

ASWELL, EDWARD C. "A Note on Thomas Wolfe." In Thomas Wolfe's *The Hills Beyond*. New York: Harper and Brothers, 1941. Pp. 349-86. (Partly reprinted as the introduction to *You Can't Go Home Again* [Harper's Modern Classics, 1949] and in Holman and Field.)

———. "En Route to a Legend." *Saturday Review* 21 (1948): 7, 34-36. (Also published as the introduction to Wolfe's *The Adventures of Young Gant* [New York: New American Library, 1948] and in Walser.)

BERNSTEIN, ALINE. *The Journey Down*. New York: Alfred Knopf, 1938.

———. *Three Blue Suits*. New York: Equinox House, 1933.

BISHOP, DONALD E. "Thomas Wolfe." *The New Carolina Magazine* (1942): 28-29, 35, 47-48. (Reprinted as "Tom Wolfe as Student" in Walser.)

BISHOP, JOHN P. "The Sorrows of Thomas Wolfe." *Kenyon Review,* 1 (1939): 7-17. (Reprinted in Edmund Wilson, ed., *The Collected Essays of John Peale Bishop* [New York: Charles Scribner's Sons, 1948]; John Crowe Ransom, ed., *The Kenyon Critics* [Cleveland: World Publishing Company, 1951]; John W. Aldridge, ed., *Critiques and Essays on Modern Fiction* [New York: Ronald Press, Co., 1952]; Philip Rahv, ed., *Literature in America* [New York: World Publishing Co. (Meridian Books), 1958]; A. Walton Litz, ed., *Modern American Fiction: Essays in Criticism* [New York: Oxford University Press, 1963]. Partly reprinted in Holman.)

BRASWELL, WILLIAM. "Thomas Wolfe Lectures and Takes a Holiday." *College English* 1 (1939): 11-22. (Reprinted in Walser.)

BURGUM, EDWIN BERRY. "Thomas Wolfe's Discovery of America." *Virginia Quarterly Review* 20 (1946): 421-37. (Reprinted in Walser.)

CANBY, HENRY SEIDEL. "River of Youth." *Saturday Review of Literature* 11 (1935): 529-30. (Reprinted in Walser.)

CARGILL, OSCAR. "Gargantua Fills His Skin," *University of Kansas City Review* 16 (1949): 20-30. (Reprinted in Field.)

CLEMENTS, CLYDE C. "Symbolic Patterns in *You Can't Go Home Again*." *Modern Fiction Studies* 11 (1965): 286-96. (Reprinted in Field.)

COLLINS, THOMAS LYLE. "Thomas Wolfe." *Sewanee Review* 50 (1942): 487-504. (Reprinted in Walser.)

CHURCH, MARGARET. "Thomas Wolfe: Dark Time." *Publications of the Modern Language Association* 64 (1949): 629-38.

COWLEY, MALCOLM. "Thomas Wolfe." *Atlantic Monthly* 200 (1957): 202-12. (Reprinted in Holman.)

DANIELS, JONATHAN. "Poet of the Boom." In *Tar Heels*. New York: Dodd, Mead and Co., 1941. (Reprinted in Richard Walser.)

DEVOTO, BERNARD. "Genius is Not Enough." *Saturday Review of Literature* 13 (1936): 3-4, 14-15. (Reprinted in Walser and Field.)

DODD, MARTHA. *Through Embassy Eyes*. New York: Harcourt, Brace and Co., 1939.

FIELD, LESLIE A. *Thomas Wolfe: Three Decades of Criticism*. New York: New York University Press, 1968.

FISHER, VARDIS. "My Experiences with Thomas Wolfe." *Tomorrow* 10 (1951): 24-30. (Reprinted in Pollack and Cargill, *Thomas Wolfe at Washington Square* [New York: New York University Press, 1954] and as "Thomas Wolfe as I Knew Him" in *Thomas Wolfe as I Knew Him and Other Essays* [Denver: Alan Swallow, 1963].)

FROHOCK, W. M. "Thomas Wolfe: Of Time and Neurosis." *Southwest Review* 33 (1948): 349-60. (Reprinted as "Thomas Wolfe: Time and the National Neurosis" in his *The Novel of Violence in America*, 2d ed. [Dallas: Southern Methodist University Press, 1957] and as "Of Time and Neurosis" in Walser.)

GEISMAR, MAXWELL. "Thomas Wolfe: The Unfound Door." In his *Writers in Crisis: The American Novel Between Two Wars*. Boston: Houghton Mifflin Co., 1942. Pp. 187-235. (Partly reprinted as "Diary of a Provincial" in Walser.)

HARTLEY, LOIS. "Theme in Thomas Wolfe's 'The Lost Boy' and 'God's Lonely Man.'" *Georgia Review* 15 (1961): 230-35. (Reprinted in Field.)

HOLMAN, C. HUGH. "'The Dark, Ruined Helen of His Blood': Thomas Wolfe and the South." In Louis D. Rubin, Jr. and Robert Jacobs, *South: Modern Southern Literature in Its Cultural Setting*. Garden City, New York: Doubleday-Dolphin Books, 1961. Pp. 177-97. (Reprinted in Field.)

———. "Europe as a Catalyst for Thomas Wolfe." In Max F. Schulz, *et al., Essays in American and English Literature*, Athens, Ohio: Ohio University Press, 1967.

———. "Thomas Wolfe: A Bibliographical Study." *Texas Studies in Literature and Language* 1 (1959): 427-45.

———. *Thomas Wolfe*. University of Minnesota Pamphlets on American Writers. Minneapolis: University of Minnesota Press, 1960. (Reprinted in William Van O'Connor, *Seven Modern American Novelists: An Introduction* [Minneapolis: University of Minnesota Press, 1964], pp. 189-225, and partly reprinted in Holman.)

———. ed. *The World of Thomas Wolfe*. New York: Charles Scribner's Sons, 1962.

JOHNSON, ELMER D. *Of Time and Thomas Wolfe: A Bibliography with a Character Index of His Works*. New York: Scarecrow Press, 1959.

JOHNSON, PAMELA HANSFORD. *Thomas Wolfe: A Critical Study*. London: William Heinemann Ltd., 1947. (Published in America as *Hungry Gulliver: An English Critical Appraisal of Thomas Wolfe* [New York: Charles Scribner's Sons, 1948] and reprinted with a new preface as *The Art of Thomas Wolfe* [New York: Charles Scribner's Sons, 1963].)

KENNEDY, RICHARD S. "Thomas Wolfe at Harvard, 1920-1923." *Harvard Library Bulletin* 4 (1950): 172-90, 304-19. (Adapted as "Wolfe's Harvard Years" in Walser.)

———. *The Window of Memory: The Literary Career of Thomas Wolfe*. Chapel Hill, North Carolina: University of North Carolina Press, 1962.

KENNEDY, WILLIAM F. "Economic Ideas in Contemporary Literature —The Novels of Thomas Wolfe." *Southern Economic Journal* 20 (1953): 35-50. (Partly reprinted in Holman.)

MALONEY, MARTIN. "A Study of Semantic States: Thomas Wolfe and the Faustian Sickness." *General Semantics Bulletin*, nos. 16-17 (1955), pp. 15-25. (Reprinted in Field.)

NORWOOD, HAYDEN. *The Marble Man's Wife*. New York: Charles Scribner's Sons, 1947.

NOWELL, ELIZARETH. *Thomas Wolfe: A Biography*. New York: Doubleday and Co., 1960.

PERKINS, MAXWELL. *Editor to Author, The Letters of Maxwell Perkins*. Edited by John Hall Wheelock. New York: Charles Scribner's Sons, 1950.

———. "Thomas Wolfe." *Harvard Library Bulletin* 1 (1947): 269-77. (Adapted as the introduction to *Look Homeward, Angel* [New York: Charles Scribner's Sons, 1952], and reprinted in part in Holman.)

POLLOCK, THOMAS CLARK and CARGILL, OSCAR. *Thomas Wolfe at Washington Square*. New York: New York University Press, 1954.

REAVER, J. RUSSELL and STROZIER, ROBERT I. "Thomas Wolfe and Death." *Georgia Review* 16 (1962): 330-50. (Reprinted in Field.)

REEVES, PASCHAL. "Thomas Wolfe: Notes on Three Characters." *Modern Fiction Studies* 11 (1965): 275-85. (Reprinted in Field.)

ROTHMAN, NATHAN L. "Thomas Wolfe and James Joyce: A Study in

Literary Influence." In Allen Tate, ed., *A Southern Vanguard*. New York: Prentice-Hall, 1947. Pp. 52-77. (Reprinted in Welser.)

RUBIN, LOUIS D. *Thomas Wolfe, The Weather of His Youth*. Baton Rouge: Louisiana State University Press, 1955. (Extracted in Holman.)

———. "Thomas Wolfe: Time and the South." In *The Faraway Country: Writers of the Modern South*. Seattle: University of Washington Press, 1963. Pp. 72-104. (Reprinted in Field.)

STEARNS, MONROE M. "The Metaphysics of Thomas Wolfe." *College English* 6 (1945): 193-99. (Reprinted in Walser.)

TURNBULL, ANDREW. *Thomas Wolfe*. New York: Charles Scribner's Sons, 1967.

VOLKENING, HENRY T. "Tom Wolfe: Penance No More." *Virginia Quarterly Review* 15 (1939): 196-215. (Reprinted in Walser.)

WALSER, RICHARD, ed. *The Enigma of Thomas Wolfe: Biographical and Critical Selections*. Cambridge, Mass.: Harvard University Press, 1953.

WARREN, ROBERT P. "A Note on the Hamlet of Thomas Wolfe." *American Review* 5(1935): 191-208. (Reprinted in Walser and Field.)

WHEATON, MABEL WOLFE, and BLYTHE, LEGETTE. *Thomas Wolfe and His Family*. New York: Doubleday and Co., 1961.

WOLFE, THOMAS. *From Death to Morning*. New York: Charles Scribner's Sons, 1935.

WOLFE, THOMAS. *The Hills Beyond*. New York: Harper and Brothers, 1941.

WOLFE, THOMAS. *Look Homeward, Angel*. New York: Charles Scribner's Sons, 1929.

WOLFE, THOMAS. *Of Time and the River*. New York: Charles Scribner's Sons, 1935.

WOLFE, THOMAS. *The Story of a Novel*. New York: Charles Scribner's Sons, 1936.

WOLFE, THOMAS. *The Web and the Rock*. New York: Harper and Brothers, 1939.

WOLFE, THOMAS. *You Can't Go Home Again*. New York: Harper and Brothers, 1940.

WOLFE, THOMAS. *The Letters of Thomas Wolfe.* Edited by Elizabeth Nowell. New York: Charles Scribner's Sons, 1956.

WOLFE, THOMAS. *The Notebooks of Thomas Wolfe.* Edited by Richard S. Kennedy and Paschal Reeves. Chapel Hill, North Carolina: University of North Carolina Press, 1970.

WOLFE, THOMAS. *The Short Novels of Thomas Wolfe.* Edited by C. Hugh Holman. New York: Charles Scribner's Sons, 1961.

WOLFE, THOMAS. *Thomas Wolfe's Letters to his Mother.* Edited by John Skally Terry. New York: Charles Scribner's Sons, 1943.

WOLFE, THOMAS and WATT, HOMER ANDREW. *The Correspondence of Thomas Wolfe and Homer Andrew Watt.* Edited by Oscar Cargill and Thomas Clark Pollock. New York: New York University Press, 1954.